The School Counselor's Guide to Surviving the First Year

The School Counselor's Guide to Surviving the First Year offers a comprehensive look into the first-year school counseling experience.

This practical guide includes topics from internship to professional development from an intimate perspective within the context of real-life scenarios. Drawing from personal experiences, journal articles, textbooks, and excerpts by numerous professional school counselors, it fuses what a school counseling trainee learns in their graduate program and the field experience they get into one unique guide. Emphasizing hands-on approaches, this volume offers personal as well as professional steps toward success in the ins and outs of counseling.

This book is a valuable toolkit for the developmental journey of school counselors in-training and beginning school counselors.

Heather M. Couch is a school counselor in Greater Cincinnati, USA, and an active member in her community.

The School Counselor's Guide to Surviving the First Year

Internship through Professional Development

Heather M. Couch

Routledge
Taylor & Francis Group

NEW YORK AND LONDON

First published 2020
by Routledge
52 Vanderbilt Avenue, New York, NY 10017

and by Routledge
2 Park Square, Milton Park, Abingdon, Oxon, OX14 4RN

Routledge is an imprint of the Taylor & Francis Group, an informa business

© 2020 Taylor & Francis

The right of Heather M. Couch to be identified as the author of the
material has been asserted in accordance with sections 77 and 78 of
the Copyright, Designs and Patents Act 1988.

All rights reserved. No part of this book may be reprinted or
reproduced or utilised in any form or by any electronic, mechanical,
or other means, now known or hereafter invented, including
photocopying and recording, or in any information storage or
retrieval system, without permission in writing from the publishers.

Trademark notice: Product or corporate names may be trademarks
or registered trademarks, and are used only for identification and
explanation without intent to infringe.

Library of Congress Cataloging-in-Publication Data
A catalog record for this title has been requested

ISBN: 978-1-138-36426-4 (hbk)
ISBN: 978-1-138-36432-5 (pbk)
ISBN: 978-0-429-43143-2 (ebk)

Typeset in Bembo
by Deanta Global Publishing Services, Chennai, India

I dedicate this book to my parents, Rick and Karen Couch. You have never stopped believing in and supporting me, for that and so much more I am eternally grateful!

Contents

Acknowledgements

A book does not get published by the author alone, it takes a number of people to make it all come together. First, I thank the Lord for blessing me with the opportunity to write this book. Writing this book has taught me a lot about myself as a school counselor and given me tools to be a better counselor. I would like to thank all of my family and friends for their support from the beginning of this journey to the end. I couldn't have done any of this without the love of my mom and dad, Karen and Rick Couch!

At the very beginning when this book was just a proposal, Sheila Gray reviewed and edited my chapter abstracts. I'm very grateful for her time and expertise! I hope all of my Oxford commas are in the correct place.

Thank you, Amanda Devine, my editor, for believing in this book from the first email I sent. She took my dream and turned it into a reality. I can't thank you enough for answering all of my questions and guiding me through the publishing process!

I would also like to thank my professor from graduate school, Brent Richardson. His guidance and wisdom have helped me in my career as a counselor. I will never forget his saying, "you have to hear their story from their heart, their mind, and their eyes". He teaches his students what it truly means to be an empathetic counselor.

Thank you, Vince Rahnfeld for your encouragement and mentorship as I navigated internship and the first year of being a school counselor. It's folks like him who sharpen the iron when it's needed and are the listening ear.

It really does take a village to accomplish one's goals in life, and for those who helped me with achieving this goal I say thank you! I am eternally grateful for the outpouring of love and support I receive.

Part I
Before Graduation

1 Internship

Internship is a time to learn the profession with a safety net. It is a great opportunity to sharpen your strengths and work on your weaknesses. However, deciding where to do your internship can be half the battle. Starting out in an internship placement that is the right fit is crucial. It's important to have a supportive supervisor that helps you grow as a counselor and mentors you through the entire process.

The **First Step** in finding a placement is to talk with your university's counseling program about schools they have had students intern at before and what the supervisor's leadership style is. Not everyone's leadership style is compatible with everyone. So, it's good to meet with your potential supervisor before starting internship. Ask them to give you an example of how they will supervise you, how your advising meetings will be structured, what their expectations are for you, and how assignments will be given. You want to have as much information as possible before making the site your placement. Also, every site might not be a good learning environment. There will inevitably be schools or supervisors who do not regularly have interns and/or are not a good place to have interns. Attending your university's internship fair, if they have one, is a good way to meet with supervisors who want interns and have been vetted by your professors.

The **Second Step** is to do research. Make sure you know the school environment before you start interning. How many school counselors do they have? What are their school counselors required to do? Do they follow the ASCA National Model? These are important questions to get answered before you choose a school. Another thing to keep in mind is what level of education you want to work in. You might not know whether or not you want to be in an elementary, middle, or high school before starting internship and that's okay. The important aspect of internship is learning to become a full-time school counselor. Yes, what a school counselor does looks different at the elementary, the middle, and the high school levels but the foundation is the same. Reach out to the school counselors at a school you're interested in and ask them questions about their program. Let them know who you are, what university you're from, and that you're looking for an internship site. They will want to learn about you to know if you're a good fit in their department.

It might be good to shadow a counselor at the school you're interested in before making a commitment.

The **Third Step** is to secure an internship site. Once you've done your research and talked with the head of the counseling department, you will secure your internship placement. Then, you will follow your internship class requirements. It is important to remember that you are not employed by the school and you are there to learn. Therefore, you shouldn't be treated as an employee by your supervisor. There are things you should not have to do unless it is for learning purposes. You should have open lines of communication and regular supervision meetings.

Tips for Internship Placement:

1. Make sure the school has a comprehensive school counseling program. Note: not every school has the ASCA RAMP certification. *Be realistic with your expectations.*
2. Meet with your potential supervisor to know their leadership style, expectations, and how involved they will be during internship.
3. Research what type of school you would like to work in when you graduate.
4. Remember you are not alone if a placement isn't the right fit; talk to your professor about it.

Navigating Internship

When you first start interning it can be overwhelming, because you're the 'new person'. A good supervisor will help you adjust and learn the ins-and-outs of the school. If you've never worked in a school before it can be an adjustment getting used to how a school operates. Take it one day at a time, it gets easier! While you're in internship there are a few things to keep in mind.

Number One: Communication

In any aspect of life, communicating is important. When you're interning you need to build a good rapport with your supervisor. Sometimes this happens naturally, but that isn't always the case. Communication doesn't just happen and don't expect your supervisor to take all of the initiative. They are still working a full-time job and being your supervisor. It is part of your responsibility, as an intern, to be open with communicating. You need to ask questions, even if they seem trivial, and talk to him/her about the experiences you're having. There might be times when you're unsure of what to do. Communicate this to your supervisor about more responsibility and collaboration. Don't wait until they notice you aren't doing anything and ask if you're finished! If you're working individually with a student and there is something that you feel uneasy about, talk to your internship supervisor right away. They are there for you! Your internship class professor is also there for you. Make sure you are communicating with him/her about how your internship placement is going. If you don't feel like there is a good relationship between you and your internship supervisor, let your professor know. As in any relationship, a good relationship means there is an open line of communication.

The article "Simple Keys to Effective Communication" suggests these few tips for effective communication (Lazarus, 2011):

1. Try to send clear messages that are congruent in both verbal and nonverbal dimensions.
2. Say what you mean and mean what you say. Be direct and honest; don't dance around the issue or play games.
3. Ask for feedback to ensure the message you sent was accurately received.
4. Wait for the person to complete a thought without interrupting to express your own ideas.
5. If you're not sure you understand the message, ask questions and seek clarification.
6. Paraphrase what you heard so the sender can be sure you got the right idea.

These are helpful tips even if you are communicating via email. Miscommunication can easily happen when communicating via email. It's best to keep emails concise and brief. Anything important should be discussed in person when miscommunication is less likely to happen.

Number Two: Flexibility

Flexibility is an essential quality to being a school counselor (don't worry, it's a skill that can be learned). Working in a school can be very frustrating. There are different bell schedules in place for different days when there might be an assembly, mass, house system, or faculty meetings. There are endless reasons for schools to have shortened periods on varying days. Most of the time the faculty knows in advance but that's not always the case. The interruption of a daily schedule tends to happen a lot. For a school counselor this may mean you aren't able to meet with the students you planned on, go into a classroom to have a guidance lesson (or shorten that lesson), or run a group. There have been many times when I have been frustrated by a disruption in my plans for the day. It's best to 'roll with the punches' rather than fight against the inevitable. There will be days when students interrupt your schedule and you have to put their needs first. I teach a sophomore guidance class and there have been times when I had to have a substitute teacher because I had to meet with a student. A school counselor's day can be unpredictable. Leila Christenbury, author of the article "The Flexible Teacher" in *The Education Educator*, said "good teaching comes not from following a recipe, but from consistently putting student needs first" (Christenbury, 2010). That is very true for school counselors as well!

Another aspect of flexibility is in terms of multiculturalism. People come from different macro and micro cultures. Even those who seemingly come from the same religion, ethnic group, and socioeconomic status will have different micro cultures based upon their environment in the home. It's important to be flexible in our worldview, because our students may have a very different one. It is important that school counselors are willing to acknowledge any bias they may have and seek guidance for themselves. As an intern, you have the great advantage of being able to seek mentoring from your professors. They can provide you with additional counseling resources and help you work through the issues you might face.

When I completed my internship, I saw both ends of the spectrum with student diversity. My first job after internship was at a small Catholic, coed mixed middle/high school. It is an accelerated gifted school where the students test in and skip at least one grade level. My seniors were between the ages of 14–17 upon graduating. The dynamic between my internship placement and my first job was vast. Not only were the worldviews of the students and parents drastically different, but so were the principal and faculty. It took a bit to adjust, but I learned to be flexible. It didn't happen overnight, but with mentorship I broadened my own worldview.

Number Three: Initiative

The biggest fear with putting forth initiative is failure. My principal at the first school I worked at did not discourage failure. He said often that the only way not to fail was to do nothing. We can be afraid to start any project, because of how others may perceive it. When you're interning, most supervisors won't have the time to hand-hold you through the entire process. Their job will be to support you, offer advice, and provide guidance. You'll collaborate on a project that you will be fully responsible for. Of course, that won't completely fill your eight-hour day, so you will have other duties to perform.

Examples of Internship Duties

- Creating and implementing guidance lessons
- Meeting with students individually
- Creating, facilitating, or co-facilitating student groups
- Organizing awareness days
- Attending counseling department, faculty, intervention, and parent/teacher/student meetings
- Helping implement parent information nights
- Collaborating on a career or college fair
- Sending out informational newsletters to students and parents

This is a short list of possible activities you could perform as an intern. What you do will be determined by you and your supervisor and what programming the school already has in place. It's an exciting time to be an intern and there are a lot of opportunities to learn. If you're really passionate about self-esteem in girls, then run a small group. This is the time to run a group with the help and guidance of your supervisor. When you get into your first school–counselor position there won't be as much support. Finally, take personal initiative by setting goals for you to achieve during internship.

Number Four: Self-Care

In one of your counseling classes, you probably wrote a self-care plan as an assignment. Self-care is arguably the most important aspect of preventing burn out. This is not only for your benefit but for your students. If you go into the school with a bad attitude the students will know it. There will be bad days and you need to have a self-care system in place. Giving of yourself every day is mentally, emotionally, and physically exhausting. You have to let yourself have time to rest and recharge. There are a lot of different activities you can do for self-care. The American Counseling Association identifies four types of self-care: physical, cognitive, emotional, and spiritual activities. Some examples are (Pearlman & Saakvitne, 1996):

Physical

- Exercising
- Maintaining a healthy diet
- Getting enough sleep
- Drinking plenty of water
- Taking vacations
- Wearing clothes you like
- Taking time off when you need it

Cognitive

- Attending personal counseling
- Journaling
- Reading materials unrelated to work
- Doing things you enjoy
- Self-reflecting
- Saying 'no' to extra responsibilities

Emotional

- Spending time with people you love
- Giving yourself affirmation
- Loving yourself
- Allowing yourself to cry

Spiritual

- Contributing to a cause you believe in
- Meditating or praying
- Being a part of a spiritual community or church
- Singing
- Spending time in nature

It can be hard to take time for self-care. Many interns are working another job during internship, might have to take care of their children, or just have other responsibilities that require their attention. This is also why it's important to make room in your day for self-care. Start with taking at least one hour a week that is solely dedicated to caring for yourself. As mentioned with the list of activities, it doesn't have to be something you do every day. It can be simply journaling and self-reflection. I know that going to the gym isn't always relaxing for me or something I considered self-care. I know it's good for me and I hate when I can't go, but I make sure that I do something once a week that I really love.

The following are some questions from the article "The Importance of Self-Care" on the blog *Confident Counselors* that suggests you ask yourself to help determine if you're making your well-being a priority (Kiddie Matters, 2017):

1. Are you able to take time for yourself without feeling guilty?
2. Do you believe you deserve self-care?
3. Do you know the difference between self-care and self-indulgence?
4. Do you realize self-care does not equal weakness?
5. Are you OK with slowing down sometimes?
6. Do you have a go-to list of activities?
7. Do you make leisure time a priority?
8. Have you made self-care a habit?
9. Do you have a basic self-care plan, preferably in writing?

There is a lot of research and books out on self-care. If you're in internship, start making self-care a habit now! If you're a school counselor and haven't made self-care a priority, it's never too late to start. Start with something simple, add it to your calendar, and keep that commitment! Don't try to do more than you're able to and exhaust yourself with self-care, that would defeat the purpose.

Last Thoughts...

Below are two reflections from school counselors during their internship experience. The purpose is to give you real insight into what internship can be like. An excerpt from Robert J. Zeglin, M.A. and Tyler J. Andreula, M.A. states (Zeglin & Andreula, 2012),

One of the main purposes of internship is to gain experience in the field with a wide variety of clients and situations. When you first begin, things can be overwhelming, and I wish I would have known that this is a completely normal feeling. I found that my site was very different from what I was accustomed to (the controlled environment in which I conducted sessions on my campus). I believe that this is something that all interns need to be prepared for and, of course, they need to understand that, at some point or another, we all feel this way.

I learned very quickly that, if you do not know how to work with a given client or how to remedy a particular situation, you need to admit that you need help, and you need to seek it out. At your site, asking for help is one of the best ways to learn. For me, the moment in which I let go of the belief that I needed to be a perfect counselor was the moment in which my counseling skills grew in leaps and bounds. Being mindful and engaging in self-reflection about your thoughts and feelings, along with what occurs during your sessions, is a wonderful way to know exactly what to reach out to colleagues about and how to provide better services to your clients.

It took me some time to feel confident at my site and, in the beginning, I was a bit hard on myself for not feeling more confident. A wise colleague of mine told me one day: 'It will all come in time. At some point, we all feel this when we first begin. I promise you that, in time, this feeling will go away and you will be comfortable.' At the time, it felt as though this would *never* happen. However, after having some client breakthroughs, learning many of the procedures, and being given my own caseload to work with, this feeling dissipated very quickly. It is crucial to not forget to reach out to those individuals who are instrumental in supporting you on campus, as well. As counseling trainees, we should become fluent in self-counseling, as well. After all, we cannot enter internship expecting to be experts on the first day, but we can, however, expect to learn a great deal and get to this point someday.

Jessica Radmaker Reichardt blogged about her experience as a first-year counselor and internship experience. Here are a couple of paragraphs taken from her reflection (Reichardt, 2014),

> Looking back through my work and reflecting on my strengths and weaknesses when compiling my portfolio has helped me to see where I have really excelled and what areas I still need to work on. It was reassuring for me to look at my strengths and take time to appreciate what I have done well. It was also helpful for me to look at my weaknesses and come up with a plan to work on these areas. If I could simplify my plan for improvement into a couple words it would be: continued education. I am well aware that I will *never* know everything there is to know about school counseling. I cannot and should not ever stop learning if I want to be a successful school counselor.

I will continue to seek out professional development opportunities as well as experiences to make myself a more well-rounded individual. I need to learn to take care of myself first before I am able to do my best in my career. This, I believe, is the most profound, and hardest to digest, lesson I've learned over the past three years. Putting yourself first is not always the easiest concept for people in the helping profession to grasp, but it's one that is essential for our success and our sanity.

I have felt extremely well cared for and supported by my professors and I have learned so much in the past three years through this program.

As an individual without a teaching license, I was required to take a classroom management class as well as an exceptional learner class. I believe these classes helped me to learn more about education but there are still major gaps in my knowledge when it comes to how the whole education system works. I believe more emphasis on how things actually work in a real world setting and *how* to get this to the ideal model that ASCA describes, instead of focusing on what *should* be done would be helpful for students as we begin our careers as school counselors. Anything to ease that shock of going from graduate student with all the best intentions to actual, working school counselor with all the real world limitations and setbacks, would be beneficial.

Wrap Up

Ultimately, what you get out of internship is dependent upon how much you invest into it. Internship is an exciting time! Feed off that enthusiasm and pour into your internship placement. There will be times when you feel overwhelmed with assignments from class and the demands of your supervisor, but remember to breathe and be in the moment. It can be easy to get bogged down with the academic calendar but make it a priority to talk to your supervisor. Get constructive feedback and make adjustments. Seek mentorship from your supervisor or professor. We all are working on being the best counselor we can for our students.

Here are a few last helpful tips (Diaz, 2009):

1. Ask a lot of questions
2. Be prepared at your internship site
3. Make internship a priority
4. Take this opportunity to learn and grow in the profession
5. Make sure that you are keeping track of your internship hours
6. Document everything!
7. Don't be afraid of failure
8. Be yourself

Lastly, I want to reiterate that you are not alone! Internship can make you feel like you're on an island by yourself. However, you might find support from your peers in the internship class. Reach out to them about what they're doing at their placement, ask them what is and isn't working, and get to know them better. You have a lot of people in your cheering section that want to see you succeed. Take advantage of all their support and guidance. Maintaining these relationships will benefit you long term.

References

Christenbury, L. (2010, December). *The Flexible Teacher.* Retrieved from Educational Leadership: www.ascd.org/publications/educational-leadership/dec10/vol68/num04/The-Flexible-Teacher.aspx

Diaz, J. (2009, September 8). *Tips for Practicum and Internship Students.* Retrieved from American Counseling Association: www.counseling.org/news/aca-blogs/aca-member-blogs/aca-member-blogs/2009/09/08/tips-for-practicum-and-internship-students#

Kiddie Matters (2017, May 8). *The Importance of Self-Care.* Retrieved from Confident Counselors: https://confidentcounselors.com/2017/05/08/importance-practicing-self-care/

Lazarus, C. (2011, July 26). *Simple Keys to Effective Communication.* Retrieved from Psychology Today: www.psychologytoday.com/us/blog/think-well/201107/simple-keys-effective-communication

Pearlman, L.A., & Saakvitne, K.W. (1996, October). *Self-Care Assessment Worksheet.* Retrieved from Mentoring: www.mentoring.org/new-site/wp-content/uploads/2015/09/MARCH_2015_Self_Care_Assessment.pdf

Reichardt, J.R. (2014). *Final Entry Reflection Paper.* Retrieved from Jessica Radmaker: https://jessicaradmaker.weebly.com

Zeglin, R.J., & Andreula, T.J. (2012, April 3). *700 Hours Later: What I Wish I Knew Before my Internship in Counseling.* Retrieved from Clinically Psyched: http://clinicallypsyched.com/700-hours-later-what-i-wish-i-knew-before-my-internship-in-counseling/

2   Networking

If you Google 'networking' you will find endless videos, articles, books, events, and groups on the subject. The business world thrives on networking. It's all about who you know and how they can help you achieve your goal. Networking is essential to the longevity of your career. For some people, networking might be a dirty word, but if we look at its definition and not how some people use it then it isn't dirty at all! Merriam-Webster defines networking as, "the exchange of information or services among individuals, groups, or institutions; specifically: the cultivation of productive relationships for employment or business". I really like the last part of the definition stating that networking is the "cultivation of productive relationships". That is exactly what networking is!

Why is Networking as a School Counseling Intern Important?

For the rest of this chapter, we are going to use the definition, "cultivation of productive relationships", as we talk about networking. When we think about it from this definition then we better understand why it is vital to our careers. As a school counselor, you will be building relationships with everyone in your school building. From the students to the principal, you will be working with them intimately. It's good to get practice in before you start your first job. As an intern, it's important to network because you're going to be looking for your first job. Then, you're going to need those contacts when you're at your first job. Networking doesn't end when you're in your school counseling position. It's just as important to maintain those connections after you have secured a position. An article from "A Girl's Guide to PM" states six reasons why networking is important (Harrin, 2019),

1. **Networking is Spotting Opportunities**

   Networking is not sales. Put that thought out of your head. In fact, it's the opposite. Networking is about spotting opportunities, so you want to spend time asking questions about the person you are talking to and their business, to try to see whether they have any problems that you can help with.

2. **Networking Builds Relationships**
3. **Networking is Expected**
   This is my favorite reason. "Even if your role isn't explicitly to bring in new business or to market the company," Kintish writes, "you are probably expected, as most people are, to meet new people and understand the market place as part of your role."
4. **Networking is Good For Your Projects**
   Kintish says that it's a way to learn more about the business, understand the industry better, and hear about the challenges faced by your contacts.
5. **Networking Can Further Your Career**
6. **Networking is a Virtuous Circle**
   "If done right, meeting more people leads to more business and career opportunities, which leads to meeting more people and more business, and so on," Kintish writes.

The Basics of Networking

Before we dive into what networking looks like in the school counseling profession, I want to go over some networking basics. An article by Chi Sigma Iota, Counseling Academic, and Professional Honor Society International highlights key components to effective networking (Networking Tips, 2018).

- "Networking is a reciprocal relationship so expect to take out as much as you put in." Networking is mutually beneficial for both parties involved. You'll need to exchange information that the other person needs as well. If you're not willing to share your knowledge and experiences, then you're not going to gain much from the other person.
- "Networking is completely legal, and it is an established and essential aspect of conducting". Networking is expected and, in some cases, required from you. Networking events are sponsored by many businesses and sometimes by local Chambers of Commerce.
- "Networking is not the same as nepotism." One of the great things about networking is you form relationships outside of your intimate circle. You don't have to worry about favoritism among relatives.
- "In networking, who you know matters as much as what you know." Information is commerce when networking. Your knowledge is valuable to others and theirs is valuable to you. You may have spent your internship focusing on grief groups with elementary students. This is knowledge and experience that another person would find valuable.
- "You are part of many networks already that you use on a daily basis." Did you recently buy a new phone or need to get a groomer for your dog? You most likely asked someone for their opinion on what to buy

and where to go. These are just two simple examples of how we network in our everyday lives.

- "Everyone is a potential networking connection." From going to the grocery store to walking your dog, you never know who you're going to meet. My family has a food catering business and our neighbor helped us be a vendor at an event. She also works for a printing company that designs shirts. So, not only is she a good neighbor but a good network.

Know your network. Ask yourself a few questions: what do I want to gain from this network? What will I add to this network? Do you want to join an existing network or create your own? When you're networking it can feel artificial if you don't know why you're networking. If the only reason is to know an influential person, then it's not mutually beneficial to both parties. Neither parties will gain anything from a network that doesn't serve a purpose.

Build rapport. We hear the term 'building rapport' with clients/students a lot in the counseling profession. However, it isn't just for the counseling profession. Counseling has given us the tools to build great positive relationships. Use those skills when networking to build trust with the other person. Then that person will be more willing to share your information with people in their network. Networking isn't always about individual relationships but extending your connections.

Give more than you take. Think about networking as an investment. You're not going to make a return on your investment if you don't put any money into it. The more money you put into your investment the most return you're going to get. This basic economics principle is the same with networking. I had a fellow school counselor, who had many more years of experience than me, refer her assistant principal to me about an issue that came up in their school. I was humbled that she had that much faith in me. That same school counselor is someone I refer to others for advice and guidance.

Keep in contact with your network. Be proactive and keep a balance when keeping in contact. You don't want to harass them, but you do want to contact them on occasion. Whether that's to wish them a happy birthday or congratulate them on a promotion. It's important to keep in touch in order to maintain your relationship. Emails are quick and convenient. Use them to your advantage! Remember names, dates, location, and special expertise. Some other things to know about your network are:

- What are the important aspects of your network contacts? Businesses?
- What are their professional needs?
- What are their professional strengths?
- How do they spend their professional and leisure time?

Be open to new situations and new relationships. You're going to attend workshops, conferences, and meetings. These are great ways to network and build your professional relationships. When you're at these events take the opportunity to reach out to people. There are usually opportunities to network with other professionals at these events during a cocktail hour or luncheon. Plan on attending a few of these network opportunities.

Lastly, follow through with any meetings you set up with people and follow up after meeting with them. Be prepared with questions and talking points. As a school counselor, you might want to talk to a person about what Social Emotional Learning curriculums they're using. Do research about the current trends of Social Emotional Learning and what curriculum is available. This can be applied to anything you want to know more about. When you're looking for a job after graduation, you will benefit from your network. Sometimes you have to adjust the focus of your network. Right now, your focus might be on building a network that helps you obtain a job after graduation. When you get your first job, your network will focus on obtaining resources and support during your first year. Think about networking as wraparound services for yourself. Your network is important to your own well-being in providing the best care for your students.

Build Your Brand

Part of networking is building your brand. When you're networking, you are marketing yourself to an individual. Whether you are meeting a potential supervisor for internship or colleague that will help you land your first-year job, you market yourself to every person you come in contact with. So, it is important that when you're networking that you're projecting the correct impression to the person you're interacting with. An article from "Inspiring Interns & Graduates" states (Thiefels, 2018),

Maintain an active LinkedIn presence
This social media platform was built for professionals of all kinds, and being active on LinkedIn could prove you with opportunities to connect with leaders and similar brands and businesses.

Cultivate relationships over time
To build sustainable connections, you have to invest in getting to know them. The relationships with staying power are those which develop through a gradual, intentional process that can take months or even years of consistent engaging with one another.

Try different networking events
Backing away from the computer screen and attending actual events is critical if you want to build your network. While standard networking events are valuable, they can also be stuffy and unfocused.

Make a point of attending networking functions through local businesses and industry chapters of business clubs. This will allow you to meet people relevant, and likely more valuable, for your brand and career.

Don't forget to check out non-traditional networking opportunities through sites like MeetUp.com, which has a wide variety of groups that host niche mixers for everyone from writing professionals to retired teachers.

Be the first to offer

Relationships should not be one-sided. Rather, they should equally benefit each person involved. Before asking for something from a potential contact, consider how you can be of use to them. Offer your services first. Networking should be based on reciprocal relationships, not one-way ones.

Show the real you in your content

Blogs, social media and other web-based content are effective networking channels, but coming across as self-promotional is not helpful to your personal brand—and can turn potential connections off.

The idea is to *serve* your contacts, not to continually toot your own horn—at least not all of the time. Instead, produce and share content that's both valuable and related to your line of work and personal beliefs.

Start networking to build your brand

When done tactfully and effectively, networking can take your personal brand to the next level, which in turn can boost your career. Step outside your comfort zone, be intentional about meeting others in the same industry and be of value to your connections whenever possible. It could lead to a relationship that might change the direction of your life.

Networking with Specific Professionals

School Counselors

Networking with other school counselors is extremely vital to our profession. We are in a helping profession that deals with a lot of personal and intimate situations. It can wear down our own mental health and we can't keep our own emotions bottled up. School counselors need each other to have a shoulder to cry on, build professional development, and to get advice from. In later chapters, we will talk about the importance of having mentorship in your career. Right now, in internship, is the time to start building those relationships with fellow school counselors. You know that you're not the sole expert in the field and there is a lot to learn.

There are a lot of school counselors and narrowing down who to network with can be daunting. The first place to start is with those in your school and district. They will be able to guide you through what they have experienced with your principal, superintendent, faculty, and school board. The education field is a small world and a lot of people move positions within the same district. Other school counselors in your district are going to be able to help you with the best practices, climate, and policy and procedures. You will find that each school district is different and building your network within is important to developing your counseling program.

Networking with school counselors at other schools is good because it gives you breadth. You can learn from what they are doing within their school and their entire district. Other districts might be able to get all of their school's RAMP, Recognized ASCA Model Program, certified. It would be good to get support and advice from their school counselors on your own program. Do some research and see what other school counselors are doing. You will have opportunities to meet colleagues at professional development events. Don't hesitate to even introduce yourself to a presenter.

During my first few years as a school counselor, I liked to meet colleagues who were seasoned in the profession. They have had more time to specialize in an area of counseling and focus on a specific population. As a school counselor, we have to be well-rounded in all of counseling but there are opportunities to specialize. Due to the nature of my first-year school counseling position, I found an interest in the social-emotional needs of gifted students. Other school counselors focus on suicide prevention and awareness, self-harm, or another mental health topic. These folks have most likely spent a lot of their professional development on a specific topic that makes them a resident expert. It is good to network with them and learn from them. Especially, if you're experiencing it in your school and you're new. Don't be afraid to reach out and ask for help!

Like those school counselors who have taken the time to become specialized, learn from those school counselors who have specialized programming within their schools. Often times, school districts will give out a needs assessment for the district and implement programming based upon the results. You might hear about a school district implementing a mental health curriculum, a campaign against bullying, or a diversity and inclusion policy. These are just a few examples of district-wide needs that will affect the school counselors. They will be expected to possibly create new programming, adhere to policy, and collect data on the programming. As a new school counselor, this can be overwhelming. Reach out to colleagues about best practices and general advice. The old saying, "don't reinvent the wheel" is a motto to live by.

It was during a time of crisis at my school when I reached out to all of my networks. As the sole school counselor, I was the resident expert on the crisis. I had a lot of support from my principal who had provided me with outside counselors and put me in touch with another school counselor in our district. I have realized that our profession is great about being supportive of one another in times of need. So, don't hesitate to reach out when a crisis happens, and you need help.

Network with school counselors who have experience in the areas you need help in. Whether that's during a time of crisis, running a group on self-harm, guidance lessons on social-emotional learning, or becoming a RAMP certified school. It's important to know who has experience in what areas. Not all school counselors are able to be experts in every area and they will put you in touch with someone who has the knowledge you're looking for. Don't feel like you're alone in this profession. There are a lot of colleagues willing to help you, all you have to do is ask!

Educators

Internship is a great time to network with not only other school counselors but school educators. In later chapters, we will talk about collaborating with educators but I wanted to briefly discuss it in this chapter. My first piece of advice with teachers is to be empathetic. You're the school counselor and that doesn't limit your clientele to the students. There are going to be teachers that do not want you to take students out of their class or give up their class time for guidance lessons. Their teaching time is valuable! Get to know teachers and listen to their concerns. Building a healthy rapport with teachers is important to do our job successfully.

Take time to understand the role of the teacher. They have spent at least four years in college preparing to teach high school History, for example, and they are given standards by the state that each of their students must meet. Some are given a curriculum they must go by and premade assessments they have to give. Then their students are expected to meet benchmarks throughout the year and at the end of the year. There is a lot of pressure on teachers and they feel underappreciated. Arguably, they have one of the most important jobs. Where would we be without teachers?

When we have teachers in our network, we are better connected to what the students are experiencing in the classroom. Part of our job is helping students be ready to learn in the classroom. Teachers are able to provide you with classroom performance and behaviors concerning a student. Seasoned teachers are able to provide great advice on what they have learned throughout the years. They often have intimate relationships with students and speak to parents regularly. The school community is trying to achieve the same goals and we have to work together to do so. Make an effort to network with teachers!

There inevitably will be schools where the faculty doesn't know what the school counselor does on a day-to-day basis. Be an advocate for yourself! Teachers will be more willing to give up their time when they know it's going to be beneficial to the student. Be proactive about networking with teachers. Try to make it a priority to eat lunch with them during lunch when you have time. Be involved in faculty meetings and teacher in-services. If there are social events that the teachers are attending, try to attend those. Go out of your way to thank them for all they do for the students. Be someone they can rely on and trust.

Administrators

The education field is a close community and one never knows who will end up being his/her principal or colleague. I still have a colleague relationship with the principal from the school I interned at. When you're interning, the administration of a school can be intimidating. Know that they are working towards the same common goals of meeting the needs of the students. However, how the goals are implemented might not be the same for the school counselor and the administration.

As with educators, know the role of the administration and what each one does within the school. Networking with the administration is essential in advocating for your program. They can provide you with outside resources and support. Forming these networks during internship can help with obtaining a job position. They'll know what job opportunities are available, and they might be willing to serve as a reference for you. I was able to be a chaperone on a retreat with the assistant principal during my internship placement. It was a great opportunity to learn from him because he had been a teacher. He was able to relate his experience with building relationships with students and give guidance on maintaining boundaries.

The administration doesn't have to be the 'big brother' who is making sure you follow the rules. If you network with the administration and build a rapport, they can serve as supervision for you. Depending on your school district, you might be considered a part of the administration team. I know from experience that it can be intimidating to voice your opinions and concerns among the administration. Once I started building a relationship with the principal and assistant principals, I felt more confident in being a part of the conversations and asking for help.

Other Professionals

As a school counselor, you will work with people outside of the education community. You're going to want to have a resource list for your parents and students of professionals in the mental health community. It helps to have a network in your area of trusted mental health professionals you can refer students to. You might need a better understanding of a mental health disorder, want to have an organization come in to speak to your students, or know how to run groups. Networking with mental health professionals will provide with support in those areas.

I work with an outside mental health awareness organization that comes in to meet with my seniors once a month. The organization provides mental health workshops to small and large groups. I've also reached out to mental health counselors about working with students who are on the autism spectrum, and suffer from self-harm, anxiety, and other disorders. It has helped me professionally to have those folks in my network.

If you are, or plan on, working in a high school, you will spend a lot of time setting up college representative visits. Building a relationship with college admission counselors is important in helping your students know the admission requirements for particular colleges. Your college admissions representatives are eager to help you and your students. Your local admission counselors might be willing to come to talk to the students in a panel format or help give students advice on their college admission essays. I have built great relationships with the college admission counselors that come to my school. They have come to host luncheons for my students, attended my college fair, and invited me to fly-in programs.

Wrap Up

As you read through this chapter, I hope you have understood the importance of networking as an intern and when you get into a first-year counseling position. There are a plethora of ways to network. The American School Counselor Association should be your number one resource. They have a separate site called ASCA SCENE where school counselors can post on discussion boards. This is a good way to network with school counselors outside of your area without having to travel. As an intern, attend any meet and greet your college might set up. If you're a member of the counseling honor fraternity, be active and attend meetings. Be proactive with networking and take advantage of opportunities! If you're not extroverted, it can be hard to get out of your comfort zone and meet new people, but the more you network the better you get at it. Always reach out to the people in your inner network. They will help you build more connections. Even though networking has been a term used in Fortune 500 companies, it is applicable to every profession.

Network Opportunities:

- College admission fairs
- Create and update a LinkedIn account
- Job fairs
- Local chamber networks
- Professional conferences and organizations
- Professional Interest Network (PIN) facilitators promote collaboration among members and support the development of school counseling resources in their work setting. PINs are designed to provide support, share ideas, and raise awareness of school counseling resources (ASCA, 2019)
- Regional school counselor workshops
- Special Interest Network (SPIN) facilitators promote collaboration among members and support the development of school counseling resources around a special-interest topic important to school counseling and education. These networks are designed to provide support, share ideas, and raise awareness of school counseling resources (ASCA, 2019)

References

ASCA (2019). *Special Interest Networks*. Retrieved from ASCA: www.schoolcounselor.org/school-counselors/about-asca/special-interest-networks

Harrin, E. (2019, January 27). *Importance of Networking*. Retrieved from A Girl's Guide to PM: www.girlsguidetopm.com/6-reasons-why-networking-is-important/

Networking Tips (2018). Retrieved from Chi Sigma Iota: www.csi-net.org/page/Networking_Tips

Thiefels, J. (2018, January 12). *5 Ways To Build Your Personal Brand With Networking*. Retrieved from Inspiring Interns & Graduates: www.inspiringinterns.com/blog/2018/01/5-ways-to-build-your-personal-brand-with-networking/

3 Testing and Licensure Requirements

During your internship class, you'll also work on the final preparations for your licensure. The process can be lengthy and it's good to start on it early. There will be an application for your state and fees you'll have to pay. This will all vary per your state's department of education. Also depending upon your state, you may or may not have to take a comprehensive examination. It can be helpful to take the licensing exam, if your state requires it, the first semester of your last year. That way if you have to retake the exam you'll have time. In this chapter, we will go over the basics for the school counseling licensure.

State Licensing Exams

Praxis

Per the American School Counselor Association (ASCA, 2019), there are 22 states that require school counselors take the Praxis Test. This is an online, comprehensive exam that lasts two hours and costs $120. All questions are selected response-questions and test on the four foundations of the ASCA National Model. This test is created and scored by Education Testing Services (ETS). You will have a required score you must get in order to pass. This will not necessarily be the same for every state. You can check your state's passing score at www.ets.org/praxis/states. If you're going to be applying for licensure in multiple states, make sure you check the passing score for both states.

Praxis constructed-response tests do not all use the same scoring procedure. There are two scoring models used for scoring Praxis tests (Educational Testing Service, 2019):

- The first model requires that two scorers rate your response to each question independently. If the two ratings disagree by more than a specified amount, a third scorer rates your response.
- The second model requires that each constructed-response item be rated independently by a different scorer. Under no circumstances does your total score depend entirely on one individual scorer.

You can learn more about how the test is scored at www.ets.org/praxis/scores/understand/how/. The ETS website has everything you need to know about the test and a free study guide to help you prepare.

The following are five sample questions taken from the Praxis School Counselor Study Companion (Educational Testing Service, 2018):

1. A school counseling program is to be established in a new public school that has just opened in an expanding school district. The first step in developing the program is to
   (A) survey the guidance and counseling needs of the student body.
   (B) devise behavioral objectives for classroom management.
   (C) decide on minimum competency levels for student progression to higher grade levels.
   (D) gather appropriate counseling and guidance materials, such as tests and occupational information.

2. A professional school counselor faxed a copy of an attendance contract to the school principal to assist with an intervention for a chronically absent student. The school counselor's input is an example of
   (A) collaboration.
   (B) responsive services.
   (C) prescriptive mode.
   (D) facilitation.

3. In consulting with a teacher about disciplinary problems in the teacher's classroom, a high school counselor demonstrates keen interest in the teacher's various concerns by listening and empathizing with her. By doing this the counselor is assuming the role of
   (A) a supervisor.
   (B) an evaluator.
   (C) a collaborator.
   (D) a helper.

Table 3.1 Praxis Overview

Test Name	Professional School Counselor	
Test Code	5421	
Time	2 hours	
Number of Questions	120	
Format	Selected-response questions	
Delivery	Computer	
Content and Approximate Percentage of Exam	Foundations	18%
	Delivery of services	45%
	Management	15%
	Accountability	22%

4. A student and her family lost all their possessions in a recent tornado. The student reports difficulty sleeping, recurrent nightmares, and loss of appetite. The student is most likely suffering from
   (A) schizophrenia.
   (B) obsessive-compulsive disorder.
   (C) oppositional defiant disorder.
   (D) posttraumatic stress disorder.

5. Several students in a middle school setting have experienced significant losses within a school year. Teachers and family members are asked to identify students who might benefit from a counseling group based on grief and loss. Once these students are identified, the professional school counselor's next step should include which of the following?
   (A) Inviting all students suggested for the group to join.
   (B) Choosing students with whom the counselor is familiar.
   (C) Asking the teachers and family members to complete a survey to determine which students should be part of the group.
   (D) Conducting brief individual interviews with the students to determine whether each of them will be a good candidate for the group.

6. Which of the following is in compliance with the Family Educational Rights and Privacy Act of 1974 (FERPA)?
   (A) An 18-year-old student can view his or her own academic records.
   (B) A noncustodial parent without any legal rights to the student can review a student's academic records.
   (C) A private psychologist who contacts the school on his or her own without the parent's knowledge can review a student's records.
   (D) Colleges and universities that are seeking information about a student can obtain a student's records without student or parental consent.

A few tips on specifically studying for the Praxis (Drexler, 2017):

1. **Practice Constantly.** Train yourself to handle each problem of the test at a time. Learn how to observe time. To master the skills, having time constraints that are self-imposed ensures you utilize your time appropriately even during the final examination. Study every area and read through the test carefully to ensure you give the most appropriate answer.

2. **Learn How to Tackle Questions.** No Praxis tutor can forget to emphasize the importance of carefully reading and understanding questions. It is advisable to read questions twice before answering if time allows.

3. **Do Not Overlook Keywords.** As a result, while tackling the test, you ought to underline important words and understand their impact on the meaning of the overall meaning. Also, paying close attention to learn how the tests use a particular language through your tutors or published books comes in handy.

4. **Avoid Jumping to Hasty Conclusions.** Like every other examination, Praxis questions require careful analysis and evaluation before answering. Most answers are formulated in such a way that they appear to be correct if you read without internalizing the actual meaning.

5. **Dealing with the Answers.** It is an almost impossibility to have all the answers even after adequate preparation for your Praxis exams. In such instance, it is wise to understand the examiner's tricks. If you are not sure of your answer to a specific question, the longer test answers are highly probable to be the correct answers.

6. **Set Your Attitude Right.** Whether something is achievable or not largely depends on your attitude. Being positive and having confidence as you prepare for your Praxis exam is a vital factor for passing. In the case of any imminent weaknesses, be humble enough to approach your educator for assistance.

State Exams

States may have their educational licensing exam other than the ETS Praxis. Ohio is an example of a state who uses their own exam. The Ohio Assessments for Educators (OAE) was created and is used in place of, or in conjunction with, the Praxis. Your university's school counseling program will have information on licensure. It can be daunting, because the requirements can change. There are states, such as Delaware and Kentucky, that do not require an exam at all for licensure. Check with your university, the department of education website for the state you reside in, and ASCA's website.

Testing Tips

I wanted to include a few testing tips in this chapter. They're a good reminder in case it's been a while since you've had to take a standardized test. Good test taking habits are universal! I've highlighted a few testing tips I thought were most relevant to school counselors.

1. **Spread out your studying.** It's really important to prepare for an exam as we know. Make sure you're not cramming for your license exam. People may tell you that the Praxis exam is really easy and common sense, but still take the time to look over study materials. What is easy for one person, may not be easy for another.

2. **Be aware of how you're feeling** about the exam before and during. If you're anxious about the exam before you take it, make sure you have healthy coping strategies in place. This will help you during the exam as well.

3. **Get a good night's sleep** leading up to the test. This is the 'golden rule' of all test taking! Don't get on the computer or your phone at least one

hour prior to attempting to fall asleep. Use a diffuser with an oil that is meant for relaxation. This really helps me get ready to fall asleep! Read a book not related to the test material.

4. **Eat a healthy meal** before taking the test. This exam isn't that long, but still you don't want to lose focus because you skipped breakfast. However, you want to make sure you're eating foods that will give you energy. Carb loading on biscuits and gravy with fried potatoes is not for today. You don't want to feel sluggish while taking it.

5. **Visualize success!** Before I was a school counselor, I performed in music ensembles and piano recitals. Often before I would perform, I would visualize playing the music before ever putting a finger on a key. This helped me mentally prepare for the performance and helped me relax. You have all of the information you need for this exam. You know how many questions there are, what the format will be, and what material will be on there. Now all you have to do is take it. Believe me, you're ready! So, picture yourself answering the questions correctly and coming back to trouble sections with ease.

Former or Current Educator

In the past, some states used to require a person be an educator before they could be a school counselor. If you're currently an educator or have been, check with your state's department of education about licensing. There might be a temporary license you could receive while in your counseling program or you might not have to take an exam.

Also, some states give 'provisional' licenses for the first number of years and then you have to get another license afterwards. The state of Kentucky is an example of a state who gives an initial provisional license then after two years of experience another license is required.

Out of State

Getting your out of state license can be tricky. If you live near another state, it might be a good idea to go ahead and get your license because you might get a job there. I'm an example of that scenario. I live in the 'Greater Cincinnati/ Northern Kentucky Tristate Area'. That means I live within driving distance of Ohio, Kentucky, and Indiana. Currently, I live in Ohio and work in Kentucky. I have my school counselor license in both states. The area I live in has a lot of education career opportunities. So, I didn't know where I would end up getting a job at. I received my license in Ohio and an out of state license for Kentucky. For these two states, it made the most sense because my counseling program was in Ohio and Ohio requires a state exam passage. I wanted to make sure that I passed the Ohio Department of Education's exam before graduation since I wasn't guaranteed a job in Kentucky. Getting an out of state license in Kentucky was easy with their provisional license requirements. However, not all states have the same requirements. Some states offer reciprocity for those who are practicing school counselors.

Wrap Up

One of the most stressful parts of preparing for your career is the licensure requirements. There can be barriers to overcome if you're getting your degree in Ohio but want to work in Kentucky or Indiana. This can be the case with neighboring states. Always consult with your professors and Department of Education to make sure you are filling out the application correctly and taking the correct examination. It can be stressful to have to take an examination for your licensure. Make sure you are maintaining self-care and best practices. Remember the advice that you would give your students about taking exams and practice it. Don't look at licensure as a necessary evil, but as a credential that certifies our profession.

References

ASCA (2019). *State Certification Requirements*. Retrieved from American School Counselor Association:www.schoolcounselor.org/school-counselors-members/careers-roles/state-certification-requirements

Drexler, A. (2017, November 30). *6 Great Tips For Studying For The Praxis Exam*. Retrieved from College Raptor: www.collegeraptor.com/explore-careers/articles/majors-industries/6-great-tips-studying-praxis-exam/

Educational Testing Service (2018). *School Counselor Study Companion*. Retrieved from ETS: www.ets.org/s/praxis/pdf/5421.pdf

Educational Testing Service (2019). *How the Praxis® Tests are Scored*. Retrieved from ETS: www.ets.org/praxis/scores/understand/how/

Part II
New Graduate

4 Job Search and the Interview Process

As you near the end of your program, you will have started applying for jobs. This is probably the most frustrating and worrisome task. You might want to put up a warning signing for others around you, so they know you're on the job hunt, because you may be prone to mood swings! The school counseling field is competitive. It's important to know where and how to look for jobs. It can seem daunting to look for school counseling jobs because there are many websites that post education jobs.

Before we discuss how and where to look for school counseling jobs, we are going to go over the cover letter and resume. As with everything, there is some preparation that comes with searching for a job. Just about all employers ask for a cover letter and resume. These two items let the employers know who you are on paper and whether or not they want to interview you. That is why it's important to spend time on revising your cover letter and resume.

Cover Letter

A cover letter can serve multiple purposes. It can be an overview of why of you are applying for the position, an introductory statement of who are you and what you value, or a short response essay. Sometimes the employer will be specific about what they want in a cover letter or it can be open ended. Regardless, the cover letter can really help you stand out amongst other applicants. There are a few things to remember when you're writing your cover letter (Porges, 2012):

1. **Don't repeat what's on your resume.** You don't need to explain in depth about your internship experience. When you get an interview, there will be ample time to talk about your experiences. As in the example of my personal cover letter, I use the cover letter to share with employers my professional identity statement.
2. **Keep it short.** The statement 'less is more' applies to your cover letter. Keep it to three paragraphs and one single spaced page. Depending upon where you are in your career, your resume or CV might be longer than one page. So, make your cover letter concise and to the point.

3. **Address nobody.** If you don't know who you are addressing, then don't bother with 'To Whom it May Concern' or any other generic address. Just start your cover letter without an address.

4. **Send it as a PDF.** Have you ever tried to open a document that was created with another version of Word than what you have? Sometimes technology isn't universal. If you save something as .docx or .pages it might not open on another computer. The safest way to send any document is to save it as a PDF. Also, you don't have to worry about how the receiver will see the format of the document.

5. Never ever, ever use the following phrase, "My name is ___, and I am applying for the position as ____". Don't restate something the employer already knows.

6. **Close Strong.** Talk about how your worldview or experience give you the tools to do well at the job. This is why I use my professional identity statement in my cover letter. It is concise, to the point, and effective. Make sure it is brief, because otherwise it loses its purpose. You don't want to sound like you're preaching.

As you're writing your cover letter, keep in mind who you're writing it for. Not every school is identical in their needs and desires from a school counselor. Do your research about the school counseling program you're applying to and prepare to write your cover letter based on that. You want to make sure that you are showing them on paper how you're the best candidate for the job. The following cover letter example is foundational and easy to tweak. It is usually what I start with and revise as needed.

Resumes and Curriculum Vitae (CV)

As you know from your many years of schooling and working various jobs, you will need to have either a resume or a curriculum vitae (CV). Coming straight out of graduate school, your employers aren't going to expect a CV. This is going to depend on a person's prior and current professional experience. This section will focus on writing a resume.

Resumes

Resumes will be something you write the rest of your life, because every job and other organization that requires an application will ask for one. You should be updating it a minimum of once a year depending upon what you're doing. As a recent graduate, your 'counseling' resume might not have a lot of experience outside of internship. That is okay! However, you might have been able to present at a conference or became president of your Chi Sigma Iota chapter. That needs to go on your resume.

There are key elements to writing a resume. You can think of your resume as a marketing brochure of yourself. It should be professional, informative, and concise. As a school counselor, it can be two pages long. You should maintain Times New Roman, 10–12 font for the body of your resume. However, don't feel like you have to stick with the traditional margin settings. If you think something is relevant and important to be on your resume, change the size of your font and adjust the page margins. Be careful not to squeeze too much on your resume that makes it overwhelming. Follow the best practices for writing a resume. You will have more time to expand on your resume during the interview.

Best Practices for Writing a Resume (American School Counselor Association, 2010)

1. Only have your current job and previous relative job positions. You don't need to have every internship you had in undergraduate school. If you are a current professional, maintain the same rule.
2. Put the most important content in the first 2/3 of the page.
3. Use verbs to describe your achievements.
4. Emphasize skills that are related to the field in which you are applying.
5. Avoid self-serving or subjective descriptions.
6. Be achievement- and results-oriented in your position descriptions.
7. Proofread.

These good resume practices are universal no matter what profession you're in. Resumes are meant to be an overview of your achievements, not a bibliography. The minimum should be put on paper and the rest discussed in person. The foundational elements that will go in your resume are:

1. A heading with your name, address, home phone, and work phone
2. Objective or skills summary
3. Education
4. Certification
5. Counseling experience (listed from most recent to earliest experience)
6. Related work experience
7. Professional memberships/affiliations
8. Special skills (computer, foreign language, etc.)
9. Honors and awards
10. Extracurricular interests
11. References (separate sheet)

The Job Search

No doubt while you are writing your cover letters and resumes you are looking on websites for available positions. It can be confusing looking for school counseling positions on education sites. Not all listings are posted on the school's website and you have to go to the district site. I have found district websites to be the best go-to place for listings. However, they're not always current. When I was in the first initial stages of my job search I emailed every principal or head counselor in the Greater Cincinnati/Northern Kentucky region. This may seem absurd, but I received a lot of positive responses. Even if they weren't hiring, the people I heard from did not respond negatively to my inquiry. One of the principals I emailed ended up being my employer. Making the connections and expanding your network is important! Also, when you're looking for open positions, check with your professors and professional school counseling organizations. Of course, you should always check the job sites such as Indeed.com and SchoolSpring. A lot of the positions I applied for I found on a job search engine.

Some other things you can do while you're applying for jobs are to keep gaining experience and network. Volunteer with youth and start collecting data early. When you get your first school counseling position you'll have to start using data in your program. It's good to start doing that in any professional experience you're getting. Make a portfolio of the things you've done at your internship site. This is really helpful when you're in an interview. It also shows that you took time to plan and prepare for the interview.

The Interview

Interviewing for a school counselor position was unlike any other job interview I had been in. You are given various scenarios that could happen in school and asked how you would handle them. There can be a panel with the superintendent and a school board member or just the principal. One of the interviews I had consisted of the superintendent, a board member, two principals, an assistant principal, and a school counselor. That interview was very intimidating as a school counselor fresh out of graduate school. I did my best to be prepared though. I had my portfolio ready to show them, was dressed professionally, and responded to their questions with confidence. In a different scenario, I have been in an interview with only the principal and the assistant principal. You might be in an interview where there isn't a school counselor present.

I've mentioned making a portfolio to give to the employer at the interview. I use a three-ring binder with protector sheets and divider tabs. I include a table of contents in the front for organization. Topics to include are (The Spirited School Counselor, 2016):

Professional Experience

This would include your resume, license or letter of eligibility from your state's department of education, references, and letters of recommendation. Also have extra copies of your resume to hand out at the interview.

1. Counseling Approach

    I put my counseling philosophy, counseling beliefs, and my personal statement in the portfolio. It would also be good to add a one-page summary of how your experience and the ASCA model align in this section.

2. Professional Development

3. Lesson Plans

    This section includes lesson plans that are age-specific and position-specific. For example, if I am interviewing at an elementary school then I include a classroom lesson for two different ages as well as a group lesson. I also include any examples of using data to drive my school counseling program. Put whatever items in this section that you did during your internship. These items may not be for the age-level that the interview is for, but it shows I know how to collect, analyze, and use data appropriately.

4. Coursework

    If you want to include your transcript, this is the section you would put it in. When I was interviewing for my first school counselor position, I didn't add my transcripts to my portfolio. I can't imagine a situation while being interviewed that I would need to show my transcripts.

Possible Questions Asked at an Interview

The most important part of the interview is the questions you will be asked. It can be scary going into interview and not having a sense of what types of questions will be asked of you. I was asked by a number of schools how I would handle a specific scenario. The good news is that there are lists of typical questions that schools use. A few of those questions could possibly be (Hughins, Learn How to Ace Your Interview for a School Counselor Position, 2019):

1. Why do you want to become a school counselor?
2. What do you want to accomplish on this position?
3. What did you like the most on your studies?
4. Why counseling, and not teaching?
5. Why do you want to work as a counselor at our school? Why not some other institution?
6. What is it that you like about working with (grade level) students?
7. How would you gain the trust of the students?
8. How do you handle criticism?
9. What goals would you set for yourself in this job?
10. How would you approach individual student planning?
11. How important is the paperwork for you?
12. How do you imagine a typical day in work as a counselor?
13. How will you evaluate your school counseling program?

14. What is the role of the school counselor in relation to teachers, parents, administrators, and other counselors?
15. How would you work with a difficult parent?
16. How would you work with children from orphanages?
17. What would you do if one your students told you she was pregnant?
18. What would you do if a student shared with you their suicide plans?
19. One of your students told you they were gay. How would you react?
20. One student wanted to drop out of school. What would you do?
21. Tell me about the situation when you experienced conflict with one of your colleagues.
22. Describe a situation when you felt pressure in work.
23. Describe a goal you achieved in your teaching (counseling) practice, and who helped you with achieving the goal.
24. How do you handle stress?
25. Why should we hire you, and not the other job applicants?

This isn't a comprehensive list, but it gives you the general idea of what schools are looking for when hiring a school counselor. Check ASCA's website for a complete list of questions. Many schools take their questions from their site. Also, Glen Hughins has a book out titled "School Counselor Guide, Brilliant Answers to 25 Difficult School Counselor Interview Questions". Here is a sample of a question and answer from his book (Hughins, School Counselor Interview Guide – Learn How to Succeed in Your Job Interview, 2019):

Q 9: How do you handle criticism?

Hint: School counselors often face criticism, from both students and teachers. Tell the hiring committee that you are ready to face constructive criticism, as you **believe it helps you to become better in what you do**.

You can also emphasize that you **do not take criticism personally,** and it won't affect your relationship with the colleagues, or the students. It is simply a part of your job.

Sample answers

- I try to do my job well, and I care about the results. Logically it sometimes hurts when someone criticizes my work—though they may be right. But I am aware that counselors are often criticized. I will try to understand each negative comment, and learn from it.
- Look, I am just starting in this job. I've graduated from college, I've been through internship, but I understand there's still much to learn, and improve in the way I do my job. I am not afraid of criticism, just the opposite—I am happy to hear it, and I believe that feedback should flow freely at school, in all directions. Each critical remark helps me to reevaluate my

work, and to become better in what I do. And I plan to keep this attitude in my entire career, since thing always evolve, students always change, and what works great with them today may not work in ten years' time.

Questions to Ask at an Interview

New counselors should research each school/district and come up with questions they want to ask during the interview. This lets the employer know that you took time to prepare for the interview and decide whether or not the school is a good fit for you. Thinking of questions during the interview will be hard so write a few down before you go. Here are a handful of questions for you to consider as you're preparing for your interview (Hansen, Questions to Ask in an Interview, 2015).

- About how many students would be in my case load?
- How many other counselors are on campus (or in the district)?
- How are the counseling duties divided (if there are several counselors)—meaning, does everyone have similar tasks, or does one counselor primarily handle scheduling, another career, another scholarship, and another personal counseling?
- How structured would my days be, and how much flexibility would I have in scheduling activities such as small groups, classroom presentations, parent phone calls, documentation time, etc.?
- What kind of documentation system or format does your counseling department use?
- What (if any) additional duties would I have on campus?
- When are meetings usually held (before or after school? Lunchtime? Or during the regular school day?) and how often?
- Would I be using a specific curriculum, or developing my own based on student needs?
- When does the counselors' school year begin and end? (particularly important at H.S. level)
- Are your counselors on the same salary schedule as teachers?
- Are you expecting or seeking any major changes in your counseling department in the next few years? If so, what changes do you foresee?
- How open is your staff to programs such as Peer Mediation, student retreats, and other programs designed to build community in your school?
- What do your school and the nearby community most need right now from this counseling program?

Helpful Interview Tips

One of the biggest tips I can give for the interview is to breathe. It's hard to be relaxed in an interview, because it's a stressful situation. Channel that stress to help you in the interview. Think of the advice you would give your students during a stressful time. Use self-talk to remind yourself that you have the knowledge and the skills for the job (CareerOneStop, 2019).

1. **Review common questions.**
2. **Make a list of questions to ask during the interview.**
3. **Be prepared.**
4. **On the day of the interview, remember to:**
   a. Plan your schedule so you arrive 10 to 15 minutes early.
   b. Go by yourself.
   c. Look professional. Dress in a manner appropriate to the job.
   d. Leave your coffee, soda, or backpack at home or in your car.
   e. Turn off your cell phone.
   f. Bring your sense of humor and SMILE!
5. **Display confidence during the interview**, but let the interviewer start the dialogue. Send a positive message with your body language.
   a. Shake hands firmly, but only if a hand is offered to you first.
   b. Maintain eye contact.
   c. Listen carefully. Welcome all questions, even the difficult ones, with a smile.
   d. Give honest, direct answers.
6. **Develop answers in your head before you respond.** If you don't understand a question, ask for it to be repeated or clarified. You don't have to rush, but you don't want to appear indecisive.
7. **End the interview with a good impression.** A positive end to the interview is another way to ensure your success.
   a. Be courteous and allow the interview to end on time.
   b. Restate any strengths and experiences that you might not have emphasized earlier.
   c. Mention a particular accomplishment or activity that fits the job.
   d. If you want the job, say so!
   e. Find out if there will be additional interviews.
   f. Ask when the employer plans to make a decision.
   g. Indicate a time when you may contact the employer to learn of the decision.
8. **Don't forget to send a thank-you note or letter after the interview.**

References

American School Counselor Association (2010). *Job Search Skills for the Professional School Counselor*. Retrieved from Ohio School Counselor Association: https://ohioschoolcounselor.org/Resources/Documents/ASCA%20Job%20Search%20Tips%20for%20School%20Counselors.pdf

CareerOneStop (2019). *Interviews Are Your Chance to Sell Your Skills and Abilities*. Retrieved from CareerOneStop: www.careeronestop.org/JobSearch/Interview/interview-tips.aspx

Hansen, S. (2015). *Questions to Ask in an Interview*. Retrieved from School Counseling Zone: www.school-counseling-zone.com/interview.html

Hughins, G. (2019, January 30). *Learn How to Ace Your Interview for a School Counselor Position.* Retrieved from InterviewPenguin: http://interviewpenguin.com/school-counselor-interview-questions-and-tips/

Hughins, G. (2019). *School Counselor Interview Guide – Learn How to Succeed in Your Job Interview*. Retrieved from InterviewPenguin: https://interviewpenguin.com/school-counselor-interview-guide-ebook/

Porges, S. (2012, August 29). *6 Secrets To Writing A Great Cover Letter*. Retrieved from Forbes: www.forbes.com/sites/sethporges/2012/08/29/6-secrets-to-writing-a-great-cover-letter/#2beda46d73d7

The Spirited School Counselor (2016, July 5). *Creating a Career Portfolio for Interviews*. Retrieved from The Spirited School Counselor: https://thespiritedschoolcounselor. wordpress.com/2016/07/05/creating-a-career-portfolio-for-interviews/

5 Rejected to Hired

Navigating Rejection

Not being offered a school counseling position is inevitable, but trainees are rarely prepared to handle that rejection. There are many questions that run through one's mind as he/she reads the generic email that says, "thank you but no thanks". I received a handful of the exact same email from principals that said they had filled the position within a week of interviewing me. Dealing with those emotions are hard and made me question whether I was in the right field.

It was nearing the end of July when I had an interview with the head principal and assistant principle. I was beginning to feel despair and desperate with the onset of schools getting ready to start without me working in one of them. I had numerous interviews that led to the standardized rejection email. It was something I had come to anticipate and was desperately trying to figure out what I would do if I didn't get a job in a school. This wasn't how I should be reacting to rejection, but my emotions were consuming me. My previous experiences had not set me up for success in reacting to rejection. I had spent four years of undergraduate school studying to be a music major only to come out and find the job market empty. So, I tried my backup plan and the backup to my backup plan, but they had all ended up in rejection. Needless to say, my coping skills were dull. Thankfully, I had/have a really supportive family system that helped me get through the rough times. Those moments built in me resilience and grit. These are two characteristics that will stay with me forever. After I interviewed for the school counseling position, the principal told me he would get back to me by the end of that same week. I left the interview and honestly didn't look back. It was one of those times where I had felt like giving up and just letting the 'chips fall where they may'. I was tired of being stressed and anxious about the situation. It was two days later when the principal called me back and offered me the position! Things ended up working out, but not like I had planned. I wouldn't change my experiences because of what they taught me.

Resiliency 'Grit'

Not hearing back from an interview or not landing an interview can lead you down the road of self-pity and shake your confidence. It doesn't help when you start seeing your friends and colleagues obtain school counselor positions being posted on all social media outlets celebrating. No one said rejection is easy, but you can get better at handling it. What can you do instead of drowning in self-pity and self-doubt? Or when it feels like you're a failure and that you weren't meant for the career. One thing to remember is that emotions aren't facts. They do not control you! We have been given these universal tools in our counseling programs to help others and they can also help us. Instead of focusing on the negative start focusing on building resiliency 'grit' and having a growth mindset.

> Resiliency involves meeting challenges or setbacks with a constructive approach and focusing on the opportunities created when things don't go as planned. Resilient people keep a positive, adaptable attitude when thrown curveballs. To become resilient, you must understand that success and rejection go hand-in-hand, and that you simply cannot advance if you always play it safe
>
> (Wilding, How to Move on When You
> Didn't Land the Job, 2019)

Angela Duckworth is the Founder and CEO of Character Lab and *New York Times* best-selling author of *Grit: Power of Passion and Perseverance*. She and her colleagues have sought to help students overcome behavioral issues through character development. Grit is both a skill and trait. When you see a talented athlete or musician you might say they're a prodigy. Their talent must be natural and probably comes easy to them. What you're not seeing when an athlete or musician is performing is the dedication they have given to hone their talent. They put in the work and effort to practice. They had to have grit in order to achieve success. Grit is realizing that when you fail, and you are rejected, those are opportunities to grow.

Having grit and being resilient means having a growth mindset. When you have a growth mindset you understand that you don't have a job 'yet'. Just because you didn't get the school counseling position you interviewed for doesn't mean you're not going to get one ever. You just haven't gotten one 'yet'! Growth mindset is about looking at abilities and talents from a learning perspective. What can you learn from the interview that didn't land you the job? How does this help you grow as an individual and as a professional? Using the skills you learned in your master's program, reframe your thoughts to drive away self-pity. Job rejections doesn't define who you are or determine if you're a good counselor. It doesn't decide for you whether or not you should be a school counselor. Those rejections offer you the opportunity to refine the skills that might be lacking or turn your weaknesses into strengths.

Helpful Tips

There are a lot of articles and resources on handling rejection, grit, and growth mindset. These won't just help you with handling a job rejection, but in life.

These will be tools you can give to your future or current students. I want to leave you with a few more helpful tips on how to handle rejection from *Psychology Today* (Brooks, Rejection and the Job Search Get used to it and learn from it., 2017) and *Business Insider* (Dumb Little Man, 2011):

Don't take it personally

You might be thinking how can I not take it personally? If you are fresh out of graduate school, you're probably applying for every possible position and not considering whether or not the school is a good fit for you. However, every employer is looking for a person who will be the right fit for their school. They're taking into consideration the programs they already have in place and what person will best implement those programs.

Ask for feedback

Some employers will give you honest feedback on your interview if you ask. If you're going to ask for feedback, you need to listen and accept what is being said. Don't dispute or argue with the person giving the feedback. Accept the feedback with gratitude and apply it as you see fit. Constructive criticism can help you when applying and interviewing for another position. There might have been something you missed on your resume or cover letter, or you might need to show more confidence in your interview.

Accept rejection and learn from it

Learning from rejection is the best way to ensure success in the future. If you learned from your interview that you seemed less than enthusiastic about the position, then you need to think about why you weren't enthused. Was the school the right fit for you? Were you the right fit for the school? There have been times when I was very upset about being rejected for a job position, but when I took a step back and analyzed I realized that it was the best decision. Sometimes I learned that I wasn't passionate about the mission and vision of the school, and other times I learned that leadership preferences weren't compatible. It's important to know what type of supervision leadership you want, because they will help you succeed in your position.

Maintain your focus of control

There are two types of control, external and internal. External refers to things outside of ourselves; whereas, internal refers to our own emotions and behaviors. One of those should be the main focus of control for you. If you thought internal, you are correct. We cannot control others. It can be very stressful to try to maintain external control when in reality we don't possess it. When I start to feel stressed and overwhelmed, I remind myself that I don't have external control, but I do have internal control. I try to focus on managing my emotions and my behaviors through mindfulness and Reality Therapy. Just as I don't have external control neither does anyone else, even if they think they do. When you realize that you solely have the power to control your emotions and behaviors rejections become easier to manage.

Prepare yourself psychologically for rejection

It is important to be confident when applying for a job and during the interview, but you also have to be realistic. School counselor positions can be competitive. Depending on where you're applying there could be over 50 people interviewing for the one counselor position open. Mentally prepare yourself that you might not get an interview or the job. Be compassionate with yourself and do self-talk. Remind yourself that this singular job does not define who you are as a counselor and does not determine your worth. Take time for self-care and surround yourself by people who support you.

Realize rejection is progression, not regression

This may seem like an oxymoron, because when you don't get a job that seems like regression. There are million negative thoughts that can run through one's mind. It can be easy to descend into a dark spiral of "I'll never get a job, I'm going to live in my parent's basement, I'll have to eat ramen noodles the rest of my life, I'm a disappointment to my significant other, I won't be able to put my kids through college". You know just how easily and quickly one thought can go from frustrated to 'the end of the world'. I know of a school counselor who didn't land a counseling position until two years after graduation. She worked at a courthouse doing something entirely unrelated to counseling. There were days when she felt really disappointed in not landing that dream counseling job, but she continued to build relationships and network within the schools and ended up getting a position as the college counseling at a school. It still wasn't her 'dream' counseling position, but she gave it her 110% and it paid off. She ended up getting her dream job as a school counselor at the high school she had attended. Her resiliency, grit, and growth mindset had turned her rejection into progression.

Be patient! You will get a school counseling position and will get the opportunity to impact lives. When you're hired take with you what you learned while waiting. Keep being resilient and having a growth mindset. These skills will help throughout every area of your life!

Hired!

Congratulations, you are now a first-year school counselor! This is an exciting time when you get to buy office supplies, books, and Pinterest your office décor (I did!). However, you might have mixed emotions about the school you're going to be working at. That is normal, and it can take time to get adjusted to the new environment. Starting a new job is like the first day of school again, and it literally will be for you. You will walk into the mandatory faculty and staff week before school starts to get ready for the year. There you will meet the rest of the faculty and it will be intimidating. The morale at every school is different. Depending upon what the faculty, staff, and administration have experienced you might be given the 'cold shoulder' until they get to know you. Other schools will be welcoming from the moment you walk in the door. The biggest piece of advice I can offer is to be open-minded and be yourself.

What to expect...

The first-year is exciting because your general enthusiasm for the profession and landing the job will show. The students, faculty and staff, and administration will feel your enthusiasm! Let that continue throughout the school year even when times get stressful. The year will be stressful, hard, challenging, chaotic, rewarding, fun, and frustrating. Take everything in stride and one day at a time.

As a first-year school counselor in a blended middle/high school, I was the only school counselor on staff. That was okay, because I only had 200 students. I was well under the ASCA counselor to student ratio. However, that meant I was the go-to person for every scenario. If the juniors and seniors had college questions, I was the college counselor. When the middle school girls had friendship drama, I was the personal counselor. The students who needed accommodations or supplemental resources, I was the academic counselor. I did it all! From testing to implementing new programs, I was the sole school counselor. I tried to do it all without complaint, because I knew my colleagues had higher caseloads. Regardless, I was very busy!

When I started my first-year school counseling position, I was automatically a part of the administrative team. This was something I wasn't expecting and didn't know how to navigate. I had to rely on my principal and assistant principal to guide me through being an administrator. Learn to expect the unexpected! There will be duties you will be asked to perform that aren't part of the ASCA National Model. These may be non-negotiable with your administration. Remember why you chose to be a school counselor and turn that non-counseling duty into an opportunity.

Expect there to be good days and bad days. Not every student is going to like you and that's okay. Depending on the age, they don't know if they even like themselves. Some students will only give you respect when they feel you've earned it. Try not to take it personally, because there is probably a reason why that student has a hard time trusting others. There will be days when it is fun to be a school counselor and there are days when it's heart-breaking. There will be times when parents feel like you're not doing enough for their child and teachers feel like you're against them. These are the times to have compassion on yourself and take time for self-care.

Finally, keep your expectations realistic! This includes with yourself. Don't expect to implement the ASCA National Model your first year. That is a lofty goal and you'll be disappointed when you don't obtain it. You can start with small goals that lead to becoming RAMP certified. Expect to make mistakes and to learn from them, expect to make friends with the faculty, expect to shed tears, and expect to love your profession!

What to do in the beginning...

The beginning of the year is chaotic! If you're in a high school, you might be helping the seniors with their college applications and writing recommendation letters. No matter what grade level, you might have to help with new student orientation and parent nights. If you're going to give guidance lessons, you'll be working with teachers on scheduling. The beginning of the year is generally very busy. Some things to do initially are (School Counselor Stephanie, 2017),

1. **Get a calendar and planner to maintain organization.** I spend a lot of time with my school's academic calendar and my planner at the beginning of the year. Odds are there are major events scheduled by the administration before school begins. You can get an idea of how to structure your year by starting with the all school events. I use both electronic and physical calendars to keep organized. Use whatever works for you!

2. **Prepare your office and counseling space.** I love decorating my office! I want it to be a safe space for students. I have spent hours repurposing bookshelves and decorating mason jars. The little details are important, because it will create the ambiance of the room. My large room feels like a lounge space for the students. I keep candy stocked and sometimes snacks. Then my small, personal office feels warm and private.

3. **Plan your guidance lessons with teachers at the very beginning of the year.** Being proactive with teachers will always work in your benefit. They don't just create lesson plans for a day or week at a time, but they prepare units for the entire semester and year. There might be days in their schedules that they know they're going to need a sub and you can teach your guidance lessons then. Class time is precious! Try to collaborate with them on what you're going to be teaching and what they're teaching. This is a great way to advocate for yourself and the profession.

4. **Introduce yourself and your role to the school.** It's important for the entire school to know who you are and what your role is. This might be something the school counseling department does at the school already, but if not make it your responsibility to introduce yourself. The fact is that there are folks who don't know who the school counselor is or what they do.

If possible, make a PowerPoint presentation to give at a faculty meeting. Go into all the classrooms and give a guidance lesson on you. This should be top priority as a new school counselor. Some items to include in your presentation are:

    a. The official characteristics and duties of our role in the school (according to the guidelines set by governing state, board, campus, national or professional organization).

    b. How we can support teachers in their work with students.

    c. How we support students.

    d. Procedures for how staff and students can utilize our services—especially in crisis situations.

5. **Meet with your administration team.** It's important to meet with your administration team those first few weeks of school. Let the principal and the assistant principals know who you are. Ask them what their goals are for the year and figure out how you can help meet those goals in the counseling office. If you have a school counseling department, there might be a school counselor who oversees the department. That person might be the liaison between your department and the administration. Let them know that you want to align your goals for the year with those of the school. Show interest in what is happening within the building.

Take a deep breath, hold it, and exhale! You will survive the first year, I promise, if you're following best practices.

Best Practices

I want to end this chapter with more general information that will help you throughout the year. These tips come from the American Counseling Association (Cordisco, 2015).

1. **Keep notes.** Whether it's electronically or on paper, it's good practice to keep notes. You never know when you'll need to reference a meeting you've had with a student, parent, or faculty member.

2. **Find a mentor.** This can be done formally or informally. Some districts assign mentors to new staff members, but others don't. I was not given a mentor, but I learned very quickly that I needed to have someone in my corner who had been around a long time and knew the ropes. This was one of the first things I did when I started my position. Since I was the only school counselor in the building I needed a seasoned school counselor to get advice from. This person really helped me through the good and bad days of counseling.

3. **Befriend the secretaries and custodians.** The secretaries are the eyes and ears of the school. When one of our secretaries is out sick, we barely

manage as a school. I rely heavily on them for help with the educational program software, office supplies, and general school information. They are some of my favorite people! I really appreciate a clean school. Not many people realize how hard it can be to keep a school clean. A school runs as a team and everyone's job is important. Don't take for granted the folks who are staff.

4. Document everything (**everything**), and never act alone. In this era of school counseling, this has become more important than ever. When sending emails, think about what you're writing and don't put anything in writing that could come back to haunt you. If you have concerns, speak to the person face-to-face or give them a call. On the other hand, put anything you may need to revisit later in writing. In a pinch, it always helps to be able to refer back to an email or a document you have kept to make sure you are on the right track. If I'm really hesitant about an email, I will have my principal or assistant principal proof my email before I send it. Don't be afraid to ask for advice or guidance!

5. Practice self-care. Self-care is important to prevent burn-out. Treat yourself to coffee or lunch once a month. I will get lunch or coffee with another teacher a few times a month. This helps me take a break from the building for short time and recharge for the rest of the day. Don't neglect to take care of yourself!

6. **Be present with the students.** This may seem obvious, but it can be hard to be present with the students when you have other things competing for your attention. I keep an agenda of what I want to accomplish for the day, but I put in time for disruptions that may come up. This helps me to be focused and present when I'm with the students. Make it your responsibility to be visible to students. Greet them in the mornings at the door and walk about the halls in between bells. Go to the sporting events, attend the school concerts, art shows, and chaperone dances. Let the students know that you are invested in them.

7. Make positive phone calls or send positive emails to parents, especially if things have been challenging for that particular student or family lately. I send out a monthly newsletter in our all school mailing. This lets the parents know what I'm doing in the classroom and what important events I'm hosting. I also like to email parents when there is something positive happening within their student's life. It's important to celebrate the successes in our student's lives!

8. Offer to cover classes for teachers for five minutes while they run to the bathroom. I often forget the amount of flexibility I have to close the door to my office and have some quiet working time, use the bathroom whenever I feel like or take lunch whenever I want to. To that end, I have found that teachers are so grateful when I offer to stay with their students for a minute or two, so the teachers can run to the restroom. I doubt that's what they were referring to when they talked about collaboration

with colleagues during new teacher orientation, but it is collaboration nonetheless!

9. Check in monthly with classroom teachers to see if there are any concerns. Don't let the teachers always come to you when they have a problem. Check in with them about student behavior and progress. This shows you're invested in the students and care enough to be proactive. This also lets them know that you care about their class.

10. **Decide your after-school workload.** This is a personal preference and something you have to decide for yourself, but as a first-year school counselor I limited my response to emails between normal business hours. I would only respond to emails after I left work if they were an emergency. If you're a person, like me, who has their email on their phone, not responding to emails can be hard. You have to decide, if it's not an emergency, if it can wait until the following day. I would try to keep this rule on weekends and holidays as well.

Refer back to these tips as you go throughout the year. Inevitably there will be times when you're overwhelmed and need a good reminder. Keep a list of resources and books to reference. Remember to read over your mission and vision statements. It can be easy to get busy with everyday duties and forget why you're doing it the first place. Write it on an index card, laminate it, and memorize it! This will help you advocate for yourself, the profession, and students.

References

Brooks, K. (2017, July 14). *Rejection and the Job Search: Get used to it and learn from it.* Retrieved from Psychology Today: www.psychologytoday.com/us/blog/career-transitions/201707/rejection-and-the-job-search

Confident Counselor Stephanie (2017, August 30). *How to Present Your Counseling Program and Role to Staff.* Retrieved from Confident Counselor: https://confidentcounselors.com/2017/08/30/present-counseling-program-role/

Cordisco, R.M. (2015, September 7). *Surviving Your First Year as a School Counselor.* Retrieved from Counselor Today: https://ct.counseling.org/2015/09/surviving-your-first-year-as-a-school-counselor/#

Dumb Little Man (2011, May 17). *How To Handle Rejection Like A Pro.* Retrieved from Business Insider: www.businessinsider.com/facing-rejection-here-are-5-key-steps-to-handle-them-like-a-pro-2011-5

School Counselor Stephanie (2017, August 30). *How to Present Your Counseling Program and Role to Staff.* Retrieved from Confident Counselor: https://confidentcounselors.com/2017/08/30/present-counseling-program-role/

Wilding, M.J. (2019). *How to Move on When You Didn't Land the Job.* Retrieved from The Muse: www.themuse.com/advice/how-to-move-on-when-you-didnt-land-the-job

Part III

The First Year

6 The Illusion v. the Reality

With Guest Writer Morgan Capucini

Starting a new job is exciting and it is easy to glamorize it. The first six months consists mainly of learning and getting acclimated to the position. This is how the first few months of my first year were. I was in the mindset of changing everything and creating a school counseling program based on the ASCA National Model. School counseling is hard, and the work can be daunting. There were times I was ready to quit and admit defeat. It was important that I had a support system that helped during this time. This chapter will discuss the reality of school counseling (i.e., not taking student's behavior personally, applying constructive criticism, and regulating one's own emotions).

When I first took the position and looked at my schedule, I thought I would have plenty of time to work on making my program RAMP certified. I started with creating lesson plans that included prep-post tests to start collecting data. I gave a needs assessment to my sophomore class. We got a new college and career curriculum that I would have to implement at the start of second semester. I worked furiously on researching what curriculum would be good for my sophomores, because I didn't want to do the same thing that the previous counselor did. I wanted to make the counseling department my own. I wanted it to reflect my vision for the school. So, I did, and I stayed busy. I still stay busy!

Those first few months I call the honeymoon phase, because everything seems to be perfect. After all, I had a job, what more could I ask for? The teachers were welcoming, and the students were friendly. I was optimistic and hopeful about the state of our school. There was nothing wrong with my perspective, but it was a bit unrealistic and naïve. I didn't have a fellow counselor to give me tips about handling frustrated teachers, students, and parents or how to navigate the environment of the school. As I have mentioned, every school is not a 'one-size-fits-all' for employment. I didn't have anyone in the school building guide me through the ins and outs of what it meant to be a counselor there. My principal did have me reach out to a seasoned school counselor at another school in our Diocese and I would meet with her at least once a quarter. That was extremely helpful in terms of consultation.

Coming out of graduate school I was ready to implement the ASCA model wherever I went and advocate for the profession with gusto. If one ends up working in a school who does not implement the ASCA model, it is hard to convince the administrators and faculty to change. It doesn't happen in a few months or even a few years, because change is hard. I realized this when I started unintentionally stepping on toes. Luckily, my principal was in favor of moving towards the ASCA model. He allowed me to do as much as I could with using Social Emotional Learning, DBT (Dialectical Behavioral Therapy) for schools, and creating my own programming. However, I wasn't going to get out of being the testing administrator. There are just some battles that won't be won. That wasn't when reality hit me.

Real Life as a First-Year School Counselor (Guest Writer Morgan Capucini)

Morgan Capucini, School Counselor at Williamsburg Middle High School, shares her experience as a first-year school counselor.

I remember being in graduate school and seeing a fellow student wearing a t-shirt that stated "WORLD'S OKAYEST SCHOOL COUNSELOR". I thought it was funny and laughed to myself, hoping that when I became a school counselor no one would ever purchase that shirt for me. Fast forward about a year later when I was sitting in my first "real" school counseling job staring at a mountain of files and reports. My eyes were tired, my head was throbbing and my heart was racing. I felt like the whole world could collapse and I wouldn't even care. As I grabbed one of the many folders in front of me to dive into the paperwork, I remembered the shirt I had seen in graduate school. In this moment, I hoped that I would even live up to being an "ok" school counselor.

I reflect back on that first year a lot and most of the memories are positive. For context you should know that I have a caseload of 600 students, grades 6–12 and am the only school counselor in my district. I am someone who loves to learn and try new things and the majority of that year was just that—trying, assessing and evolving. I learned everything from how to create and code courses for state funding to how to sit with someone when they find out their best friend in the entire world has suddenly died. Each day brought me a new adventure, some undesired and frustrating, but ultimately those adventures reminded me of the importance of the role of the school counselor.

Knowing how important I was to my school and the students I serve was the one thing I could hold onto that first year. I often got caught up in my head because it felt like I was always working so hard to meet the needs on my seemingly never ending to-do list, yet it never got any smaller. There were days where I would come into the building with three simple task related goals in my mind, only to leave eight hours later with *none* of those goals accomplished. I had to keep reminding myself that my job, as unpredictable as it could be, was important and that all important things take passion and time.

Today, I am happy to say that I am in my third year as a school counselor at the same district that I began at. As a third year, it is easier in many ways because I have confidence and experience to carry me, but, I think it is important to relay that there is always [something] unexpected thrown my way. While this can cause me frustration or sometimes throw me into a tizzy of "What do you mean the Department of Education changed that again?!", I wouldn't trade my job for the world. Being a school counselor and what it means to be a school counselor is an ever changing force—but those that do it cannot forget that it is important work. While I strive to be a great school counselor, there are days that I leave satisfied knowing I did my best and it only turned out "ok". I leave on those days remembering the t-shirt I saw during my graduate program and smile, understanding exactly what that shirt meant.

New York University's school counseling program has a series called School Counselor Stories. They published articles that school counselors submit about their experiences. Angela Bassett, an elementary school counselor, shared this in her article (Bassett, 2016):

As an elementary school counselor, I enjoy watching students and their parents walk into school each morning. They interact in a way that tells their unique story; it's interesting to observe their interactions.

Being a school counselor has helped me grow in ways I didn't realize I needed to. I had believed that becoming a school counselor was a natural, personal progression for me—first teaching, then my master's program. I knew I enjoyed helping and encouraging people, so I figured I was ready for the task at hand. However, my desire to help and encourage people was not enough to keep me motivated. I was on the fast track to burnout and knew it was time to change my thinking. I couldn't please everyone all of the time. I had to learn to delegate and let others lead. There were going to be times when I had to stand on the boundary line and not give into expectation.

Being a school counselor is rewarding and filled with rich experiences. We have the "inside look" into the nooks and crannies of people's life, gaining a deeper understanding of what makes them unique. As a school counselor, we see students, peers, and parents and the interactions between all of them. Understanding this dynamic also allows us to build a stronger case conceptualization for our students. Strong case conceptualizations are essential for school counselors. We look at all aspects of student and family life to help form opinions of how to improve academic and long-term success. We look at factors that could contribute to positive and negative behaviors. We ascertain developmental concerns and family changes for the purpose of providing feedback that will help families in treatment.

I have faced 10 years of many different kinds of conflicts and watched people go through life transitions. There have been times I needed to think about if I wanted to continue. There is no doubt I have changed. I have become stronger, braver, and capable of handling many different situations. I have learned how to let go of trying to control everything. It has been a unique gift in my life. I am honored and privileged to be in the position of leading and guiding lives. I became a school counselor to make a difference, one life at a time.

Kirstin Perry, 2018 School Counselor of the Year, gives this advice to first-year school counselors (Barrick, 2018):

I always tell my interns the same thing (which was something told to me once by a professor): 'You will learn the first third of what you need to know during your coursework; you will learn the second third of what you need to know during your internship; and you will learn the final third of what you need to know during your first year as a professional school counselor.' In other words, do not feel like you need to know everything. You are still learning, and it is okay not to know what to do sometimes.

If you are the only school counselor in your school, like I am, I recommend making a list of school counselors at other schools that you can call if you need advice, have questions, or want to share resources.

I also recommend sitting down with your principal before the school year starts, and periodically throughout the year, to discuss your program goals and expectations. This has always worked for me. Rather than wonder, I always ask to hear feedback so I can continually improve. Be open to any feedback—there is nothing wrong with making mistakes. We all do!

Finally, listen to the staff, students, parents, and your community. They will tell you what the school needs and guide your program. The first year is definitely a year of listening and taking notes. You will never have to wonder if what you are doing is right for the school, if you listen—especially to the students! They will tell it to you direct.

Brian Coleman, 2019 School Counselor of the Year, gave advice on the challenges, impact, and lessons he's learned being a school counselor (Coleman, 2019):

What are some of the challenges in school counseling today?

The most persistent challenges I see are: Imbalanced counselor-to-student ratios. The absence of school counselors in school environments. School stakeholders' confusion/misunderstanding as relates to the school counselor's role and potential in school communities. Gaps in the educational outcomes for marginalized student populations. Inconsistent buy-in for social and emotional learning and holistic student development in schools. Limited pre-professional training as relates to diverse learning supports, career and post-secondary advising. Real and perceived divestment in public education at the local, state, and national levels.

What impact can school counselors make on students today?
School counselors can impact students in a variety of ways across the academic, person/social, and college/career areas of students' lives. Impact can include everything from increased self-esteem and self-advocacy to improved attendance and access to a viable post-secondary program. More than anything, I think school counselors can give students opportunities to be seen, heard, and affirmed in ways that may be difficult for students to find in other areas of their lives.

What life lessons have you learned being a school counselor?
Be yourself. Failure is a wonderful teacher. Vulnerability is an integral part of a healthy lifestyle. Invest in activities and people that contribute to your happiness! Therapy and counseling support isn't just for the students that you serve—commit to your own work, too! Find the fun and joy in each day. Laugh often. Self-care doesn't just happen, it requires intention, patience, and action!

I want to leave you with one last article about a second-grade teacher, with a license to practice mental health, transitioning into the role of a first-year school counselor. It's important to note that you don't have to be a teacher in order to be a counselor and you can be a teacher and transition into another career. It might be hard, but follow your passion! This excerpt is from the *EduKate and Inspire* blog written by Kate (EduKate and Inspire, 2016),

> This past school year was a whirlwind. It was basically like being a first-year teacher all over again. One major advantage I had for the new position was the ability to stay at the same school where I've been teaching. I've taught 2nd grade at my school for the past six years, and when our veteran school counselor announced her retirement, I decided to apply for the job. I never expected to leave the classroom this early in my career (it feels strange writing that since I'm in year 10 of education…I guess it's not *that* early!), but I couldn't pass up the opportunity of being able to be a school counselor in a community that I love. I had already built rapport with students and staff and had a good handle on our school culture, so I was able to start the new job with a solid foundation.
>
> In case you are wondering, my educational background is a combination of teaching and counseling. I received my bachelor's degree in early childhood education and am licensed to teach pre-school through third grade. I spent 6 years teaching second grade, 1 year in first grade, and 1 year teaching a pre-primary class at a Montessori school. I've always been interested in the mental health field, so I decided to pursue graduate

coursework in counseling. My master's degree is in community counseling and I am a Licensed Professional Counselor in the state of Ohio. When I completed my internship, I was able to work with many populations. I did everything from play therapy with children, individual counseling with adults, group counseling with at-risk teenagers, and even some marital counseling—nothing like providing marital counseling when you are a 20-something single counselor! Throughout my coursework, I specialized in play therapy and art therapy and would like to become a Registered Play Therapist one of these days. Although I am not currently practicing at a mental health agency, my community counseling degree gave me a great foundation in counseling.

Because I wanted to stay in the schools full-time (for now!), I decided to pursue my school counseling license. The University of Toledo has a great endorsement program that allows you to add on a school counseling degree to a previous counseling license. I completed a few more classes and did an internship at my school, and finally became dually licensed.

Wrap Up

As you begin your first year as a school counselor, be realistic about the job. I love being a school counselor! However, it is a bed of roses with thorns. There are things about the job that are hard and aspects I don't enjoy. When we are taught in graduate school to counsel and not give AP tests, it is a hard to love giving AP tests. I was fortunate at my first school that I didn't have to do scheduling. Many high school counselors spend a lot of time working on student schedules. The extra duties that school counselors get assigned are the ones I don't love. It takes away from our time with the students. However, we have to do them. I try to look at it from a Growth Mindset and see how I can use those duties to help further my work with the students. Take every opportunity you are given and be the best at it.

Final Tips

I leave with you tips from Anne Perrone (Perrone, 2016):

Surviving your 1st year as a school counselor:

1   Understand how to use the ASCA Model
2   SWOT Analysis
3   Interview Administration and Gate keepers
4   Needs Assessments for Faculty, Students, Parents
5   Use model to set SLTs
6   Invest

First-Year Elements:

Important anchors to a successful first year

- Individual Counseling
- Classroom Lessons
- Data

Using the foundation of graduate school to develop a preventative and responsive school counseling program:

- Small Group Counseling
- SWOT Analysis
- Admin & Gate keeper Interviews
- Needs assessments
- Creating SLTs
- Time Management
- Strengths
- Weaknesses
- Opportunities
- Threats

Questions to ask yourself:

- What is going well for the school counseling program?
- What are some barriers to making the counseling program better?
- What are the hidden gems of the school counseling program?
- What systemic barriers might slow down growth of the school counseling program?

Conduct a mini SWOT analysis in your admin interview

- What would your admin like to see out of the school counseling program?

Schedule a follow up meeting to share your SWOT results!

- Quarterly
- Pulse checks
- Conduct after counselor introduction
- Use technology when possible
- Avoid recreating the wheel!

What stuck out from your SWOT Analysis and Interviews?
What are the expectations from your school administration or local school board?

Are your SLTs realistic?

- Plan
- Prepare
- Perform
- Reflect

Mindsets and Behaviors Curriculum

- Pre/Post test—you mean ALL the time?
- Serious topics can be fun, too!
- Schedule these every day
- Make it work with the students' schedules as much as possible
- Maintain library of activities
- Seem always available (even when you have a French fry hanging out of your mouth)
- SLT magic
- Can be driven by needs assessments (school culture), teacher (or parent) feedback, quarterly pulse checks
- Same group across multiple grades with little manipulation
- Marketing
- Use a system that works with your school
- Use Pre/Post tests
- Use data to support SLTs targets
- Schedule meetings with your administration to review data
- Adjusting personal goals from data
- Identify ways admin can support you
- Identify new opportunities for growth
- Teacher Team meetings: attend quarterly (if not more often) for specific student needs or identifying school culture changes
- Admin check-ins to bridge the island feeling
- Self-care
- Be realistic with personal expectations
- Do take personal time, daily

References

Barrick, C. (2018, January 2). *An Interview with Kirsten Perry, 2018 School Counselor of the Year.* Retrieved from College Board: www.collegeboard.org/membership/all-access/counseling/interview-kirsten-perry-2018-school-counselor-year

Bassett, A. (2016, July 20). *School Counselor Stories: Angela Bassett.* Retrieved from NYU: https://counseling.steinhardt.nyu.edu/blog/school-counselor-stories-angela-bassett/

Coleman, B. (2019, March 16). *Guest Blog: An Interview with the 2019 School Counselor of the Year.* Retrieved from ACT: https://equityinlearning.act.org/equity-in-action/guest-blog-an-interview-with-the-2019-school-counselor-of-the-year/

EduKate and Inspire (2016, June 7). *Goodbye 2nd Grade, Hello Counseling.* Retrieved from EduKate and Inspire: https://edukateandinspire.blogspot.com/2016/06/goodbye-2nd-grade-hello-school.html

Perrone, A. (2016, September 23). *Surviving Your 1st Year as a School Counselor.* Retrieved from Prezi: https://prezi.com/zsyczopprche/surviving-your-1st-year-as-a-school-counselor/?webgl=0

7   Crisis and the Resident Expert

As school counselors in training, we take a course on crisis but when it happens in the field it is a humbling experience. I say humbling, because you realize that all of your head knowledge couldn't have given you enough preparation for application. How does the school counselor deal with his/her own emotions? How does one detach themselves emotionally, so he/she doesn't wither under the pressure? The entire school building relies on the school counselor for answers. After a crisis happens the school counselor is considered the resident expert. They are the ones that the faculty and students will go to for advice. This chapter will discuss post crisis interventions and prevention resources.

What is a Crisis?

First, I want to define 'crisis' with how it will be used in this chapter. Students will come to you on a daily basis with what they consider a personal crisis. This chapter isn't to diminish any students' experience, but to help you as a first-year counselor have an inside look at a school-wide crisis. We will be using the term crisis when defining traumatic events.

A traumatic event that may occur in the school can be a suicide, national disaster, school shooting, or man-made disaster. I want to note that this list is not excluding other tragedies that students may face within the school. This chapter is to serve as a resource and that further continuing education is encouraged.

What Does the School Counselor Do During a Crisis?

It might seem like there are different ways to help students during these crises, however they are universal concepts that can be applied to every scenario. As first responders during a crisis, your responsibility is to the students. Your school and district will have information regarding the specific details of how you implement your role.

Your school and district may have policies and procedures on what to do during a crisis. If they do, it should be your number one resource. The principal is also a good resource on getting this information. Their number one priority is providing a safe environment at the school. The policy and procedures manual includes information about a crisis team, how to utilize the crisis team, who to contact (if not a crisis team), how to activate a response to crisis in the building, who to direct the media to, and the immediate steps to take. If your school or district does not have a policy or procedure manual for you to reference take the initiative to help create one. This will help you understand what to do and be invaluable to the school/district.

Schools and districts may offer ongoing school safety training. This is something you should invest in even if it's not required. The more training you get the more prepared you'll feel when a crisis happens. Ask your principal or superintendent what school training programs the district implements and how you can further your education. Your state department of education will also have information on statewide initiatives and protocol.

There are fundamental roles that school counselors have in addition to what your schools' policies and procedures outline. According to an article from *Counselor Today* (Bray, 2016) those roles are to:

- **Be a visible presence.** It is extremely important that we get to know our students and they get to know us. Make it a priority to go into classes and introduce yourself as the school counselor. Tell them your role, where your office is, the reasons to come see you, how to contact you, what they should report, and explain confidentiality. Take every opportunity to step away from the office and be amongst the students.
- **Reaching those who are at risk.** Our training extends to assessments. We are able to screen students who may be at risk for suicide, depression, and anxiety. These assessments can help with making referrals to outside mental health counselors.
- **Fostering a safe environment.** How you go about fostering a safe environment is going to be based on the needs of your school. You can create and give a needs assessment survey at the beginning or end of each school year. The responses you get can range from social emotional to feeling safe within the school. Regardless of what the students answer, you will be able to tailor your programming based on the results.
- **Crisis intervention and threat assessment.** A school counselor can create and maintain a safe environment by providing trainings to staff and faculty, collaborating with the school resource officer, and parent outreach. They can implement social emotional learning curriculums or more specific target programs to students.
- **Resiliency and response.** As part of intervention or postvention, school counselors can implement a program that builds resiliency. They can go into classrooms to teach guidance lessons or lead small groups. There are a lot of resources available on empirically based curriculum. Dialectical Behavioral Therapy Skills Training for Emotional Problem Solving for

Adolescents (DBT STEPS-A) developed by Dr. Mazza is designed for schools. It provides detailed lesson plans on the fundamental components of DBT. This program is great for intervention or postvention.

- **Parents as part of the safety equation.** There is a significant amount of research that connects student achievement and parent involvement. The author of the article interviewed school counselors and they stated that they saw similar results with parent involvement and school safe environments. When parents/guardians are able to take an active role in their child's education and safety there is oversight, a sense of security, and accountability.

How Do School Counselors Help Students during a Crisis?

As school counselors, we are trained to counsel students and make sure they are ready to learn. It isn't within our scope of practice to do ongoing therapy, but we can provide brief immediate counseling. When there is a crisis at the school we can first respond by using our counseling skills. We can use techniques from Solution Focused Therapy, Reality Therapy, Cognitive Behavioral Therapy (CBT), or another theory. It's important to use active listening skills and show empathy. Not every student is going to respond to a crisis the same way. The Red Cross Association identifies these common reactions and responses to crisis (The American National Red Cross, 2018):

- Feeling physically and mentally drained
- Having difficulty making decisions or staying focused on topics
- Becoming easily frustrated on a more frequent basis
- Arguing more with family and friends
- Feeling tired, sad, numb, lonely, or worried
- Experiencing changes in appetite or sleep patterns

We can help students during this time by helping them keep their routines as normal as possible. Students get security from a predictable routine. Stress the importance of limited television and news access to parents and faculty. If the crisis becomes public, the constant exposure via social media, news, and TV can make it harder on the student. Be honest with the students about what is happening and share with them as much information as they are developmentally able to handle. We are there to listen to their concerns and be a pillar for them. Reassure them that the school is going to do everything it can to ensure it is a safe place. It's best to be honest with students and not give them false assurances. Depending upon the grade level, there can be a good discussion on morality and ethics. First deal with and assess your own response to the crisis before helping students. You're not going to be able to help students if you are in crisis mode with them. We can also rebuild and reaffirm attachments and relationships (American School Counselor Association, 2018).

An article from the Child Mind Institute talks about how to send a child back to school after a crisis. When there were multiple school shootings in 2017 and 2018, it was hard for parents to send their children and adolescents to school. The article said to take cues from your child, give them ample opportunity to ask questions, acknowledge their feelings and remain calm, emphasize school safety, give extra reassurance, listen when they're not talking, and know who else can help (Child Mind Institute, 2018). Although this article was for parents, I think it is beneficial for school counselors as well. I know personally, my students had concerns about coming to school and were scared even though the crisis hadn't been at our school. The high school students were vocal about their concerns, but my younger middle school students were less likely to speak out. For elementary school counselors, it's especially important to recognize the nonverbal cues. Those students might not have the language to articulate their emotions.

Preventions

Prevention for varying types of crises can be different, but there are universal designs. Creating a positive school climate, having assessments, ensuring that students are monitored at all times, and using best practices within the school are all preventative measures that are universal. Our school counseling program should be an integral part of prevention within the school. When it comes to school counseling programming, there are a lot of ways that it can happen. This is going to reflect on the needs of your school and district. I have listed different school counseling programming that I have used as prevention.

Monthly Curriculum

There is a plethora of curriculums out there for school counselors to use. If you want to teach Growth Mindset, Social Emotional Learning, Kindness, or Mindfulness there are numerous valid and realizable curriculums to choose from. When thinking about what curriculum to use in my own school, I looked at the population of the students and what their needs were. The students at my first school were considered gifted. They had to achieve a certain score on the entrance exam in order to be accepted into the school. I looked for curriculums that were for students who are gifted. I did a lot of research and reading on the subject that lead me to using Christine Fonseca's "I'm Not Just Gifted" Social Emotional Learning curriculum. I used this curriculum for my Prep 7 and 8 grades because they were newest to the school. For my Freshmen, I used MindUP which goes more in depth about mindfulness and SEL.

Monthly Workshops

After the initial year of using DBT STEPS-A with my juniors and seniors, I decided to do mental health 'workshops' with them instead. I had SEAS the

Day Foundation come in once a month to talk about cyber-bullying, anxiety, stress, relationships, and college life. We also held a school-wide inspirational t-shirt creation that students could wear during exams. I have SEAS the Day Foundation come into my beginning-of-the-year orientation for Preps and Freshmen. We have put Post-It notes on lockers with inspirational quotes, talked about the importance of kindness, and healthy relationships. I've brought in emotional support dogs during exam week as well.

Here is more information about the curriculum I have used. There are more resources and information in Part IV.

"I'm Not Just Gifted" by Christine Fonseca is designed to help gifted children explore their giftedness, develop resiliency, manage their intensities, face adversities and tough situations, and cultivate their talents and passions. Including lesson plans, worksheets, and connections to Common Core State Standards, I'm Not Just Gifted is the practical guide necessary for anyone serving and working with gifted children.

(Fonseca, 2018)

"MindUP" by The MindUP Foundation is a research-based curriculum features 15 lessons that use the latest information about the brain to dramatically improve behavior and learning for all students. Each lesson offers easy strategies for helping students focus their attention, improve their self-regulation skills, build resilience to stress, and develop a positive mind-set in both school and life. The lessons fit easily into any schedule and require minimal preparation. Classroom management tips and content-area activities help you extend the benefits of MindUP throughout your day, week, and year.

(Scholastic, 2018)

Random Acts of Kindness Foundation, RAK, program includes a variety of online lessons and activities with intent to build SEL opportunities and student character, to create positive classroom and school environments, and to encourage service learning in the outside community. As such, it reflects an ecological framework—viewing the student from multiple contexts including as an individual as well as a member of a classroom, family, culture, and society. The curriculum design concepts and learning objectives are based on the "kindness paradigm," and this paradigm provides the basis for the scope and sequence of the grades K–8 lesson plans (Exhibit 1). Methods employed in the core activities are designed to inspire, empower, promote action, and provide opportunities for sharing.

(Random Acts of Kindness Foundation, 2018)

Small Groups

I haven't run small groups at my school due to the amount of time I spend going into classrooms and running two other programs. However, if I weren't the only school counselor or counselor in the building I would definitely run small groups. They can be very beneficial when working with a targeted need. There are curriculums that work well for small groups or you could create your own. From creating positive relationships to overcoming anxiety, you can run groups on every topic. The benefit of small groups is that you are screening students to be in them. Instead of doing an entire guidance lesson on coping with divorced parents and blended families that might only relate to handful of students, you can have a small group with just those students.

School-wide Campaigns

School-wide campaigns could fall under either prevention or invention. They tend to happen after a school crisis. There have been numerous campaigns on bullying. One program was developed by a police officer for anonymous reporting called STOP IT. Our school used this for a year and a half. It did help us in some bullying that was happening, but our students abused it. There will be students who use these tools for their intended use and those who will abuse it. I do think anonymous reporting is a great idea and this program is a good tool.

As part of my school-wide campaign, we implemented the "Whole Child Initiative". This is something many schools have adapted to ensure they are meeting the needs of the entire child. This includes physical and mental health within the school. A way to measure the mental and physical needs of the child is through the School Health Index by the Center for Disease Control and Prevention. The CDC describes the School Health Index as follows:

The *School Health Index (SHI): Self-Assessment & Planning Guide* was developed by CDC in partnership with school administrators and staff, school health experts, parents, and national nongovernmental health and education agencies to

- Enable schools to identify strengths and weaknesses of health and safety policies and programs.
- Enable schools to develop an action plan for improving student health, which can be incorporated into the School Improvement Plan.
- Engage teachers, parents, students, and the community in promoting health-enhancing behaviors and better health.

The SHI has two activities that are to be completed by teams from your school: a self-assessment process and a planning for improvement process.

- The **self-assessment process** involves members of your school community coming together to discuss what your school is already doing to promote good health and to identify your strengths and weaknesses. The SHI allows you to assess the extent to which your school implements the types of policies and practices recommended by CDC in its research-based guidelines for school health and safety policies and programs.
- The **planning for improvement process** enables you to identify recommended actions your school can take to improve its performance in

areas that received low scores. It guides you through a simple process for prioritizing the various recommendations. This step will help you decide on a handful of actions to implement this year. Finally, you will complete a School Health Improvement Plan to list the steps you will take to implement your actions.

The SHI currently addresses seven health topic areas, including:

- Physical activity and physical education.
- Nutrition.
- Tobacco-use prevention.
- Alcohol and other drug use prevention.
- Chronic health conditions (e.g., asthma, food allergies).
- Unintentional injury and violence prevention (safety).
- Sexual health, including HIV, other STD and pregnancy prevention.

It also includes cross-cutting questions, which address policies and practices that apply to all seven health topic areas.

Completing the SHI is an important first step toward improving your school's health promotion policies and practices. Your school can then act to implement the School Health Improvement Plan and develop an ongoing process for monitoring progress and reviewing your recommendations for change. Your school's results from using the SHI can also help you include health promotion activities in your overall School Improvement Plan (Center for Disease Control and Prevention, 2018).

As you consider your options for prevention, remember to seek advice from more experienced school counselors. This information is not meant to substitute any additional courses or trainings. Please seek your district's policy on gaining additional training.

Interventions

As with preventions, there are many interventions you can implement in your school. The important key to picking an intervention is making sure you make an assessment. After assessing my students, I found out they were having a hard time with emotional regulation. They were experiencing a lot of anxiety and perfectionism but didn't know what to do with those feelings. With that knowledge I researched programs that had been successful with emotional regulation. That is when I chose DBT STEPS-A. Dialectical Behavioral Therapy had resonated with me in my graduate program and I really like the holistic approach it brings to therapy. The following information about DBT STEPS-A comes from Mazza Consulting.

DBT Skills Training for Emotional Problem Solving for Adolescents (DBT STEPS-A) is a Social Emotional Learning (SEL) curriculum developed by Dr. Mazza, Dr. Dexter-Mazza, and colleagues to be implemented in middle and high schools in order to teach all adolescents effective emotion regulation, decision making, and problem-solving skills. DBT STEPS-A can be implemented at Tiers 1, 2, and 3 in schools using a Multitiered Systems of Support (MTSS).

The DBT STEPS-A curriculum includes 30 lesson plans that are designed to fit within a general education curriculum. Each lesson is 50 minutes long. The curriculum was adapted from the skills training program in Dialectical Behavior Therapy developed by Dr. Marsha Linehan, a professor at the University of Washington. The 30 lessons cover skills from each of the DBT skills modules including:

- Orientation and Goal Setting
- Dialectical Thinking
- Core Mindfulness Skills
- Distress Tolerance Skills
- Emotion Regulation Skills
- Interpersonal Effectiveness Skills

DBT STEPS-A has been being used in several middle and high school programs around the country (Mazza Consulting, 2018).

Another program that is an empirically based program that focuses on emotional regulation is I Can Problem Solve. This program is for elementary to middle school grades, whereas DBT STEPS-A is better suited for high school. I wanted to provide you with two examples of intervention programs for all grade levels.

I Can Problem Solve for Schools. The I Can Problem Solve (ICPS) is a school-based intervention that trains children in generating a variety of solutions to interpersonal problems, considering the consequences of these solutions, and recognizing thoughts, feelings, and motives that generate problem situations. By teaching children to think, rather than what to think, the program changes thinking styles and, as a result, enhances children's social adjustment, promotes pro-social behavior, and decreases impulsivity and inhibition. The program was originally designed for use in nursery school and kindergarten, but it has also been successfully implemented with children in grades 1 to 6 (Shure, 2018).

I want to leave with you my own personal experience with crisis as a first-year school counselor. I have intentionally left out any personal information about students and information about the school at which the crisis happened to protect the identity of those students. This is solely for educational purposes.

Vignette

My first-year experience was difficult in the beginning, because I had a student who had attempted suicide. This attempt led to multiple students in the class saying that they had suicidal thoughts, had attempted suicide in the past, or were going to commit suicide. It was clear that there needed to be invention and postvention. As it was my first year, I didn't have the resources to know what curriculum or assessments to use. We didn't have a school policy and procedure manual. I felt like a ship without a captain. My principal, at the time, was the person I relied on for help. We created a crisis team that included the superintendent and a psychiatrist. We met to create an initial mental health intervention program for the year that I would spearhead. This would lay the foundation for starting our "Whole Child Initiative". This was an overwhelming undertaking, but I met with the psychiatrist to help create a plan for a school-wide intervention. We used SEAS the Day Foundation to come in and talk to the school about suicide and the signs of suicide. I went into the junior and senior classes using DBT STEPS-A, DBT Social Training for Emotional Problem Solving for Adolescents, because it was empirically based and specifically designed for schools. That was the initial intervention program. The next steps were to identify the underlying needs of the students. We created a homework policy, implemented a new college and career program that met twice a month for grades 9–12, needs assessments through parent and student surveys, and Social Emotional Learning for all grades. This took two years to fully implement. During the initial crisis, we brought in outside mental health counselors to help me meet with students one-on-one and in small groups. This lasted for a couple of weeks and then it was on an as need basis.

During this time, I accepted the challenge of being the sole counselor in the building and went hard to work. I didn't stop to think about my own emotions. This was my way of coping with the situation. Being new, I think it was easier to separate myself from the situation and look at it from an objective point of view. I consulted with my professors from my graduate program and met with a school counselor in our district. Getting consultation from other professionals who had been the field longer than me really helped me handle the crisis. They gave me an outlet to share my concerns and emotions about it while giving advice when I asked for it. It's something that no counselor wants to happen with their students, but unfortunately it does, and we have to be prepared. It's important to know what and who your resources are. Whether it's someone to get consultation from or who to ask about the school/district policy. Don't feel like you are alone in a crisis! Reach out to other school counselors in your district or that you know from graduate school. I have found that our profession is the best for helping each other.

References

American School Counselor Association (2018, August 23). *Helping Students During Crisis*. Retrieved from ASCA: www.schoolcounselor.org/school-counselors/professional-development/learn-more/helping-kids-during-crisis

Bray, B. (2016, August 24). *The Counselor's Role in Ensuring School Safety*. Retrieved from Counselor Today: https://ct.counseling.org/2016/08/counselors-role-ensuring-school-safety/

Center for Disease Control and Prevention (2018, August 27). *Using the School Health Index*. Retrieved from Center for Disease Control and Prevention: www.cdc.gov/healthyschools/shi/introduction.htm

Child Mind Institute (2018, August 23). *Going Back to School After a Tragedy*. Retrieved from Child Mind Institute: https://childmind.org/article/going-back-school-tragedy/

Fonseca, C. (2018, August 26). *I'm Not Just Gifted*. Retrieved from Christine Fonseca: www.christinefonseca.com/i-m-not-just-gifted

Mazza Consulting (2018, August 25). *Mazza Consulting*. Retrieved from DBT STEPS-A: www.mazzaconsulting.com/dbt-steps-a/

Random Acts of Kindness Foundation (2018, August 26). *School Pilot Study*. Retrieved from Random Acts of Kindness Foundation: https://downloads.randomactsofkindness.org/RAK_SRI_School_Pilot_Study_2013-14.pdf

Scholastic (2018, August 26). *MindUP*. Retrieved from Scholastic: http://teacher.scholastic.com/products/mindup/

Shure, M. (2018, August 27). *Thinking Child*. Retrieved from I Can Problem Solve: www.thinkingpreteen.com/icps.htm#schools

The American National Red Cross (2018, August 23). *Recovering Emotionally*. Retrieved from I Can Problem Solve: Retrieved from American Red Cross: www.redcross.org/get-help/disaster-relief-and-recovery-services/recovering-emotionally.html

8   Balance, Boundaries, and Transference

School counselors are unique, because they get to see students in a variety of settings. This can allow school counselors to have a close relationship with their students. Sometimes boundaries are grey due to the nature of the school setting. There needs to be a balance with maintaining a mentoring and professional relationship with students. The balance is of them feeling comfortable to be open about their personal problems and understanding that the school counselor is a professional. If there is no balance, then boundaries can be crossed. Crossing boundaries can happen easily in the first year of counseling. This isn't in reference to ethical issues but being seen as a friend or mentor instead of a professional.

Balance

If you think about your motivations for becoming a school counselor, it was probably similar to a lot of other people: to help students. When building relationships with students it's good to ask yourself: is this professional relationship helping the student succeed inside and outside the classroom? As school counselors, we don't provide ongoing therapy and we don't have guidelines as strict as mental health professionals. A mental health counselor might not acknowledge a client if they see them at the grocery store or mall due to confidentiality. They're not going to be engaged with a client outside of their therapy session. School counselors can be more engaged with students due to the nature of the position. We should be involved in the school and attend school functions. A good way to observe student's social behavior is by attending school sporting events, chaperoning dances, and going to other school events. It also shows you support the students.

It is important to make sure you have balance in your relationship with students. There needs to be a clear understanding with students that they're not your friend. As a first-year school counselor it can be hard to create a balance, because you don't know the students. They will try you and overstep boundaries. Your responsibility is to teach and to model good boundaries. How well students maintain boundaries is going to depend on their age. I had discussed this with my principal during my first year. It is always recommended that you consult with your supervisor if you have a question about something that happens with a student. Don't try to deal with it alone! When you take action to consult with your supervisor, that is modeling good boundaries. That student came back to me and said I broke confidentiality by telling the principal what he had said. Within the context of the situation, I had not because I felt uncomfortable by the comment and it was inappropriate to say to an adult. It was within my professional judgement to let another administrator know and proceed with discipline.

It takes time to build relationships with students on a professional level. They see the school counselor as the 'cool' adult in the building. They feel comfortable talking to you about anything they have on their mind. That can be confusing for them until you start reinforcing those professional boundaries. It can be a joke they make in the hallway trying to look cool with their friends and you have to talk with them in private. You don't want to reinforce negative behavior or break their trust, but you don't want to let the behavior continue.

As you're building relationships, it's important to note that you don't have to be the only person a student comes to see. This is part of maintaining balance within your program, prevent burnout, and prevent crossing boundaries. The article from *The Counseling Geek* talks about the importance of knowing your strengths and weaknesses as a counselor and not being everything for all students (Ream, 2017),

It's About Finding a Balance

I have zero research-backed data on this, let's call it a hunch, but from the anecdotal evidence of talking with colleagues and following along on the school counselor Twitter and Facebook haunts, I notice we all desire to be all things for all people. It is our tendency as school counselors and helping professionals. The problem with not having balance in your school counseling program is that you (the school counselor) gets absolutely worn out. A worn out counselor is not good for anyone. We get extra testy, short with parents, students, and colleagues, and we lose the fire we very much need to be effective.

While I know that I may not fit the typical school counseling "mold", I know that my own set of skills, strengths, and attributes bring a ton to my kids and school. I also know that my colleagues and friends that do fit the "mold" are incredible. They are able to connect with students in a totally different way than I do, create different programs that are perfect for their kids and our world is better because of them. If you are reading this and feel like you don't fit the "mold" – be aware of your areas of strength AND your areas that are not your strength. Because those areas of strength are where you not only need to practice but also where you need to network.

Making the Connection

Being the only school counselor (until next year!) at my school has been challenging but made easier because of "my" team. I say "my" because I am not supervising them or responsible for them – but having a team allows me to capitalize on my areas of strength and the areas that my team-mates have. It just so happens that their strengths complement my weak-nesses. For example – Hilary is our school's wellness center liaison. Our wellness center is a great space comprised of a comfy, welcoming interior with a caring adult to talk with students on a more casual way. Hilary is GREAT with the kids. She is younger and they really connect well with her. In fact – in a recent student connections survey (I am planning a future blog post on this) – over 50% of the students reported having her as a connection they trust on campus.

Boundaries

Setting boundaries and keeping boundaries isn't just to ensure the safety of the students, but for your own mental health. It's important to remember that we're not an emergency room and that there will be more important tasks than talking to a student. Your office should not be used to get out of class or another activity they should be doing. The students need to know that there are times for them to talk to you informally, but you have a job to do. You're not an individual counselor to a handful of students, you are the school counselor for the entire building. This will help prevent burn out and feeling overwhelmed.

Dual relationships need to be avoided. As I mentioned, the school environ-ment allows for more opportunities to support students. A school counselor should support their students, but also consider positive and possible risks with attending events outside of the school. I formed a close professional relation-ship with a student who studied ballet outside of school. It was important to her that I attend one of her performances at the end of the year in early June. I spoke with the assistant principal and found out if any faculty were going before deciding. The assistant principal thought it would be good for me to attend. A large group of students went with their parents and another teacher was in attendance. I didn't sit with my students or their parents in the audience. Afterwards, I stayed to congratulate my student and then left. I wanted to be clear that I was there to support her but wasn't going to overstep profession-alism. This one exception was made with consultation and weighing up the possible risk and benefit.

In a society driven by social media, it's vital that school counselors stay cur-rent with what is happening virtually. However, it goes without saying that you should never friend, follow, like, message, or engage with a student on social media. There are some schools that allow their counseling department to have a social media platform. That is up to the discretion of the school but be careful with how you are using it. Due to the nature of our interaction with students, I would stray away from connecting with them virtually. They don't need to follow us on Instagram or Twitter. There is no reason for them to contact us on any personal email or social media messaging platform. Everything we do should be sanctioned by the school and endorsed by the district.

It might seem like there is a lot of grey area when it comes to boundaries as a school counselor. There might be a situation where a school counselor has a family member as a student or is close friends with their parents. A school counselor doesn't have to stop being friends with the student's parents, but there does have to be boundaries set with that student. Consult with your supervisor or principal about any concerns you might have. Keep the student's best interests in mind. We are in the school to help students succeed academically, socially, and emotionally, and in their college and career path. If we are ignoring boundaries then we cannot help our students reach their full potential.

The best resource for maintaining boundaries is the ASCA Ethical Standards for School Counselors which states:

A.5. Dual Relationships and Managing Boundaries

School counselors:
   a. Avoid dual relationships that might impair their objectivity and increase the risk of harm to students (e.g., counseling one's family members or the children of close friends or associates). If a dual relationship is unavoidable, the school counselor is responsible for taking action to eliminate or reduce the potential for harm to the student through use of safeguards, which might include informed consent, consultation, supervision and documentation.
   b. Establish and maintain appropriate professional relationships with students at all times. School counselors consider the risks and benefits of extending current school counseling relationships beyond conventional parameters, such as attending a student's distant athletic competition. In extending these boundaries, school counselors take appropriate professional precautions such as informed consent, consultation and supervision. School counselors document the nature of interactions that extend beyond conventional parameters, including the rationale for the interaction, the potential benefit and the possible positive and negative consequences for the student and school counselor.
   c. Avoid dual relationships beyond the professional level with school personnel, parents/guardians and students' other family members when these relationships might infringe on the integrity of the school counselor/student relationship. Inappropriate dual relationships include, but are not limited to, providing direct discipline, teaching courses that

involve grading students and/or accepting administrative duties in the absence of an administrator.

d. Do not use personal social media, personal e-mail accounts or personal texts to interact with students unless specifically encouraged and sanctioned by the school district. School counselors adhere to professional boundaries and legal, ethical and school district guidelines when using technology with students, parents/guardians or school staff. The technology utilized, including, but not limited to, social networking sites or apps, should be endorsed by the school district and used for professional communication and the distribution of vital information.

(American School Counselor Association, 2016)

I would like to make a short comment about maintaining clear boundaries with other faculty members before moving on to transference. It is important to keep boundaries with yourself and other faculty members because of your role with the students. I'm not saying you shouldn't be friends with the other faculty members but be cautious when going to non-school functions. It can lead to negative talk about other faculty members, administration, parents, and students. As a school counselor you have to stay unbiased towards students. If you're hearing how another teacher perceives a student, it can affect your own judgment. Don't give in to gossiping or venting about others to the faculty you work with. You are there to create a positive school environment.

Transference

Transference and counter-transference came from Sigmund Freud's psychotherapy. Transference is "the process whereby clients project onto their therapists past feelings or attitudes they had toward their caregivers or significant people in the lives" (Corey, Corey, Corey, & Callanan, 2015). When a school counselor allows a dual relationship to happen or doesn't keep strict boundaries there is the risk for transference and counter-transference to happen. Sometimes transference happens when the counselor is doing their job correctly, because the client's feelings are rooted in past relationships and are directed toward the counselor.

Types of Transference

There are different types of transference that clients can experience. Some of the more common types of transference include (Good Therapy, LLC., 2015):

- **Paternal transference,** when an individual looks at another person as a father or an idealized father figure. The person may be viewed as powerful, wise, and authoritative, and an individual may expect protection and sound advice from this person.

- **Maternal transference** occurs when an individual treats another person as a mother or idealized mother figure. This person is often viewed as loving and influential, and nurture and comfort is often expected from them.
- **Sibling transference** can occur when <u>parental</u> relationships are lacking or when they break down. Unlike parental transference, this type of transference is generally not represented by leader/follower behavior, but by peer or team-based interactions.
- **Non-familial transference** can be seen when individuals treat others according to an idealized version of what they are expected to be rather than who they actually are. <u>Stereotypes</u> can form in this manner. For example, priests may be expected to be holy in everything they do, while policemen may be expected to uphold the law at all times, and doctors may be expected to cure any ailment.

Sometimes, transference is seen in everyday situations, such as when:

- One is easily annoyed by a classmate who looks a bit like one's often-irritating younger sibling.
- A young person treats a much older female coworker with tenderness because she brings back memories of that person's now-deceased mother.

Dealing with Transference

As school counselors, students may associate you with a sister, aunt, or mother depending upon their age. It's good to follow these steps to know how to deal with the transference (Counselling Connection, 2014):

1. Take a step back and disassociate with the affective reaction and view it more objectively.
2. Identify the client's affective state.
3. Establish the significance of the client's message.
4. Decide how most effectively to use what has been learned.

After you have analyzed the transference, you should talk about it with your student. The student might have resistance to talking about the transference. These might be due to a number of reasons (Counselling Connection, 2014).

1. Ignoring real life concerns
2. Identifying the transference
3. Refusing to consider transference a possibility
4. Avoiding responsibility, fear of autonomy

Depending on the age of your student, they might not be able to articulate their resistance to talking about the transference. It might take building a stronger professional relationship with the student before they are able to open up to you or for you to understand them.

Counter-Transference

Counter-transference involves the therapist's emotional response to a client.

Counter-transference can be damaging if not appropriately managed. With proper monitoring, however, some sources show that counter-transference can play a productive role in the therapeutic relationship.

There are multiple manifestations of counter-transference (Corey, Corey, Corey, & Callanan, 2015):

1. Being overprotective with a client can reflect a therapist's fears. As a school counselor, you may be in the right with being overprotective of a student. We are mandated reporters and it's our duty to let the proper authorities know if there is neglect and abuse in the home. There might be students who live in a neighborhood where violence and substance abuse are prevalent. There may be justified reasons for being overprotective of our students, but you have to understand your own fears and not let them hinder your counseling.
2. Treating clients in benign ways may stem from a counselor's fear of clients' anger. This can happen without intention. If you have had a negative student reaction from a previous counseling meeting, then you might create a bland atmosphere the next time. Seek advice from your supervisor on how to build a better relationship with the student.
3. Rejecting a client may be based on the therapist's perception of the client as needy and dependent. Students know how to take advantage of a situation. They know which teachers will let them go see the school counselor whenever they want and the teachers who will want the school counselor to touch base with them. I have sent a student back to class when they genuinely needed me, because on previous accounts they had used me to get out of class. That is when a conversation needs to be had with the student about what the correct use of your office is.
4. Needing constant reinforcement and approval can be a reflection of counter-transference. As a new school counselor, it can be easy to get caught up in making sure your students like you and want to come talk to you. When you put the focus on the students liking you versus meeting their needs, you are setting yourself up for disappointment. You'll feel like you're not doing a good job, you'll get angry, and you'll get discouraged. Set measurable goals for yourself in terms of your school counseling program. You don't need the students' approval in order to be an effective counselor.
5. Seeing yourself in your clients can be another form of counter-transference. "I remember when I was your age…" is something their parents tell them and every other adult, but you should not unless it has a genuine purpose. I have found that students don't want to know what I did when

I was their age or how I handled a situation, they want to know how they should handle the situation they're in now. Don't live vicariously through your students' lives.

6. Developing sexual or romantic feelings toward a client can exploit the vulnerable position of the client. Keep in mind that as a school counselor this is unethical and illegal.
7. Giving advice can easily happen with clients who seek answers. As school counselors, these aren't necessarily wrong. They might need advice on how to write a college essay, apply for college, what classes they should take, etc. When it comes to handling confrontation with their peers or standing up for themselves, just to name a few, we should encourage them to come to conclusions on their own though with guidance.
8. Developing a social relationship with clients may stem from counter-transference, especially if it is acted upon while therapy is taking place. As mentioned previously in this chapter, follow your school/district's policy.

Counter-transference is especially common in novice counselors. It's important to pay attention to your response to students and seek supervision regularly. When you're a school counselor, remember that you're not the student's parent. Counter-transference may look like you 'parenting' the student versus guiding them. These parental feelings aren't bad, but they can be used better than scolding or lecturing the student. A few warning signs of counter-transference for dealing with children and adolescents are (Fritscher, 2018):

- Fantasies of rescuing the child from his/her situation
- Ignoring the child's deviant behavior
- Encouraging the child to act out

Understanding our own emotions is vital to our well-being. It might feel like the weight of the world is on our shoulders and we have to solve all of our students' problems. Our job is to empower them to change their own world! We are to give them resources and support to go out and make their world a better place. Sometimes that means we make the hard decisions for them. These should always be done around the parameters of the ASCA Ethical Standards for School Counselors and with supervision and by using an ethical decision-making model. I encourage school counselors to attend workshops and presentations on the ethics and laws in our profession at least once a year. Also, if you ever have questions call ASCA. They will give you advice on what steps to take.

Wrap Up

As you go through your first year, make sure you have support and a mentor to guide you through the tough scenarios and to answer any questions you have. You're going to have scenarios that you feel inexperienced in and need the guidance of another school counselor. That is okay, we have all been there. You are not alone! It is better to admit that you need guidance from an experienced school counselor than to try to handle the situation on your own. We are a community. The school counseling profession is a small world and I have found that other professionals are more than willing to help. Even though everyone is busy, don't hesitate to reach out to your colleagues or professors. These can be scary topics to digest, but remember they are for the well-being of the students and to keep them safe. I know when I was taking a class on ethics it made my palms sweat! It isn't to make the new school counselor nervous, but cautious and aware. Be mindful in all that you do and practice self-care. I cannot stress enough the importance of a mentor in our profession. In order to 'First Do No Harm', we have to be vigilant in taking care of ourselves.

References

American School Counselor Association (2016). *ASCA Ethical Standards for School Counselors*. Alexandria, VA: American School Counselor Assoication.

Corey, G., Corey, C., Corey, M.S., & Callanan, P. (2015). *Issues and Ethics in the Helping Progessions*. Stamford, CT: Cengage Learning.

Counselling Connection (2014, August 4). *Dealing with Transference*. Retrieved from Counselling Connection: www.counsellingconnection.com/index.php/2014/07/04/dealing-with-transference/

Fritscher, L. (2018, June 27). *Counter-Transference*. Retrieved from Very Well Mind: www.verywellmind.com/counter-transference-2671577

Good Therapy, LLC (2015, August 28). *Transference*. Retrieved from Good Therapy: www.goodtherapy.org/blog/psychpedia/transference

Ream, J. (2017). *Finding the Balance – What is Your School Counseling Style?* Retrieved from The Counseling Geek: www.thecounselinggeek.com/2017/05/finding-balance.html

Part IV

The Ins and Outs of Counseling

9 Individual and Group

Depending upon the school setting, a school counselor will either do more individual or group counseling. As a first-year school counselor in a new school that only had one counselor, my students were used to what the previous had done. They were used to individual counseling and guidance classroom lessons, but not group counseling sessions. This was something that I tweaked to fit the students' needs. I have found that running a group counseling session is challenging at my school with its strict schedule, but students will come in clusters to see me. You might have students come together in a group to talk about a problem one of them is having. In the middle school grades, I've seen this happen quite a bit. They feel more comfortable sharing when they have their friends' support. In elementary schools, one-on-one counseling may happen more often than groups. In all three settings, there can be a combination of both individual and group counseling. This chapter will discuss the varying aspects of counseling students individually and in groups.

Individual

Elementary

When counseling elementary students, it can be hard for them to engage individually. They might not have the vocabulary or be timid. It's good to have a strategy that isn't just the student sitting in the chair and you questioning them. Individual counseling can be more interactive with elementary students. You want your students to feel comfortable and engaged when they're with you. You can make your office decorations reflect that as well.

Some activities you can do with students are (Haas, 2018):

- **Who is your support system?** This activity can be done a variety of ways. One way is showing students a chart of their inner and outer circles that include family (most inner), friends (middle circle), and people in the community (their most outer circle). This can spark a great conversation about the relationships they have with others. It can give you a good understanding of who they trust and want in their inner circle.

- **Time management table.** Helping students manage their time is something I do a lot. Creating a visual graph with them can be a fun way to get to know your students and see their creative side.

- **Helping a student with organization.** Some students have a hard time with being organized. Take your individual counseling session outside of the office and help the student come up with a system to organize their locker.

- **Helping the student deal with different situations.** You can help your students understand what is in and out of their control. By helping them understand what they can control and what they can't, you're helping them develop numerous skills.

- **Setting goals with your students.** Teach your students how to set Specific, Measurable, Achievable, Relevant, and Time Bound (SMART) goals. This will help with short-term and long-term goals. It applies to all situations too!

- **Using Post-It notes.** You can use Post-It notes to help reluctant students to talk and prioritize what to talk about. A student might not know what they're feeling or know how to start talking about what they're feeling. You could write down a list of emotions to show them and then have them write down the emotions they're feeling on a Post-It note. After they write down their feelings they can choose which one they want to talk about.

- **Using a protective shield.** You can use the protective shield as a metaphor when discussing self-esteem with students. Their positive words about themselves is a shield against negativity others might try to hurt them with.

- **Journal.** Journaling is a great way for students to get out what they're feeling. You can give your students prompts that they have to write about. They can reflect on what they're feeling or write about how they would resolve a conflict.

- **Goal charts.** A goal chart is a good way to help students keep track of their goals. You can work with a teacher to help by rewarding the student when they complete a goal. This will be different from student-to-student, but they could receive positive praise for completing their goal.

- **Self-esteem.** There are a lot of self-esteem activities you can do with your students. One activity is having them write on an outline of a person. They write five things they like about themselves on the inside of the person. Then, they write five things they dislike about themselves on the outside. They can do this monthly or weekly to work on areas they like/ dislike about themselves.

- **Family changes.** There can be a lot of changes within the family over the course of a student's early life. We can help them with divorce, death, blended families, siblings, etc.

- **Jenga.** Jenga can be used in many different sessions. You can have each student ask a question as they pull out a block. Or you can write a question on each block. For example, if you have a self-esteem group, you can write:

- Tell the person to your left what your favorite thing about them is.
- What is your favorite thing about yourself?
- What are you best at?
- What is the person to your right best at?
- What are you most proud of?
- What do you value in a friendship?
- **Balloons**. Balloons can be used in many ways. Balloons can be used to make stress balls to help students calm down. Balloons can also be used to work though the death of a loved one by having a balloon release. You spend time talking about their feelings, the stages of grief and the memories of the loved one. On the last session, allow the student to write a letter and attach it to the balloon to release it. This also gives a closure to the sessions.

Middle School

Middle school can be a hard time during a student's life. Depending on what grade level your school district starts middle school, students will be starting puberty. Their bodies are developing, and they are dealing with some emotions for the first time. There are a lot of resources available for helping girls navigate self-esteem, body image, and relationships. When working individually with students, it's important to be empathic and understand what they're going through developmentally. *Queen Bees and Wannabes* by Rosalind Wiseman is a great book on what girls go through with their peers. She discusses the different friend roles that girls put themselves into in order to survive the social hierarchy within their friend groups.

The 'drama' that seems to be prevalent in middle school is important because of their development. *Development through Life* authors, Barbara and Philip Newman, discuss the different developmental tasks that early adolescents go through from ages 12 to 18. Their developmental tasks are physical maturation, formal operations, emotional development, membership in the peer group, romantic and sexual relationships. The authors state that if students do not go through these developmental stages then they will have a psychosocial crisis of group identity versus alienation. The reason I talk about this in the individual counseling session for middle school is because it's a good reminder to know where the students are coming from when they are having relationship and friendship problems. Boys are not excluded from peer pressure and bullying. Rosalind Wiseman also wrote a book called *Masterminds and Wingmen, Helping Our Boys Cope with Schoolyard Power, Locker-Room Tests, Girlfriends, and the New Rules of Boy World*. Understanding what our young adolescent students are going through is crucial to helping them on an individual level.

When you're counseling students at the middle school and high school level remember to use the Nine Empathic Responding Skills and Phrasing from *Individual Counseling* by Mei-whei Chen and Nan J. Giblin (Chen & Giblin, 2014):

1. Paraphrasing: "Wendy, it seems that the situation between you and your friend is effecting you negatively."
2. Reflecting thoughts: "Sandi, you seem to believe as a fact that 'No one really cares about my feelings'."
3. Reflecting needs: "Ed, I can see that deep down you have a strong need for connection with your father, but there is more and more frustration as time passes because your father hasn't shown much interest in responding."
4. Reflecting feelings: "I have the sense, Susan, that you feel angry at your mother (reflecting feelings) but you think to yourself, 'it's awful to feel angry at my parents' (reflecting thoughts)."
5. Reflecting meaning and values: "It sounds like you're torn between two sets of conflicting values: one, to comply with your parents' expectations, and the other, to trust your own instincts."
6. Checking perceptions: "I was wondering if breaking up with your boyfriend/girlfriend is what you really want. I heard some doubt in your voice. Did I hear you right?"
7. Affirming: "Sam, I appreciate how hard it must have been for you to go through this. Your resiliency is commendable."
8. Summarizing (tracking): "It sounds like you're torn two ways..."
9. Advanced empathy: "Although you didn't talk much about your feelings, each time we discuss your mother's verbal abuse, your head hangs down and your fist clenches, and I can sense a strong feeling of shame and tension inside of you."

High School

Individual counseling at the high school level is one of the largest roles for the school counselor. A school counselor will see students about college, vocation, mental health, relationships, academia, and whatever else is on their mind. Establishing rapport with these students is important due to the fact that you see students more often one-on-one. Since school counselors have many roles within the high school, the opportunity to go into classrooms can be scarce. Instructional time is fought for in the high school, because of the number of programs that are run. So, building rapport with students and having a firm counseling foundation is key. There are different activities you can do with students if they're reluctant or forced to come see you.

'Walk and Talk' is a way to get out of the office and get out of the traditional therapy session. Students can be intimidated or closed off with the environment of a traditional setting. They relate this to going to the principal's office or to their personal counselor. There might be negative experiences tied to the setting and that can inhibit your ability to help them. Getting outside and walking has many benefits (Morton, 2018):

1. Walking promotes cognitive functioning by releasing a protein that is crucial for sustaining memory and higher thinking.
2. Walking decreases low mood by releasing endorphins that energize the brain. In fact, just after five minutes of walking, a feel-good effect begins to take place.
3. Walking distracts from worry because the brain is able to immerse itself in an enjoyable activity.
4. Walking increases energy levels and is more beneficial than consuming an energy drink which most students pick up when feeling lethargic.

When you do an activity that is outside the office make sure you ask the student's permission, re-establish rules of confidentiality, respect the student's physical limitations, set boundaries, and debrief.

You can have students take self-assessments and use that as a way to talk about careers, strengths and weaknesses, and social-emotional learning. They can be used for every counseling domain that we help students with. There are many activities that you can do with students. You can do motivational interviewing or ice-breaker-type activities. Especially when you are first getting to know your students, it is important to make sure they feel comfortable in your office. Depending on your school, you might have more students than ASCA recommends and you might not get a lot of time to spend with them one-on-one. So, make the most of your time with the students that you do have.

Group

Small groups can be very effective and a great way to see a handful of students at once. There are different of types of groups you can run within your school. There are task groups that develop curriculum, individual, or social learning plans. Psycho-educational groups promote typical growth or prevent/remediate transit difficulties in personal/social, academic, and career development. Counseling groups address problems in the lives of students. Psychotherapy groups address consistent patterns of dysfunctional behavior. Some things you want to keep in mind when you're creating your small groups are:

1. Structure of your small group.
2. Number of sessions is typically six to eight, and whether that is weekly or monthly is up to you.
3. Length of session. The grade levels and ages of your students will determine the length of time you spend together.
4. The schedule of when the group will meet. This can take coordinating with teachers if you don't have a built-in advisory/club/free bell in your

school's schedule. Before or after school, or during a lunch period might be a time you have to meet.

5. Will the groups be heterogeneous or homogenous groups? Will the participants be experiencing the same problems/characteristics or not?
6. How will you screen the students to be in the group?
7. What are the ages, diversity, genders, and compatibility of the students in the group?

As you're creating your small group you will want to first give out a needs assessment to the school in order to know what type of small group would be good for your students. You might think a girls empowerment group would be a good fit, but after you give a needs assessment you find out that isn't what the students need. After you know the results of your needs assessment, you can organize your group. Make sure that you obtain informed consent and create participant rules. Collect pre-group data that is objective about your students. Subjective data can be useful when screening students for the group. Parental and teacher input can help you with understanding those who are in your group. We live in a data-driven world, so as you're giving your lessons within the group, give out pre- and post-surveys. This will help with knowing how the group is progressing from session to session. You'll want to give a post-group survey to help compare student growth from the first session to the last. It's important to assess your group for its effectiveness and to help support your counseling program (Missouri Comprehensive Guidance and Cousenling Program: Responsive Services, 2015).

Elementary

As an elementary school counselor, you have a wonderful opportunity to run small groups with your students. There are a plethora of small group lesson plans available through books, blog sites, and online resources. I would like to highlight a few great resources that are available to use.

Vanessa Green Allen has her own book *The No More Bullying Book for Kids* and is well known for her blog *Savvy School Counselor*. On her site you can find children's books that have lesson plans included with them. She keeps an up-to-date blog on various lesson plans and activities that are current. Her book addresses the various forms of bullying that occur in today's world and includes (Green, 2018):

- **An overview of bullying** to help kids understand what bullying is, reasons why people bully others, and the different types of bullying——physical, verbal, emotional, and cyber.
- **Practical tips for specific words and actions** kids can use to deal with bullies, as well as advice for getting help from others when they need it.
- **Strategies for becoming 'bully proof'** which focus on helping kids build the resilience to bounce back from bullying.

- **Real-world examples and anecdotes** that illustrate a variety of real-life bullying instances and encourage kids to practice making judgment calls.

There are many children's books on social-emotional, mental health, and relationship topics. The following is a short list of topics you could use in small group lesson plans and an example of a lesson (Rex, 2018).

- **Anger management:** One small group activity you can do when teaching anger is *Angry Birds*. This is an interactive way for students to understand anger. You can show the consequences of our actions by using the characters from the game. Then, you can teach coping strategies.
- **Anxiety:** You can have a 'stress buster' group by creating stress relief boxes. The student starts with a blank pencil box that you could spend your first session decorating. Then, week after week students put items in the box that relieve stress. By the end of the group, students will have an entire box full of strategies to help them when they feel anxious or overwhelmed.
- **Divorce:** When helping students deal with divorce, it's important to help them identify the emotions they associate with the divorce. You can have students in your group pick objects that symbolize various feelings or situations they experience at school. Then, they share their interpretation with the group.
- **Grief:** An activity to help with students grieving is to have them create a memory or pillow bag. Students draw pictures or place special objects in a bag to help them remember the person who died.
- **Making and keeping friends:** Depending on the grade you're working with, there a number of movie activities you could use with your group. There are flash cards to discuss the judgments we make about other people called 'Animal Flash Cards'.
- **Self-esteem:** Books are a great way to discuss self-esteem within a group. *Cupcake* by Charise Mericle Harper is a book about a plain vanilla cupcake that isn't picked to eat. Students might be able to relate to this story from not being picked first to play on teams at recess.
- **Social skills:** *My Mouth is a Volcano* by Julia Cook is a great way to discuss self-control. The image of a volcano is clear to students, who often describe their actions or feelings as "explosions". Students can have discussions about their behaviors and the consequences by reflection using a worksheet.

Middle School and High School

Middle school and high school are together because the lessons for them can be similar. Small groups in these grades can be very beneficial to help students feel less isolated. In these grades, it's less about educating students on what skills are and more about helping them use the skills they have. Topics that work well with middle and high school students are:

- Anger management
- Coping with life changes
- Relationships
- Self-esteem
- Study skills
- College and career readiness
- Social-emotional learning

The North Carolina Public School has free online lesson plans for elementary through high school small groups. Their lesson plans also include an evaluation and worksheets. The West Virginia Department of Education also has free online lesson plans that come with everything you need to implement the lesson. It can be hard to create your own lesson plans as a first-year school counselor.

A Day in the Life...

As you're thinking about what your counseling implementations might look like, I want to give you a couple examples of what your day might look like. As much as you want to spend more time on individual and group counseling, it might not be possible due to the schedule.

Elementary

The life of an elementary school counselor can be hectic and stressful. For the lucky schools who have a school counselor, you might be the only one for 500+ students. It can be a nonstop day as shown by this elementary school counselor's schedule (Schiavone, 2017):

7 a.m. = I get ready for work with my mind racing. When I arrive at school, I have an hour to check email, consult with teachers, plan, and gather materials for my individual sessions and classroom guidance lessons.

9:05 a.m. = I am either in the lobby or outside greeting students. These 15 minutes allow me to say "Hello" to hundreds of students. I walk to homerooms and check in with a few students, and then head to the TV studio to be on the morning announcements and talk about the character trait of the month.

9:30 a.m. = I check my email. I grab my materials for a classroom guidance lesson, just as a student in tears shows up at my door. I stop and talk through the problem. Then, I rush down to the classroom (a few minutes late) and teach a lesson about conflict resolution to enthusiastic third graders.

10:30 a.m. = Back to my office. The nurse calls. A second grader has shown up in her office for the fourth consecutive day with no fever or sickness. I scurry to pick up a student for a scheduled counseling session. A teacher pops in to follow up on a parent email, and we schedule a parent conference.

11:30 a.m.–1:30 p.m. = I run social lunch bunches and group counseling sessions each day. The students and I use this time to explore topics such as friendship, social skills, test anxiety, and anger. In the midst of my lunch groups, a student bursts in and plops on my sofa. I take a pause from my group to address her needs.

1:35 p.m. = From the back of a classroom, I quietly observe a student for the IEP (Individualized Education Program) team process. I will report my observations from this lesson at the next team meeting. I'm off to my other classroom guidance lesson, and I get sidetracked for a few minutes talking to another teacher and parent volunteer about an upcoming Career Day.

2:15 p.m. = Students pop by to check in. I put my coat on, check on the Safeties, and then go outside for afterschool duty. Afterschool, I have a parent-teacher conference.

4:45 p.m. = I sit back at my desk and write some notes, respond to emails, and think about how students are different as a result of my program.

Middle School

A middle school counselor's day can look similar to a high school counselor's day. In the following excerpt, a middle school counselor talks about what her job entails versus her specific schedule (Schmitt, 2012):

> That's a difficult question to answer because our jobs are so complex. School counselors have lots of variety in their days, and they spend a lot of time working with people either one-on-one or in groups.
>
> The most important part of my work is providing direct services to the children. That can mean individual counseling, running groups, and providing classroom guidance. I work hard to protect a large part of my time for students. My role in consultation work – whether with teachers, administrators, or mixed groups – is also rewarding and effective. This can sometimes mean lots of meetings, but it's not time wasted if I can develop outcomes and goals for each step of the process.
>
> School counselors provide valuable connections between groups who have to come together to support student success. For instance, it's important that I assist parents as they navigate school processes. When parents come in to meet with teachers or special education facilitators, I can assist the group by providing insight into the student's needs, I can make sure parents understand the processes, and I can advocate for best practices.

This year I've also spent a good deal of time working with student data. I assist with class registration and scheduling, but the more valuable work is in data analysis that leads to improved programs or policies. I also use student data to develop and follow a 'counselor's watch list'. Students on this list warrant careful monitoring to make sure they achieve their personal, behavioral, or academic goals. I will also play a role in the coordination of our standardized testing. I appreciate the valuable data that the testing provides, but I worry about the time I won't have for the kids because I'm managing testing.

High School

The day in a high school counselor's life can vary from day to day and school to school. I, as a high school counselor, love it! I enjoy the balance of providing direct and indirect services. This article excerpt from *The Harvard Crimson Admissions Blog* states (Pak, 2014),

> Andi O'Hearn from Beijing City International School, and Susan Baker from Johnston High School in Iowa agree that there is no typical day in the life of a high school counselor. Their day can start at 8:00 a.m. and go all the way into midnight with no break.
>
> 'I start every day with a list of what should and needs to be done, but if a student is in a crisis, that will take precedence over everything else.' Baker said. 'What I try to focus on during application season is meeting with every one of my assigned seniors to make sure they are on course for graduation and what they intend to do after high school. This varies from student to student; most will be going on to some type of schooling, four year, two year or vocational. A few will enter the military and others may enter the workforce or take a gap year.'
>
> On top of a high school counselor's regular responsibilities, as a counselor in China, O'Hearn also works with the students' parents, some of whom may not speak English. She also prepares her students for the ACT and SAT, which are not as accessible in China, in addition to the TOEFL or IELTS.
>
> Each counselor has her own way of approaching the application process. O'Hearn said that she tries to begin working with students as early as grade 9 'to help them understand that they will be telling a four-year story, not a one-year story.'
>
> Baker, on the other hand, becomes most involved with the students in their senior years, focusing on application-specific advising, materials, and essays.
>
> Both O'Hearn and Baker are driven by the ultimate goal of all their work.
>
> 'I believe the purpose of my position is to support students and help them make good choices as they prepare for the next step in their lives,' O'Hearn said.

'I am here to help them by answering questions, filling out forms and following up as an admissions counselor when needed. But since students are about to go out into the world on their own, I hope they have learned the skills to navigate and advocate for themselves,' Baker added.

O'Hearn and Baker feel that the most rewarding thing is to get to know their students, see them grow and mature through the process, and finally achieve their dreams.

Wrap Up

As you plan your school counselor year, don't feel like you have to run small groups. If one of your fellow colleagues runs a small group, I encourage you to co-lead it. It is good experience if you have not run one before. Don't feel like you have to create your own from scratch. Utilize the resources available online and from other school counselors. There are books that have lesson plans that can be used for small groups. If you're creative it's a great opportunity to use your strengths, but it isn't necessary. As you think about your schedule and plan your year, try to keep in my mind that you're going to have to be flexible. Regardless of whether you are in an elementary, middle, or high school, you will have situations come up that will take time away from your plans. That is all part of being a counselor in a school! We work with a very unpredictable variable as school counselors. As I end this chapter, I leave you with a few more resources!

Resources

http://savvyschoolcounselor.com/category/small-groups/
www.elementaryschoolcounseling.org/individual-counseling.html
www.schoolcounselingfiles.com/individual-counseling.html
www.ncpublicschools.org/docs/curriculum/guidance/resources/programs-study.pdf
http://wvde.state.wv.us/counselors/group-lessons.html
https://onlinecounselingprograms.com/resources/school-counselor-toolkit/student-development/middle-school/

References

Chen, M.-W., & Giblin, N.J. (2014). *Individual Counseling Skills and Techniques*. Denver, CO: Love Publishing Company.

Green, V. (2018). *The No More Bullying Book for Kids*. New York: Rockridge Press.

Haas, C. (2018, September 13). *Individual*. Retrieved from Counseling with Callie: https://counselingwithcallie.weebly.com/individual-counseling.html

Missouri Comprehensive Guidance and Counseling Program: Responsive Services (2015, May). *Professional School Counselor Small Group Counseling Guide*. Retrieved from Missouri Department of Education: https://dese.mo.gov/sites/default/files/guid-respon-serv-small-group-counseling-guide-2015.pdf

Morton, C. (2018, August 25). *Talk and Walk: Getting Out of the Office to Help Students' Mental Health*. Retrieved from For High School Counselors: http://forhighschoolcounselors. blogspot.com

Pak, S.M. (2014, February 27). *Life as a High School Counselor*. Retrieved from The Harvard Crimson Admissions Blog: www.thecrimson.com/admissions/article/2014/2/27/ high-school-counselors/

Rex, M. (2018, September 17). *Small Group Counseling*. Retrieved from Elementary School Counseling: www.elementaryschoolcounseling.org/small-group-counseling.html

Schiavone, C. (2017, February 3). *A Day in the Life: School Counselors*. Retrieved from Baltimore County Public Schools: https://deliberateexcellence.wordpress. com/2017/02/03/a-day-in-the-life-school-counselors/

Schmitt, D. (2012). *An Interview with Middle School Counselor, Phyllis Farlow*. Retrieved from Teaching: http://teaching.org/resources/an-interview-with-middle-school-counselor-phyllis-farlow

10 Guidance Lessons or Skills Classes

Whether an elementary teacher, middle, or a high school teacher; as a school counselor you will create and implement lessons in the classroom at some point. This can seem daunting on top of everything else a school counselor does, but there are many resources and ready-to-implement lesson plans. Even though they can be time consuming, there are benefits to guidance lessons. It's a great way to implement a school-wide program. Some schools have themes for each year that build upon the previous year. The entire school is on board with implementation. This includes teachers using specific curriculum in their instruction, outside resources coming into the school, and counselors going into classrooms. I recently met with a principal at an elementary school who is implementing a character development model in the school that spans 3–5 years. This year they are focusing on social-emotional learning. The teachers will have instruction about SEL built into their traditional lessons. When implementing a program, getting the faculty and administration to be a part of the execution is important.

As you start your first year, go into classrooms as much as your schedule and school allows. Don't feel like you have to go in twice a month in every grade. That might not be feasible in your school and can be burdensome when you're new. Make time to go into all the grades a handful of times for them to know who you are. Then think about a theme you would like to address and go into classrooms once a quarter. That way you are able to manage the lessons with your other responsibilities. In this chapter, I have provided resources and materials for implementing guidance lessons that have been invaluable to me when I was a first-year counselor.

Elementary

At the elementary level, there are many small group activities that you could use as guidance lessons. The ones mentioned in the previous chapter could easily be modified to do in a classroom. I have listed a couple of resources that are empirically based and come with a scripted lesson plan and all of the materials.

MindUp

MindUp is a Pre-K through High School curriculum that is available to purchase through major booksellers. The curriculum features 15 lessons that focus on the brain to help improve behavior. There are additional lesson materials for incorporating other disciplines into the lesson. They can be as short as ten minutes and work well as a beginning class activity or taught as a full class period. "Each lesson offers easy strategies for helping students focus their attention, improve their self-regulation skills, build resilience to stress, and developing a positive mind-set" (MindUp, 2018).

Merrell's Strong Kids

Merrell's Strong Kids K–12 curriculum teaches social-emotional competencies. *Strong Kids* is an easy way to help your students develop the social-emotional skills they need to manage their challenges and succeed in school and life. Developed by a team of educational and mental health experts, this evidence-based, age-appropriate curriculum is (Merrell's Strong Kids, 2018):

- Low cost and low tech
- Proven to help increase students' knowledge of social and emotional concepts and decrease their emotional and behavioral problems
- Easy to implement with no mental health training required
- Brief enough to use with any program

Middle School

My school has a middle school program connected to the high school. Due to my students skipping a grade upon entering, they are younger than the traditional middle school and high school student. Because of their age and social development, I use the middle school curriculum in the high school grades as well. Both of the curricula I mentioned in the *Elementary* section of this chapter, I have used in my middle school and high school grades. This is why I've only listed two resources.

I use I'm Not Just Gifted by Christine Fonseca for my Prep 7 and 8 students. They are newer to the school and understand what the term 'gifted' means. What I like about this curriculum is that it is especially designed for students who are gifted. It helps students answer the following questions:

- What does it mean to be a successful person?
- What traits and characteristics define successful people?
- Why do gifted children, in particular, need a strong affective curriculum in order to maximize their potential?

These questions and more are explored in this guide to helping gifted children in grades 4–7 as they navigate the complicated social and emotional aspects of their lives. This curriculum is designed to help gifted children explore their giftedness, develop resiliency, manage their intensities, face adversities and tough situations, and cultivate their talents and passions. Including lesson plans, worksheets, and connections to Common Core State Standards, I'm Not Just Gifted is the practical guide necessary for anyone serving and working with gifted children (Fonseca, 2018).

Random Acts of Kindness Foundation

The Random Acts of Kindness Foundation (RAK) is an internationally recognized nonprofit whose mission is to inspire a culture of kindness in schools, homes, and communities. Their goal is to provide engaging, accessible, high-quality resources to support schools, homes, individuals, and communities in acting to develop a culture of kindness. Their lessons are grounded in Social Emotional Learning (SEL). The goal of their lessons is to help students to (Random Acts of Kindness Foundation, 2015):

- Develop an increased awareness of their own emotions, feelings, and identities as caring individuals.
- Use appropriate emotional vocabulary, communication, and listening skills.
- Increase awareness of others' emotions and understanding of how kind and unkind actions impact others.
- Act kindly toward themselves and peers in the classroom, school, home, and community.
- Improve the ability to apply problem-solving strategies in many social situations.
- Increase the ability to participate in the classroom productively, contribute to discussions, ask questions, and share experiences, engage in learning, listen, follow directions, take risks, and play a role in the larger group.
- Improve academic performance and achievement.

High School

In this section, I would like to give you another social-emotional resource and a number of college/career resources. I spend a good portion of my time planning and implementing my school's college and career readiness program. The resources I've listed are ones I use as the foundation of my lesson planning.

Social Emotional

Rosalind Wiseman is well known for her book *Queenbees and Wannabees*, but she has also established a curriculum titled *Owning Up*. This curriculum is part of her organization called Cultures of Dignity that works with communities to shift how we think about adolescents' physical and emotional well-being (Cultures of Dignity, 2018).

Owning Up is a 17-lesson curriculum that examines the cultural constructs that influence young people's socialization. It incorporates cultural definitions of gender, sexism, racism, classism, homophobia, and other forms of 'isms' that affect young people's beliefs and decision-making around self-esteem, friendships, group dynamics, and social and physical aggressions (Wiseman, 2017).

Mastering Test Anxiety is a curriculum for small groups but can also be used in guidance lessons. It is a comprehensive guide that addresses test anxiety and math anxiety. Each lesson starts by giving students the opportunity to be held accountable with respect to their specific goals and ends with positive self-talk or affirmation. The purpose is for students to learn new skills and to help increase self-awareness of reactions and feelings related to tests (Knight & West, 2012).

College and Career

CollegeEd is the College Board's free, standards-based college planning and career exploration program for middle and high school students. The CollegeEd program builds on the College Board's more than 100 years of experience in guiding students on the path to college. It provides lessons and activities designed to help students develop the skills to meet their goals in life. CollegeEd offers flexible options for teaching, implementation, and family involvement. The program consists of three levels, each with its own student workbook and accompanying educator guide. CollegeEd materials are provided as PDF files. They can be downloaded and used online or printed out by districts, schools, and families for noncommercial, educational purposes. CollegeEd includes self- and career-exploration activities (College Board, 2018).

Counseling 21st Century Students for Optimal College and Career Readiness A 9th–12th Grade Curriculum is a guide for how to structure your college and career counseling program. You can use the chapters to do individual counseling or as a guidance lesson. There is a CD included with the tables, exercises, and charts that are contained in the book. Topics included in the curriculum are:

- Making the transition to ninth grade successful.
- Using technology in the advising process, such as online resources for college and career research, assessing interests, and structuring advising sessions.
- Preparing for standardized testing and using it to motivate students about the college application process.
- Assisting students in researching careers and colleges, making the most of college visits, applying for college, and writing the application essay.

NACAC has combined the Guiding the Way to Higher Education: Step-by-Step to College Workshops for Students curricula with resources from the Families, Counselors and Communities Together (FCCT) manual to create the **Step by**

Step: College Awareness and Planning for Families, Counselors and Communities. Revised in 2017, the curricula—presented in four sections, for elementary school students (grades K–5), middle school students (grades 6–8), early high school students (grades 9 through first semester 11), and late high school students (grades 11–12)—offer training for counselors and others who work with underrepresented and underserved students to provide comprehensive tools for meeting the needs of first-generation students and their families (National Association for College Admission Counseling, 2018).

Wrap Up

I hope this chapter has given you a foundation for implementing your guidance lessons. These curricula really helped me plan my lessons for each grade level and give me a central focus. I teach a guidance class to the sophomores that meet once a week and having a curriculum that is empirically based is important to me. My first year, I was overwhelmed by the class and had to do a lot of revising. These revisions were due to starting a new college and career curriculum and a needs assessment. In the appendix of this chapter, I have included my syllabus for my sophomore class, an example of a guidance lesson, and an example of a pre-post test. Your professors at your graduate programs spent time talking about the importance of data. ASCA has a lot of resources on having a data-driven school counseling program. Take every opportunity to gather data to support what you are doing in the school. Show the results of these pre-post tests and how you are impacting the students. They can be great for creating new goals for the next year. You're not always going to get the data you want, but it will help you to know what to do differently or what to continue to do. Take advantage of guidance lessons or teaching a class that is within your role. It's a good way to meet the needs of many students in one setting. Try to collaborate with teachers to reinforce the skills and concepts you are teaching. Social Emotional Learning is relevant in all educational domains. Educate your faculty and administration on the importance of well-being for academic success. Treat each task you're given as an opportunity! You might not want to teach a class, but it's the opportunity to capitalize on being in front of students and meeting their needs.

Appendix A. Personal Example of a Syllabus

Department of Counseling

Course Title:	Guidance Class
Semester:	Fall 2016 and Spring 2017
Day and Time:	Friday 2nd and 3rd period
Instructor:	Heather Couch, MA
Office/Phone:	Counseling Office, ext. 2330
E-mail Address:	heather.couch@covingtonlatin.org
Website:	www.covingtonlatin.org/guidance
Office Hours:	7:30–8:00 am, 3:00–3:30 pm, or drop in

Course Description

This class is a full class that will be separated into personal/social the first semester and career/college the second semester. The class will educate sophomore students on the personal and social issues that arise (such as drinking, drugs, cyberbullying, etc.). They will learn about relationships and how to navigate peer pressure. Students will learn about suicide prevention and self-harm. The second semester will focus on career development and college readiness.

Objectives

Code key (S = School Counseling Standards) based on the ASCA Student Standards.

Students will:

Personal/Social Standards

1. PS:A1.2 Identify values, attitudes, and beliefs
2. PS:A1.4 Understand change is a part of growth
3. PS:A1.5 Identify and express feelings
4. PS:A1.6 Distinguish between appropriate and inappropriate behavior
5. PS:A1.7 Recognize personal boundaries, rights, and privacy needs
6. PS:A1.8 Understand the need for self-control and how to practice it
7. PS:A1.9 Demonstrate cooperative behavior in groups
8. PS:A2 Acquire interpersonal skills
9. PS:B1 Self-knowledge application
10. PS:C1 Acquire personal safety skills

College and Career Standards

1. A:A3.5 Share knowledge
2. A:B2.7 Identify post-secondary options consistent with interests, achievement, aptitude, and abilities
3. A:C1.6 Understand how school success and academic achievement enhance future career and vocational opportunities
4. C:A1.1 Develop skills to locate, evaluate, and interpret career information
5. C:A1.2 Learn about the variety of traditional and nontraditional occupations
6. C:A1.3 Develop an awareness of personal abilities, skills, interests, and motivations
7. C:B1.1 Apply decision-making skills to career planning, course selection, and career transition
8. C:B1.2 Identify personal skills, interests, and abilities and relate them to current career choice
9. C:B1.3 Demonstrate knowledge of the career-planning process
10. C:B1.4 Know the various ways in which occupations can be classified

11. C:B1.5 Use research and information resources to obtain career information
12. C:B1.6 Learn to use the Internet to access career-planning information
13. C:B2.5 Maintain a career-planning portfolio
14. C:C1.3 Identify personal preferences and interests influencing career choice and success

Required Textbooks:

Methods of Instruction

The following methods will be used to facilitate learning in this course:

- lectures
- small group activities, including discussions and interactions
- cooperative learning via group projects and activities
- media, including video tapes, audiotapes, visual aids
- simulation via role play
- critical thinking exercises—'thinking outside the box'
- writing via reaction papers, evaluation of assessments

Course Requirements and Assignments

1. **Class Attendance and Participation**—This is a pass or fail class and much of the learning in this occurs in the context of discussion, demonstrations, and experiential activities; you are expected to be 'present' (ready to learn) for all classes. Factors used to assess your grade include *attendance, informed participation in class exercises and discussions, and brief reaction papers.* A grade of incomplete will be given until such assignments are completed. Please see attendance policy below for additional information.

Signature Assignment

Assignment MET(100–85pts)	PARTIALLY MET(84–70pts)	NOT MET(69–0pts)
1. Small Group Full participation to the best of your ability. Full engagement during the group process by active listening and discussion.		Unwilling to participate in group with the minimum requirement of a feeling check or active listening to peers.
2. Life Plan Exceptional work was put into the portfolio. Worksheets were completed with thought-out answers.	There was proficient amount of work put into the portfolio. Worksheets were completed, but not with thought-out answers. The minimum requirements were met.	Limited amount effort put into project. Portfolio was missing items or not completed in its entirety.

Writing Expectations:

Professional writing is expected. Students should turn in quality work that reflects the academic standards of CLS. All papers are to be typed, double-space, using 12 font in Times New Roman. Follow APA Style, referring to the APA Manual.

Evaluation:

1. Attendance and participation
2. Reaction essays
3. College/career plan

Policies and Expectations

- The classroom format is largely experiential. It is not possible to make up the experiences of discussion, demonstration, and practice done in class.
- Attendance and participation constitute a significant portion of your final grade. Participation means preparing for class by reading required materials and entering into class discussions.
- *Punctuality*: being on time is expected. Consistent tardiness will also add up and become inclusive as an absence. Additionally, leaving class significantly early two times will be equivalent to one absence.
- *Late work*: When a student accumulates three missing homework assignments—not due to illness or absence:
    - The teacher will assign the student to *academic jug* (held in the jug room). The jug assignment card will be special to indicate that it is an *academic jug*.
    - Parent(s) will be informed by email or phone of the jug and the reason for the jug:
        - Deans shall be carbon copied into the email (CC:).
    - The homework policy is continuous. After every three missing assignments in a subject area, students are assigned to academic jug; however, each new quarter starts the student with a fresh start.
        - Unless a particular student has been expressly exempted by the Dean of Studies, teachers will enforce the homework policy for all prep and freshman students.
        - Teachers will maintain a form provided by the Dean of Studies to track the academic jugs of prep and freshman students. This form will be turned into the Dean of Studies at the end of each quarter.
- *Academic Honesty*: All issues of academic dishonesty will be handled according to the student handbook guidelines.
- *Behavior:*Vulgar behaviors, whether via speech or action, will not be tolerated and may result in a jug or further disciplinary action. Due to the nature of this class, please be mindful of others' opinions/emotions/views. There will be open discussion and respect is expected at all times! There may be times

when confidentiality is requested, please be mindful to not gossip or share with other peers. Confidentiality will be explained in the class.

Tentative Course Schedule *(specific topics are subject to change)*

Date	Topic/Reading Assignment	Readings and Assignments
Week 1 (Aug 19)	Introduction, Review of Syllabus, Class Assessment, APA, and Warrior Run	Take field trip information home to parents
Week 2 (Aug 26)	Cliques, Stereotypes, Self-Exploration, Values and Beliefs	
Week 3 (Sep 2)	Relationships and Boundaries	
Week 4 (Sep 9)	Bullying Part 1	
Week 5 (Sep 16)	Bullying Part 2, Cyberbullying, Social Media, Inappropriate Texting	
Week 6 (Sep 23)	**Sub Teacher (out for PD)**	Reaction Essay
Week 7 (Sep 30)	Self-Harm Part 1: Substance Abuse	
Week 8 (Oct 7)	Self-Harm Part 2: Physical and Emotional	
Week 9 (Oct 14)	Suicide Prevention and Awareness Part 1	
Week 10 (Oct 21)	Suicide Prevention and Awareness Part 2	
Week 11 (Oct 28)	**Sub Teacher (out for PD)**	Reaction Essay
Week 12 (Nov 4)	Group, Week 1 = Introduction to Group	
Week 13 (Nov 11)	Group, Week 2	
Week 14 (Nov 18)	Group, Week 3	
Week 15 (Dec 2)	Group, Week 4	
Week 16 (Dec 9)	Group, Week 5	
Week 17 (Dec 16)	Group, Week 6	

Appendix B. Personal Example of a Lesson Plan:

Lesson 1

Introduction

This Personal/Social Development Unit is designed for seventh, eighth, and ninth graders to serve as a foundation for understanding interpersonal skills, starting the process of self-exploration, learning about relationships and conflict, and team building. In order to increase seventh, eighth, and ninth graders' social skills, this unit plan will have them do icebreakers, worksheets about respect, and team building games. This topic is important because it will help set a framework for students to understand the importance of getting to know their peers and understanding their own uniqueness. This lesson will be taught to all Prep 7/8 and Freshmen at Covington Latin School. On two different days a week for two weeks, counselor will spend time in each of the 7/8/9 classes.

Title of Lesson: Getting to Know Others and Myself

ASCA National Standards and Competencies:
★**AA.S.7** Student will acquire the knowledge, attitudes, and interpersonal skills to help them understand and respect self and others.
★**PS:A1.1** Develop positive attitudes toward self as a unique and worthy person.
★**PS:A1.10** Identify personal strengths and assets.
★**P/SD A.** Students will acquire the knowledge, attitude, and interpersonal skills to help them understand and respect self and others.
★**PS:A2.8** Learn how to make and keep friends.

Indicators:
AA. PSD.6.7.10 Develop a sense of belonging to a group to establish group cohesiveness.

Learning Goals and Objectives:
★Students will be able to work together to identify what makes them similar and different.
★Students will be able to identify their strengths and weaknesses.

Lesson #1: Getting to Know Others and Myself (50 minutes roughly)
Participants: Developmental Level: Middle/High School; Grade level: 7th–9th grades
Materials Needed: Blank paper and writing utensils.

Learning Activities:
Group Activity (15 minutes)

1. The instructor should introduce the lesson by pointing out that students sometimes feel alone even in a large group. Some students may also feel very different from others without realizing how much they have in common with their fellow classmates.
2. Distribute the 'We're Alike Bingo' handout and review the directions at the top. The goal is for students to complete typical bingos such as vertical, horizontal, sideways, or four corners. Asking students to

complete at least two bingos encourages them to meet more students and potentially learn more about their classmates.

3. Allow the students adequate time to do the activity.

Open discussion about the following questions: (15 minutes)

a. Were you surprised to find so many students with similar likes?
b. What are some ways that you discovered similarities of which you were not aware?
c. Why is it good to know how you are similar to other students?
d. Is it OK to also be unique in some ways?
e. Why is it interesting to know how other students are unique from us?
f. How does this activity help you?

Discuss: Understand Myself (20 minutes)

1. Discuss the statement: "Too much of anything is not a good thing." Have you ever been in a group with all leaders? All followers? All fun people? How can teams increase productivity? We need a variety of individual strengths when working as a team.
2. Students will be given a worksheet to identify their strengths and weaknesses.
   a. After filling out the worksheet, students will discuss their different strengths and weaknesses with the person next to them. Then they will bring the discussion to the entire class.
   b. Do others have similar or different strengths and weaknesses?
   c. What strengths or weaknesses seem to be more unique to you?
   d. Why is it important to know this information? How can it be helpful to you in the future?

Post Test (5 minutes)

Assessment/Evaluation: There will be a pre-post test given to the students. Discussion will allow for me to hear that the students are able to restate what they have learned in their own words.

Appendix C. Pre/Post Test

Knowing Others and Myself   Pre-test or Post-test (circle one)

Please rate how much you agree or disagree with the following:

1. I am comfortable making new friends.

1	2	3	4	5	6
Strongly Disagree	Disagree	Slightly Disagree	Slightly Agree	Agree	Strongly Agree

2. I understand that everyone is both unique and similar.

1	2	3	4	5	6
Strongly Disagree	Disagree	Slightly Disagree	Slightly Agree	Agree	Strongly Agree

3. I know what my strengths and weaknesses are.

1	2	3	4	5	6
Strongly Disagree	Disagree	Slightly Disagree	Slightly Agree	Agree	Strongly Agree

4. I know how to improve my weaknesses.

1	2	3	4	5	6
Strongly Disagree	Disagree	Slightly Disagree	Slightly Agree	Agree	Strongly Agree

References

College Board (2018, September 20). *What is College Ed?* Retrieved from Big Future: https://bigfuture.collegeboard.org/get-started/educator-resource-center/collegeed-college-planning-program/what-is-collegeed

Cultures of Dignity (2018, September 20). *About.* Retrieved from Cultures of Dignity: https://culturesofdignity.com/dignity-about/

Fitzpatrick, C., & Costantini, K. (2011). *Counseling 21st Century Students for Optimal College and Career Readiness.* New York, NY: Routledge.

Fonseca, C. (2018, September 20). *I'm Not Just Gifted.* Retrieved from Christine Fonseca: www.christinefonseca.com/i-m-not-just-gifted

Knight, A.M., & West, L.C. (2012). *Mastering Test Anxiety.* Alexandria, VA: American School Counselor Association.

Merrell's Strong Kids (2018, September 20). *About.* Retrieved from Merrell's Strong Kids: https://strongkidsresources.com/about/general

MindUp (2018, September 20). *MindUp for School.* Retrieved from MindUP: https://mindup.org/mindup-for-schools/

National Association for College Admission Counseling (2018, September 20). *Step by Step: College Awareness and Planning for Families, Counselors and Communities.* Retrieved from NACAC: www.nacacnet.org/advocacy--ethics/initiatives/steps/

Random Acts of Kindness Foundation (2015). *Educator Guide.* Retrieved from Random Acts of Kindness: http://materials.randomactsofkindness.org/teacher-guide/RAK_Teacher_Guide_20140407b.pdf

Wiseman, R. (2017). *Owning Up.* Thousand Oaks, CA: Corwin.

11 Family Counseling

One of the classes that many school counselors take in conjunction with mental health counselors is family therapy. I've had to meet with parents and students together about college and personal issues. Although the information I learned from my family therapy class has been helpful, it was about therapy. This chapter will discuss the topic of family counseling from the school counseling perspective.

Family Counseling in the School

Our students come from many different backgrounds. Blended families, single parent families, foster care families, or guardianship to name a few of the diverse family homes. According to the U.S. Census Bureau for children under the age of 18, 50.7 million live with two parents, 17.2 million live with mother only, 2.8 million live with no parent present, and 3.0 million live with father only (U.S. Department of Commerce, 2017). In addition to these children, are the over 400,000 that are in foster care (U.S. Department of Health & Human Services, 2017). When you take this data into consideration and the growing number of students who are Secondary English Learners, there is a lot of benefit to understanding family systems and applying it in the school counseling program.

Recently a parent came into my office to talk to me about the divorce between her and her husband. The divorce was finalized but they were still cohabitating until other arrangements were made. The parent was concerned for the daughter who had yet to talk to the parent in depth about the divorce. To the parent, it seemed like the daughter was handling the divorce well but the parent wanted me to know in case something seemed different with the daughter. The daughter is introverted and doesn't talk about her feelings often and the parent came in wanting to inform me and get resources. The parent thought that once they moved out of the house that it would affect her daughter, because the reality of it would set in. They come from a traditional, Catholic background and divorce isn't something her daughter has seen in her friends' families.

This scenario isn't uncommon considering the large number of children coping with parental divorce. It's good that the parent came into my office to inform me about the situation going on at home. The student was new to our school and I hadn't built a rapport with her. She might not have felt comfortable telling me herself that her parents had recently gotten divorced. There are risk factors that we can look for in students. These include, but aren't limited to:

- Single-parent families in the United States are increasing.
- Children of divorce have more mental health problems in comparison with their peers.
- Suicide is the third leading cause of death among U.S. youth.
- Brain regions responsible for decision-making are not fully developed in youth.
- Changes in family structure can have an effect on school grades.
- Anxiety, depression, and behavior problems are elevated after divorce.
- Children of divorce often feel a sense of instability.

An understanding of these risk points is essential for moving forward with children and families because the risk can provide direction for the work that needs to be done. For example, knowing that mental health symptoms are elevated following divorce and impulsive decision-making is greater among youth (Butler, Crespi, & McNamara, 2017).

These are things that counselors know how to address but might not always consider without an awareness of the data. In addition, parents can become defensive, or they might blame themselves for their children's difficulties. For this reason, it is imperative to educate parents on these risk points. It is also important to realize that family issues may require clinical supervision (Butler, Crespi, & McNamara, 2017).

Supervision

As school counselors we aren't licensed to practice marriage and family counseling. Seek consultation with a mental health counselor who focuses on marriage and family. They will be able to provide resources and assistance. As we meet with students, family issues will come up and we need to know how to help our students. Seek consultation and supervision from someone who has experience and training with family counseling.

Considerations

As a school counselor, you're not always counseling the student. Families are going to be involved at some point in the years you see them. As a school counselor at a high school, I frequently talk to parents about the college process. Seniors' parents come talk to me during parent teacher conferences, they email, and call me. We want the parents to be involved in their child's life. However, we have to know if the relationship between the parents and child is healthy or not.

> Family counseling offers unique and engaging ways of reframing prob-lems. Rather than blaming an individual for a particular problem, family counselors look at the family system. Perhaps a child's acting-out behav-iors allow parents to avoid looking at their relational problems. Perhaps a child's failing grades reflect more on family anxiety and stress than on individual issues. Fundamentally, family counseling takes a larger, more systemic perspective of presenting issues.
>
> (Butler, Crespi, & McNamara, 2017)

As school counselors, we have the skills to work with families. We understand the importance of building rapport, interpersonal relationships, and use assess-ments and interventions. The connection between academic success and life outside of school is undeniable. As a school counselor, you have to consider what is happening outside of school. Before ending this chapter, I would like to discuss childhood trauma. This can affect how you interact with the parents or know why certain family problems exists.

Trauma

Childhood trauma has been shown to affect students' academic achievement and their mental health. There can be a stigma that childhood trauma is only in low-income, urban schools but that isn't the case. Trauma does not have an economic or ethnicity preference. There is a lot of research surrounding the Adverse Childhood Experiences (ACEs). The ACEs is a questionnaire that asks about your childhood experiences with abuse, neglect, and other negative experiences.

The questionnaire will look similar to the following questions (Stevens, 2018):

Prior to your 18th birthday:

1. Did a parent or other adult in the household often or very often… Swear at you, insult you, put you down, or humiliate you? or Act in a way that made you afraid that you might be physically hurt?

   No___If Yes, enter 1 __

2. Did a parent or other adult in the household often or very often… Push, grab, slap, or throw something at you? or Ever hit you so hard that you had marks or were injured?

   No___If Yes, enter 1 __

3. Did an adult or person at least 5 years older than you ever... Touch or fondle you or have you touch their body in a sexual way? or Attempt or actually have oral, anal, or vaginal intercourse with you?

   No___If Yes, enter 1 __

4. Did you often or very often feel that... No one in your family loved you or thought you were important or special? or Your family didn't look out for each other, feel close to each other, or support each other?

   No___If Yes, enter 1 __

5. Did you often or very often feel that... You didn't have enough to eat, had to wear dirty clothes, and had no one to protect you? or Your parents were too drunk or high to take care of you or take you to the doctor if you needed it?

   No___If Yes, enter 1 __

6. Were your parents ever separated or divorced?

   No___If Yes, enter 1 __

7. Was your mother or stepmother:
   Often or very often pushed, grabbed, slapped, or had something thrown at her? or Sometimes, often, or very often kicked, bitten, hit with a fist, or hit with something hard? or Ever repeatedly hit over at least a few minutes or threatened with a gun or knife?

   No___If Yes, enter 1 __

8. Did you live with anyone who was a problem drinker or alcoholic, or who used street drugs?

   No___If Yes, enter 1 __

9. Was a household member depressed or mentally ill, or did a household member attempt suicide?

   No___If Yes, enter 1 __

10. Did a household member go to prison?

    No___If Yes, enter 1 __

Now add up your 'Yes' answers: _ This is your ACEs score.

   Studies have shown that there is a correlation between academic achievement, health problems, and mental health and the number of ACEs one has. According to the Child Health findings of the 2016 National Survey of Children's Health (NSCH), this included nine ACEs (Sacks & Murphey, 2018):

- Economic hardship and divorce or separation of a parent or guardian are the most common ACEs reported nationally, and in all states.
- Just under half (45 percent) of children in the United States have experienced at least one ACE, which is similar to the rate of exposure found in a 2011/2012 survey.* In Arkansas, the state with the highest prevalence, 56 percent of children have experienced at least one ACE.
- One in ten children nationally has experienced three or more ACEs, placing them in a category of especially high risk. In five states—Arizona, Arkansas, Montana, New Mexico, and Ohio—as many as one in seven children had experienced three or more ACEs.
- Children of different races and ethnicities do not experience ACEs equally. Nationally, 61 percent of black non-Hispanic children and 51 percent of Hispanic children have experienced at least one ACE, compared with 40 percent of white non-Hispanic children and only 23 percent of Asian non-Hispanic children. In every region, the prevalence of ACEs is lowest among Asian non-Hispanic children and, in most regions, is highest among black non-Hispanic children.

The ACEs do not substitute a comprehensive trauma screening, but it does aid in understanding the effects of trauma on a child. This information can help school counselors look at other outside factors that might be contributing to a student's poor academic performance or poor behavior. Another recent study looked at maltreatment and school performance. The University of Michigan conducted a study within the Michigan public schools and found 18% of third graders had been subject to an investigation of maltreatment in the home. Their sample included over 700,000 Michigan public school students who were born between 2000 and 2006. They focused their analysis on 3rd graders because it's the first year the state administers standardized assessment to all students. They looked at whether students were meeting the state defined proficiency level in reading and math. Their findings were (Jacob & Ryan, 2018):

1. Approximately 18 percent of Michigan third graders have been formally investigated by Child Protective Services (CPS) for possible exposure to maltreatment.
2. African American students, students who quality for free/reduced lunch (i.e. poor students), students living in relatively high-poverty areas, and students attending urban schools are all more likely to be investigated by Child Protective Services for suspected child maltreatment.
3. 57% of third graders with a prior CPS investigation achieve basic proficiency levels on the statewide reading exam compared with 65% of third graders with no prior CPS investigation. 44% of students with a prior CPS investigation passing the math threshold compared with 51% among

other third graders. These gaps are equivalent in size to the Black–White achievement gap that one finds after controlling for a similar set of neighborhood and school factors.

4. Referral rates vary dramatically across districts, and even across schools within the same district. It is not unusual for one-third of students in high-poverty schools to have been investigated for abuse or neglect.
5. While poorer school districts have high rates of maltreatment investigations, there are important exceptions to this pattern.

As school counselors, we can look at these studies and be better informed about the lives of our students. School counselors working in districts with high rates of maltreatment can help provide resources and implement programming to address these issues. School counselors can be trained in trauma and then provide training to faculty. It's important for school counselors to help meet the needs of their students and not overlook the factors happening in the home. Youth in foster care are among these children who are experiencing maltreatment. Helping them to navigate the foster care system is crucial to their success inside and outside the school.

Wrap Up

There are many areas within the family unit that we did not cover. It's very important to attend workshops and courses on family counseling and trauma. We make decisions to refer students to see outside mental health professionals and are mandated reporters. These decisions need to be made having the correct knowledge. We are the experts within the schools that our students, families, faculty, and administration look to for advice. When we are working with students; we have to take into consideration their environment and family structure. Meeting the needs of students cannot happen if we compartmentalize what is happening inside and outside the school.

References

Butler, K.S., Crespi, D.T., & McNamara, M. (2017, May). Bringing the family counseling perspective into schools. *Counseling Day*, pp. 54–58.

Jacob, B.A., & Ryan, J. (2018, March 22). *How Life Outside of a School Affects Student Performance in School*. Retrieved from Brookings: www.brookings.edu/research/how-life-outside-of-a-school-affects-student-performance-in-school/

Sacks, V., & Murphey, D. (2018, February 12). *The Prevalence of Adverse Childhood Experiences, Nationally, by State, and by Race or Ethnicity*. Retrieved from Child Trends: www.childtrends.org/publications/prevalence-adverse-childhood-experiences-nationally-state-race-ethnicity

Stevens, J.E. (2018, September 28). *Got Your ACE Score?* Retrieved from ACES Too High?: https://acestoohigh.com/got-your-ace-score/

U.S. Department of Health & Human Services (2017, October 20). AFCARS Report #24. Retrieved from U.S. Department of Health & Human Services: www.acf.hhs.gov/sites/default/files/cb/afcarsreport24.pdf

U.S. Department of Commerce (2017, November 17). *Living Arrangements of Children Under Age 18*. Retrieved from US Census Bureau: www.census.gov/library/visualizations/2016/comm/cb16-192_living_arrangements.html

12 Dealing with Your Own Biases

Dealing with your own biases can be one of the hardest things to teach in graduate school. Professors teach on topics that are controversial to challenge students' biases. This is good preparation for any counselor, because there will always be students who have different values and beliefs. However, there will be biases you doesn't know you have until the issue is brought up by a student. Part of dealing with your own biases is knowing what the bias is, but also knowing what to do with ones that arise.

Implicit and Explicit Bias

Before we get into how you know what your biases are, I would like to provide the definitions for two types of bias. Implicit and explicit bias are the common types that are discussed at length in our society. If you are doing any studying on diversity and inclusion, you will be discussing these two terms. They are important to understanding how we are influenced by our culture on a macro and micro level.

The Ohio State University Kirwan Institute for the Study of Race and Ethnicity provide the following information on implicit bias:

Defining Implicit Bias[1]

Also known as implicit social cognition, implicit bias refers to the attitudes or stereotypes that affect our understanding, actions, and decisions in an unconscious manner. These biases, which encompass both favorable and unfavorable assessments, are activated involuntarily and without an individual's awareness or intentional control. Residing deep in the subconscious, these biases are different from known biases that individuals may choose to conceal for the purposes of social and/or political correctness. Rather, implicit biases are not accessible through introspection.

The implicit associations we harbor in our subconscious cause us to have feelings and attitudes about other people based on characteristics such as race, ethnicity, age, and appearance. These associations develop over the course of a lifetime beginning at a very early age through exposure to direct and indirect messages. In addition to early life experiences, the media and news programming are often-cited origins of implicit associations.

A Few Key Characteristics of Implicit Biases

- Implicit biases are **pervasive**. Everyone possesses them, even people with avowed commitments to impartiality such as judges.
- Implicit and explicit biases are **related but distinct mental constructs**. They are not mutually exclusive and may even reinforce each other.
- The implicit associations we hold **do not necessarily align with our declared beliefs** or even reflect stances we would explicitly endorse.
- We generally tend to hold implicit biases that **favor our own ingroup**, though research has shown that we can still hold implicit biases against our ingroup.
- Implicit biases are **malleable**. Our brains are incredibly complex, and the implicit associations that we have formed can be gradually unlearned through a variety of debiasing techniques.

(The Kirwan Institute for the Study of Race and Ethnicity, 2018)

Defining Explicit Bias

'Explicit bias' refers to the attitudes and beliefs we have about a person or group on a conscious level. Much of the time, these biases and their expression arise as the direct result of a perceived threat. When people feel threatened, they are more likely to draw group boundaries to distinguish themselves from others (Perception Institute, 2018).

Values and Belief

An important part of knowing your biases is understanding your values and beliefs. Think about where you get your values. They are going to be influenced by your culture. Within your culture; family, religion, neighborhood, school, peers, the media, government, and personal experiences are all going to affect your values and beliefs. Ask yourself these questions to start identifying your values and beliefs:

1. What are your core beliefs? What do you believe is fundamentally right or wrong?
2. What has influenced you to have these core beliefs?
3. What do you consider to be immoral or unethical?
4. What determined your career path?
5. What are your assumptions about people?

An activity to help you understand what your biases are is to pretend you are having a dinner party. From the following list of people you have to choose three; who will you invite (Patterson, 2018)?

- Mom of two with drug addiction
- Homeless man with alcohol dependence
- Person with schizophrenia, not on meds
- Man charged with Felony Domestic Abuse
- Famous politician
- Person who makes racial slurs in public on camera

Then ask yourself, who did you decide to invite and why did you or did not you invite them? This activity is an easy way to realize your assumptions about people from different backgrounds. You don't get to choose who your clients are, and you need to know how you will respond to different situations they present to you. Continue to develop self-awareness so that you don't impose your values and beliefs onto your students.

> Self-awareness is perhaps one of the best tools you can use to avoid imposing your values on clients. This involves taking a comprehensive inventory of your feelings, values, attitudes, and behaviors and noticing your reactions to your clients' statements or actions, especially those that provoke a strong or negative feeling.
>
> (Miller, 2018)

We have an important role in helping our students and they look to us for guidance. It can be easy to tell them what they should do versus helping them come to their own conclusions. They are vulnerable when they come to talk to us and we need to stay neutral to their worldview as they're continuing to develop it.

Diversity and Inclusion

As school counselors in the 21st century, it is important that we understand our students come from many different cultures. Diversity and inclusion, and equitable education models are initiatives that many school districts are implementing. Understanding the working definitions of diversity, inclusion, and equity are important as a school counselor.

Diversity, as defined by the Merriam-Webster dictionary, is "the condition of having or being composed of differing elements: VARIETY *especially* : the inclusion of different types of people (such as people of different races or cultures) in a group or organization" (Merriam-Webster, 2018).

Inclusion, as defined by the Cambridge Dictionary, is "the act of including someone or something as part of a group, list, etc., or a person or thing that is included" (Cambridge Dictionary, 2018).

Equity, as defined by Dictionary.com, is "the quality of being fair or impartial; fairness; impartiality" (Dictionary.com, 2018).

What is the purpose of understanding these terms and definitions? These are going to continue to be initiatives that school districts are going to embrace. School districts are looking at diversity for understanding achievement gaps. As a school counselor you can have an active role in these initiatives. You can be an active voice in your school for your students.

An example of an equity policy from the Cincinnati Public Schools shows how a district-wide initiative can be implemented (Cincinnati Public Schools, 2018),

The policy commits the school board to ensuring that the principles of fairness, equity and inclusion are fully integrated into all of the policies, programs, operations and practices guiding the 34,000-student public school district, the largest in Southwest Ohio.

It also obligates the district to eliminate any policies, structures and practices that 'perpetuate inequities and contribute to disproportionality of access and outcomes.' In addition, the policy calls for equitable distribution of financial, capital and human resources through Cincinnati Public Schools' annual budget allocation process.

The policy directs the superintendent and district treasurer to develop a plan with clear and measurable accountability standards and procedures to be shared with the public and submitted to the Board annually for approval. The Board will review implementation of the plan by all district departments and school sites at least semi-annually.

How does this impact you as a counselor? This can be an opportunity to take leadership in helping close achievement gaps, being on a curriculum committee, and working with families. Judy R. Hughey from Kansas State University wrote in her article, "Meeting the Needs of Diverse Students: Enhancing School Counselors' Experience", the following information about how to help bridge the achievement gaps in diversity (Hughey, 2011):

In planning for academic counseling intervention implementation, Lee stated: 'Counseling interventions are greatly impacted by language issues and value differences that come with the cultural diversity.' Olson and Jerald provided a framework for the discussion of school contextual factors and challenges as counselors, advisors, and teachers plan appropriate interventions to communicate, collaborate, and consult for student success. The following frames the various discussions being carried out by the project team:

1. Achievement gap—Students experience difficulty achieving academic success and have difficulty transitioning to college and/or meaningful work settings.

2. Concentrated poverty—Living in poverty often means families lack resources (health insurance, health care, mental health care) that could enhance learning opportunities.
3. Teaching challenge—Schools are unable to hire adequate numbers of diverse qualified teachers and counselors. Issues that complicate the teaching and counseling of diverse learners include high absenteeism, lack of parental involvement, lack of knowledge regarding language and culture issues, K–12 and postsecondary school retention, and effective teaching strategies.
4. School climate—Significant social and academic issues (conflict resolution, academic success, and socialization) exist in teaching diverse students.
5. Access to resources—Diverse students often do not have access or awareness to the same technology or other resources as their classmates.

To help you have a better understanding of why it's important to know how to support your students, the following are two Elementary and Secondary Enrollment reports from the National Center for Education Statistics.

Between 2003 and 2013, the percentage of students enrolled in public elementary and secondary schools decreased for students who were White (from 59 to 50 percent) and Black (from 17 to 16 percent). In contrast, the percentage of students enrolled in public schools increased for students who were Hispanic (from 19 to 25 percent) and Asian/Pacific Islander (4 to 5 percent) during this time period. Enrollment of American Indian/ Alaska Native students was around 1 percent from 2003 to 2013. The percentage of students enrolled in public schools who were of Two or more races increased between 2008 (the first year for which data are available) and 2013 from 1 to 3 percent.

Between fall 2013 and fall 2025, the percentages of students enrolled in public schools are projected to continue to decrease for students who are White (from 50 to 46 percent) and Black (from 16 to 15 percent). In contrast, the percentages are projected to increase over this period for students who are Hispanic (from 25 to 29 percent), Asian/Pacific Islander (from 5 to 6 percent), and of Two or more races (from 3 to 4 percent). The percentage of students who are American Indian/Alaska Native is projected to be about 1 percent in 2025.

With this data we can see how the schools are becoming more diverse over the next several years. The purpose of this information, as a school counselor, is to know how to better help our students. As a high school counselor, we can make sure that test prep is available to those who need it for the ACT and SAT. We might have students whose first language isn't English and who need additional support for those standardized tests. In addition to the academic and college/career support, students will need the social and emotional support.

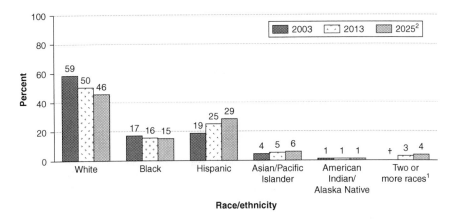

Figure 12.1 Percentage distribution of public elementary and secondary students by race/ethnicity: 2003, 2013, and 2025 (projected). [†]Not applicable. [1]In 2003, data on students of Two or more races were not collected. [2]Projected. Note: Race categories exclude persons of Hispanic ethnicity. Some data have been revised from previously published figures. Detail may not sum to totals because of rounding. Although rounded numbers are displayed, the figures are based on unrounded estimates. Source: U.S. Department of Education, National Center for Education Statistics, Common Core of Data (CCD), "State Nonfiscal Survey of Public Elementary and Secondary Education," 2003–04 and 2013–14; and National Elementary and Secondary Enrollment Projection Model, 1972 through 2025. See Digest of Education Statistics 2015, table 203.50.

Multiculturalism

As school counselors, it is our job to meet the students where they are. We have to be multicultural competent in order to meet the needs of our diverse population. It can be hard to be competent in every culture; that's why continuing education is critical. Previously in this chapter we talked about values and beliefs, and that we get our values and beliefs from our culture. One of the first steps to being multicultural competent is to understand your own culture. There are five key dimensions to culture (TESOL, 2018):

1. Culture as an element refers to how each person has their own culture but may be unaware of our cultural beliefs and understandings.
2. Culture as relative refers to the aspect of culture that is only understood in relation to other cultures.
3. Culture as group membership is the side of culture involving multiple memberships in a variety of groups in society.
4. Culture as contested refers to the challenges to culture at national and individual levels.
5. Culture as individuals (variable and multiple) refers to the representation of culture as individual and personal.

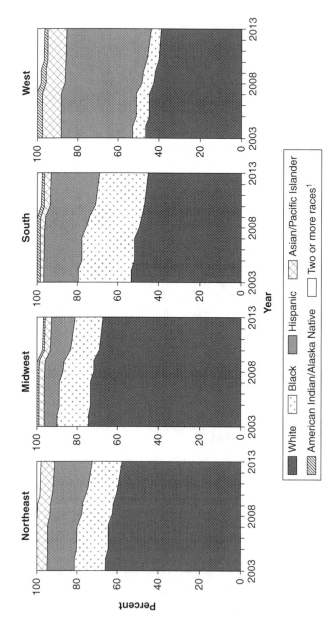

Figure 12.2 Percentage distribution of public school students enrolled in pre-kindergarten through 12th grade, by region and race/ethnicity: Selected years, fall 2003 through fall 2013. [1] Prior to 2008, data on students of Two or more races were not collected. Since data on students of Two or more races for 2008 and 2009 were reported by only a small number of states, figures for these years are not comparable to figures for 2010 and later years. Note: Race categories exclude persons of Hispanic ethnicity. Detail may not sum to totals because of rounding. Source: U.S. Department of Education, National Center for Education Statistics, Common Core of Data (CCD), "State Nonfiscal Survey of Public Elementary and Secondary Education," Selected years, 2003–04 through 2013–14. See *Digest of Education Statistics 2015*, table 203.50.

Not only is this important for you to understand about yourself, but for what your students are facing. As a school counselor in a predominately Caucasian, upper middle-class private school, I wanted to do a lesson on diversity and cultural identity to my sophomore class. I felt that it was important for my students to understand how people's cultural identity forms. This lesson was taught with good intentions, but the execution was not grade appropriate. I ended up having to apologize to my students for the miscommunication. They took the information I presented them with as offense. After reflecting, I realized that the audience was not ready for a lesson on culture identity when they hadn't figured it out on their own. School counselors have to be sensitive to where our students are at in their own cultural identity. We also have to know where we are with our own cultural identity.

The Racial/Cultural Identity Model has five phases of cultural identity (Sue & Sue, 2013):

1. Conformity: Marked by desire to assimilate and acculturate—buys in to the melting pot analogy. Accepts belief in White superiority and minority inferiority. Role models, lifestyles, and value systems all follow the dominant group.
2. Dissonancy: Breakdown of denial system. Encounters information discordant with previous beliefs in the conformity stage. Dominant-held views of minority strengths and weaknesses begin to be questioned. There is now a growing sense of personal awareness that racism does exist, that not all aspects of the minority or majority culture are good or bad, and that one cannot escape one's cultural heritage.
3. Resistance and Immersion: 'Why should I feel ashamed of who and what I am?' Begins to understand social-psychological forces associated with prejudice and discrimination. Extreme anger at perceived cultural oppression. May be an active rejection of the dominant society and culture. Members of the dominant group viewed with suspicion.
4. Introspection: Increased discomfort with rigidly held group views (i.e., all Whites are bad). Too much energies directed at White society and diverted from more positive exploration of identity questions. Conflict ensures between notions of responsibility and allegiance to one's minority group, and notions of personal autonomy. Attempts to understand one's cultural heritage and to develop an integrated identity.
5. Integrative Awareness: Develop inner sense of security as conflicts between new and old identities are resolved. Global anti-White feelings subside as person becomes more flexible, tolerant and multicultural. White and minority cultures are not seen as necessarily conflictual. Able to own and accept those aspects of U.S. culture (seen as healthy) and oppose those that are toxic (racism and oppression).

With this knowledge from my graduate coursework, I was able to analyze where my students were with understanding their cultural identity. This has helped me recognize that my students of color may be in the conformity or dissonance phases and aren't ready to talk about diversity. When we are able to apprehend this about our students we are able to meet them where they are. It's crucial that we know where we are with our cultural identity and assumptions about diversity.

> As a bottom line, culturally competent counselors and advisors will result in academic and social success experienced by students in all educational environments. Likewise, it will result in more culturally responsive counseling, improved collaboration with parents, and better data collection and interpretation for the benefit of the multicultural community.
>
> (Hughey, 2011)

Wrap Up

When I think about the issues of diversity that come up within the school building it usually is in regard to equitable education. Are we making sure we are meeting the needs of our students with taking into consideration their ethnicity, socioeconomic status, and culture? We need to be conscious of where our students are coming from and what they might be experiencing at home. Our students who are refugees are experiencing extreme stressors. They have to deal with adjusting to a new culture. They might have a dual role within their family to act as a translator if they understand English better than their parents. It's part of our responsibility to identity risk, identify who is at risk, and provide interventions. We can help encourage and empower families, focus on student strengths, and stop bullying or harassment (National Association for School Psychologists, 2018). Make sure you know the resources available for your students who are refugees.

Before closing out this chapter I would like to speak briefly to students in poverty. Socioeconomic status is not preferential to race. In addition to understanding racial diversity, we have to mindful of the financial needs of our students. What are the resources available to them and how can we ensure they are getting them? With economic barriers, families might not have access to cars or be able to drive. I had a student who wanted to participate in clubs after school, but there wasn't a late bus schedule and their only transportation was the school bus. According to The National Center for Children in Poverty, among all children under 18 years in the U.S., 41 percent are low-income children and 19 percent—approximately one in five—are poor. This means that children are overrepresented among our nation's poor; they represent 23 percent of the population but comprise 32 percent of all people in poverty. Many more children live in families with incomes just above the poverty threshold. Being a child in a low-income or poor family does not happen by chance. Parental education and employment, race/ethnicity, and other factors are associated with children's experience of economic insecurity (Koball & Jiang, 2018).

There are a lot of resources available concerning the topics mentioned in this chapter. Seek out professional development in these areas so that you are aware of what is happening in your state and nation-wide. We work in a diverse field and no two students are the same. Continuously seek supervision, consultation, and personal counseling. The more informed we are about diversity, inclusion, and equity the better we can serve our students and the community. I end this chapter with ASCA's position statement on equity. This is a good reference for what our profession dictates is our responsibility.

American School Counselor Association (ASCA) Position[2]

The School Counselor and Equity for All Students

(Adopted 2006, revised 2012, 2018)

School counselors recognize and distinguish individual and group differences and strive to equally value all students and groups. School counselors are advocates for the equitable treatment of all students in school and in the community.

The Rationale

According to the U.S. Department of Education, in 2014, the number of students of color in U.S. public schools surpassed that of white students. However, white students continue to graduate from high school at higher rates than black and Hispanic students. In addition, an achievement gap exists along socioeconomic lines.

Many students of color, first-generation, and low-income students aspire to college; however, the college application process can present significate obstacles. Some students in schools report there is no adult in the school with whom they feel they can discuss these issues, and many of these students come from underrepresented social or cultural groups. These students cannot always rely on their parents for college information and must instead turn to their high schools, where school counselors are in a position proven to increase access for students. School counselors can also play a role in assisting students in identity development contributing to their success.

Historically, underrepresented populations have faced barriers to participating in a rigorous curriculum and higher level classes. School counselors, teachers, administrators, and other school staff can be involuntary gatekeepers of access to these classrooms. Research finds that when students and school counselors are able to connect, school counselors have the potential to become empowering agents. When students feel like they are being treated in a biased or negative manner, they often exhibit self-destructive behaviors such as truancy, withdrawal, acting out, and nonparticipation in class activities. Conversely, when students believe they are treated fairly, they are more likely to be engaged in school, talk about pressing issues, and participate in class activities.

Family participation in the college-going decision-making process is critical. School counselors are in a position to seek family engagement in the college-going process to ensure students from diverse backgrounds are included. The ASCA Ethical Standards for School Counselors support this concept, stating that all students have the right to a school counselor who acts as a social-justice advocate, supporting students from all backgrounds and circumstances, and consulting when the school counselor's competence level requires additional support.

The School Counselor's Role

School counselors develop and implement a comprehensive school counseling program promoting equity and access for students. School counselors work to help close achievement, opportunity, attainment, and funding gaps in their schools, districts, and communities. School counselors are mindful of school and community perceptions of the treatment of underrepresented groups and understand the importance of collaborating with school and community groups to help all students succeed. School counselors demonstrate cultural competence.

School counselors promote equitable treatment of all students by:

- Using data to identify gaps in achievement, opportunity, and attainment
- Advocating for rigorous course and higher education for underrepresented groups.
- Maintaining professional knowledge of the ever-changing and complex world of students' culture
- Maintaining knowledge and skills for working in a diverse and multicultural work setting
- Informing school staff of changes regarding different groups within the community
- Promoting the development of school policies leading to equitable treatment of all students and opposing school policies hindering equitable treatment of any student
- Promoting access to rigorous standards-based curriculum, academic courses, and learning paths for college and career for all students
- Developing plans to address over- or under-representation of specific groups in programs such as special education, honors, Advanced Placement, and International Baccalaureate
- Creating an environment that encourages any student or group to feel comfortable to come forward with problems
- Collaborating with families in seeking assistance services for financial literacy, job skills and placement, and free services (such as childcare assistance) as well as providing parents with educational opportunities to assist them in supporting their students' education

- Acting as a liaison between home and school promoting an understanding and encouraging creative solutions for students handling multiple responsibilities beyond a typical load

Summary

School counselors recognize and distinguish individual and group differences and strive to value all students and groups equally. School counselors promote the equitable treatment of all students in school and the community.

Notes

1 Used with permission from the Ohio State University.
2 This is a paid permission from The American School Counselor Association.

References

Cambridge Dictionary (2018, October 8). *Inclusion*. Retrieved from Cambridge Dictionary: https://dictionary.cambridge.org/us/dictionary/english/inclusion

Cincinnati Public Schools (2018, October 8). *Equity Policy*. Retrieved from Cincinnati Public Schools: www.cps-k12.org/about-cps/board-of-education/equity-policy

Dictionary.com (2018, October 8). *Equity*. Retrieved from Dicitonary.com: www.dictionary.com/browse/equity

Hughey, J.R. (2011). Meeting the needs of diverse students: Enhancing school counselors' experience. *Educational Considerations*. 28(2): 20–27.

Koball, H., & Jiang, Y. (2018, January). *Basic Facts of Low-Income Children*. Retrieved from National Center for Children in Poverty: www.nccp.org/publications/pub_1194.html

Merriam-Webster (2018, October 8). *Diversity*. Retrieved from Merriam-Webster: www.merriam-webster.com/dictionary/diversity

Miller, A. (2018, October 8). *How Not to Impose Your Values on Clients*. Retrieved from Chron: https://work.chron.com/not-impose-values-clients-21470.html

National Association for School Psychologists (2018, October 10). *Supporting Refugee Children & Youth: Tips for Educators*. Retrieved from NASP: www.nasponline.org/resources-and-publications/resources/school-safety-and-crisis/war-and-terrorism/supporting-refugee-students

Patterson, F. (2018, October 4). *Personal Values and the Counseling Relationship*. Retrieved from NAACAD: www.naadac.org/assets/1959/frances_patterson_ac15_personalvalues.pdf

Perception Institute (2018, October 1). *Explicit Bias*. Retrieved from Perception: https://perception.org/research/explicit-bias/

Sue, D., & Sue, D. (2013). *Counseling the Culturally Diverse: Theory and Practice* (6th ed.). New York, NY: John Wiley & Sons.

TESOL (2018, October 8). *Knowledge of Multicultural School Counseling*. Retrieved from TESOL: www.tesol.org/docs/default-source/books/14030_sample.pdf?sfvrsn=2

The Kirwan Institute for the Study of Race and Ethnicity (2018, October 1). *Understanding Implicit Bias*. Retrieved from The Ohio State University Kirwan Institute for the Study of Race and Ethnicity: http://kirwaninstitute.osu.edu/research/understanding-implicit-bias/

Part V
Defining Who You Are

13 In the School

No two school counselors are the same. There are some school counselors who like to keep very strict relationship boundaries with their students. They will not live in the same area as their students, because they don't want to run into them at Kroger or McDonalds. They want to keep their personal life personal, and there is nothing wrong with that. Then there are the school counselors who have students 'living' in their office. They are very involved in participating in school events outside of the school day. They might have an open-door policy in addition to having office hours. Figuring out how involved one is with their students will also impact boundaries as stated in the earlier chapter. There are other things that will define one as a school counselor in the school. How much time is one going to spend on individual and group counseling, guidance lessons, testing, and mental health? This chapter will discuss the different topics associated with defining oneself as a school counselor in the school.

First, let us start off by knowing how ASCA defines the role of the school counselor.

The School Counselor and Comprehensive School Counseling Programs
(Adopted 1988; revised 1993, 1997, 2005, 2012, 2017)

The American School Counselor Association (ASCA) Position[1]

School counselors design and deliver comprehensive school counseling programs that improve a range of student learning and behavioral outcomes. These programs are comprehensive in scope, preventive in design, and developmental in nature. "The ASCA National Model: A Framework for School Counseling Programs" outlines the components of a comprehensive school counseling program. The ASCA National Model brings school counselors together with one vision and one voice, which creates unity and focus toward improving student achievement and supporting student development. This provides equitable access to a rigorous education for all students by identifying the knowledge and skills all students will acquire as a result of the K–12 comprehensive school counseling program. The Model ensures that the program

- is delivered to all students in a systematic fashion
- is based on data-driven decision making
- is provided by a state-credentialed school counselor

Effective school counseling programs are a collaborative effort between the school counselor, families, community stake-holders and other educators to create an environment resulting in a positive impact on student achievement. Education professionals, including school counselors, value and respond to the diversity and individual differences in our societies and communities in culturally sensitive and responsive ways. Comprehensive school counseling programs in both the brick-and-mortar and virtual settings ensure equitable access to opportunities and rigorous curriculum for all students to participate fully in the educational process.

One study found that schools designated as Recognized ASCA Model Program (RAMP) schools had significantly higher schoolwide proficiency rates in English as compared with the control schools. This same study also found four-year longitudinal results indicating a significant positive difference between RAMP-designated elementary schools and their control schools in math. "Findings provide support for the impact of comprehensive, data-driven, accountable school counseling programs at the elementary level…"

According to Lapan, "When highly trained, professional school counselors deliver ASCA National Model comprehensive school counseling program services, students receive measurable benefit".

ASCA also recommends that school counselors spend 80 percent or more of their time in direct and indirect services to students. These direct and indirect activities should come from the ASCA National Model rather than inappropriate duties assigned to school counselors as listed in the ASCA National Model Executive Summary. The 20 percent or less of the school counselor's time should be focused on program and management planning including:

- Developing an annual plan
- Results reports and data projects

The Rationale

A comprehensive school counseling program is an integral component of the school's mission. Comprehensive school counseling programs, driven by student data and based on the ASCA National Model:

The School Counselor's Role

School counselors focus their skills, time, and energy on direct and indirect services to students. To achieve maximum program effectiveness, ASCA recommends a student-to-school-counselor ratio of 250:1. Although ratios vary across states, school districts, and even grade levels, the growing body of research as summarized by Carey and Martin supports that implementation of comprehensive school counseling programs positively affects outcome data (e.g., student achievement and discipline referrals) at all grade levels through:

- School counseling program assessment
- Other activities as determined by the school counselor and administrator when developing the annual plan

Duties that fall outside of the school counselor framework as described in the ASCA National Model should be limited and performed by other school staff to support a school's smooth operation and allow school counselors to continue to focus on students' academic, career, and social/emotional needs. Fair-share responsibilities should not preclude implementing and managing a comprehensive school counseling program.

School counselors participate as members of the educational team and use the skills of leadership, advocacy, and collaboration to promote systemic change as appropriate. The framework of a comprehensive school counseling program consists of the following four components: foundation, management, delivery, and accountability. See "The ASCA National Model: A Framework for School Counseling Programs" for more detailed information.

Foundation

School counselors create comprehensive school counseling programs that focus on student outcomes, teach student competencies and are delivered with identified professional competencies.

- Program Focus: Developing personal beliefs, a vision statement, and a mission statement with program goals measuring the vision and mission statements.
- Student Standards: Effective school counseling programs look at three developmental domains for students as well as state and district initiatives. These three domains include:
  - Academic
  - Career
  - Social/emotional
- Professional Competencies: The school counselor competencies outline the knowledge, attitudes, and skills that ensure school counselors are

equipped to meet the profession's rigorous demands. See the ASCA Ethical Standards for School Counselors for specific information to guide school counselors' decision-making and standardized professional practices.

Management

School counselors incorporate organizational assessments and tools that are concrete, clearly delineated, and reflective of the school's needs. See the ASCA National Model for more detailed information. Assessments and tools include:

- School counselor competency and school counseling program assessments Use-of-time assessments
- Annual agreements
- Advisory councils
- Use of data to measure the program as well as to promote systemic change
- Curriculum, small group, and closing-the-gap action plans
- Annual and weekly calendars

Delivery

School counselors deliver a comprehensive school counseling program in collaboration with students, families, school staff, and community stakeholders. The ASCA National Model and the ASCA National Model Implementation Guide have specific details and examples about each of the following areas:

Direct Services with Students

Direct services are face-to-face or virtual interactions between school counselors and students and include the following:

- School counseling core curriculum
- Individual student planning
- Responsive services

Indirect Services for Students

Indirect services are provided on behalf of students as a result of the school counselor's interactions with others including:

- Referrals for additional assistance
- Consultation and collaboration with families, teachers, other educators, and community organizations

- Other activities that fall in line with the appropriate duties of a school counselor as detailed in this statement and in the ASCA National Model

Accountability

To demonstrate the effectiveness of the school counseling program in measurable terms, school counselors:

- Analyze school and school counseling program data to determine if students are different as a result of the school counseling program
- Use data to show the impact of the school counseling program on student achievement, attendance, and behavior
- Analyze school counseling program assessments to guide future action and improve future results for all students. The school counselor's performance is evaluated on basic standards of practice expected of school counselors implementing a comprehensive school counseling program. There are three sections within this component, and each section has various tools for analysis. These sections and tools as listed in the ASCA National Model are:

  - Data analysis: school data profile analysis and use-of-time analysis
  - Program results: curriculum results report, small-group results report, closing-the-gap results report
  - Evaluation and improvement: four components
  - Self-analysis of the school counselor's strengths
  - Self-analysis of the school counseling program's strengths
  - Evaluation of the school counselor's performance by administration using the school counselor performance appraisal
  - Review of the program goals created at the beginning of the school year

Trish Hatch discussed intentional guidance as "a deliberate act by a school counselor to guide, lead, direct or provide purposeful interventions for students in need academically, personally or socially". Becoming proficient at using data will help school counselors efficiently serve their students and have intentional guidance or counseling services.

Summary

School counselors in both the brick-and-mortar and virtual/online environments develop and deliver comprehensive school counseling programs supporting and promoting student achievement and standardizing the measurement of program effectiveness. As outlined in the ASCA National Model, these programs include a systematic and planned program delivery involving all students and enhancing the learning process. The comprehensive school counseling program is supported by appropriate resources and implemented by a credentialed school counselor. The ASCA National Model brings school counselors together with one vision and one voice, which creates unity and focus toward improving student achievement and supporting student development.

You might realize that not every school is implementing the ASCA model. Part of your time might be spent as the testing coordinator and lunchroom monitor. Although these roles are not part of our responsibilities as a profession, it might be part of your job. When you're new in your school counseling position, you're not going to be able to change your role to the ASCA model on day one. It will take time to change the culture and mindset of the school. In later chapters, we will talk more about implementing the ASCA model.

Guidance v. School

I do want to discuss the evolution of the term 'school counselor' versus 'guidance counselor'. Although ASCA is doing a phenomenal job at advocating for the profession and educating the community, not all schools are on board with the name change. Our profession has evolved from just doing guidance to meeting the academic, personal/social, emotional, and college/career needs of the students. We have become the general practitioner in the school that refers students to specialists.

"Historically, the term 'guidance counselor' was used to reference counselors working within the school system. These counselors' main role was to 'guide' students to college: writing letters of recommendation and sending out transcripts" (Counseling@NYU, 2017). From the Article, "With New Roles, School Counselors are More Indispensable as Ever" from *neaToday*, John Rosales states (Rosales, 2015):

> Jonathan Durr embodies the definition of what a school counselor should and shouldn't be. For example, Durr does not just sit in his office handing out college applications. He does not just change schedules for students who want to drop a class. No, no, no. That type of counselor went out with the typewriter.
>
> 'School counselors are vital members of the education team,' says Durr, a counselor at Paducah Tilghman High School in Paducah, Kentucky. 'We work with teachers, administrators and parents or guardians to help students in the areas of academic and career achievement, personal and social development, and more.'
>
> Much, much more, according to the American School Counselor Association (ASCA), sponsors of National School Counseling Week (February 2–6). This year's theme, 'Celebrate School Counseling,' focuses attention on the multiple roles school counselors are thrust in to help students from all ethnic, cultural and socioeconomic backgrounds reach

their full potential, graduate from high school, and become productive, responsible adults.

'With all that counselors do, it is sometimes necessary to deal with the most pressing issues first, then get to other items as we can,' Durr says. 'It is a constant balancing act to ensure that we are not sacrificing the important for the urgent.'

As with most high schools, Tilghman counselors audit transcripts to ensure students have the classes they need to graduate, make schedule changes as needed, verify that graduation requirements have been met before each student graduates, prepare reports for parents, and attend parent meetings to discuss issues students are having.

'We do our best to meet each student's needs,' Durr says. 'We have a great team in place to get that done.'

As school counselors, we are continuously advocating for ourselves and the profession. The evolution of our profession has come at an integral part of our society. From student mental health awareness to students who are refugees, we can meet the needs of the students while they are in school. It can be hard, as a first-year, to know how firmly you stand on the position of 'school' versus 'guidance' counselor. You may be met with opposition or be accused of being progressive.

When I was interning and when I started my first year as school counselor, my title was guidance counselor. It took time to change the language of the students, faculty, and administration. I started with my signature in my emails. Now, whenever the community received emails from me it said, "Heather M. Couch, School Counselor". I continuously use the title 'School Counselor' when I introduced myself in any capacity. Any time there is a document that comes from my office it says from the "school counselor" or "counseling department". It's been an adjustment, because there people in the administration that still call me "guidance counselor". Changing the mindset of the administration and faculty does not happen overnight. If you want to change the culture in the school when it comes to your department, you're going to have to advocate and educate the administration and faculty. Sometimes it can be discouraging, because even though you advocate and educate there will faculty and staff who will say they don't know what you do. Even when it gets discouraging remember why you are advocating. It's part of our responsibility to let the community know we are there to provide resources and meet the needs of the students.

Your Counselor Identity

What is your theoretical orientation? This answer will determine what your personality is in your office. I am a firm believer in the therapeutic relationship and take from Dr. Irvin Yalom's existential counseling theory. As a school counselor, I don't just use Yalom's theoretical orientation. I pull from Dialectical Behavioral Therapy since the components focus on a lot of what students need. Reality Therapy is another theory I use with students when helping them set goals and evaluate their progress on achieving those goals.

Since two theories I draw from focus on the therapeutic relationship, I tend to have an open relationship with my students. Of course, there are some things I don't disclose with them, but because I'm an advisor for clubs my students know me well. Not every counselor has to be that involved in student activities and there are some who aren't. This decision, for me, is based on my student-focused approach. However, this can take up a lot of personal time. I take students to a conference once a semester and I chaperone every school dance. At this point in my life I have the availability to be involved with extra-curriculars, but that might change in the future. I enjoy seeing students be involved with things they're passionate about outside of the classroom. We all came into counseling with other passions, interests, and talents. I like to share a few of mine by being an advisor for student clubs. I'm the faculty advisor for our YMCA Chapter club which is a mock government program. I was involved in this program when I was in high school and helped a student start the chapter at the school. That was how I got involved with helping oversee an extra-curricular.

Not two counselors are alike. You might decide that you're not going to oversee any clubs. Where you are in your life will decide that for you as well. There is nothing wrong with living outside the school district and keeping a clear boundary that your personal life doesn't mix with your professional life. I will add that while that is what is supposed to happen in mental health counseling it doesn't necessarily work in the school. Schools function as a family unit almost. There will be Christmas parties, recitals, sporting events, and the list goes on forever. If you want to be successful in your job at a school and want the administration/faculty to know you're invested in the school, you're going to have to attend some of these school functions. Don't feel obligated to attend every event but make it a priority to attend the big events.

Professional Identity

Knowing what type of school counselor you want to be should also include looking back at your values and beliefs to know why you want to be a school counselor. Understanding who you are will help you create your professional identity. My experiences, education, and culture have all shaped my professional identity. No doubt you created a professional identity statement in your graduate program. This should be the foundation for who you are as a school counselor and should help you shape your counseling program. Another component of your identity is what you believe as a school counselor. I have provided for you my own personal examples.

Example of a Professional Identity Statement:

As a professional school counselor, I believe that every student is entitled to the highest level of education. I will foster an environment that allows students to develop in their academic, personal, social, and personal pursuits. I am committed to providing students with the opportunity to succeed in all areas of their lives. All students have the ability to achieve success academically and personally! I am devoted to providing a holistic program that focuses on academic, personal/social, and career development to meet the needs of all students. I am dedicated to collaborating with teachers, community resources, and other stakeholders to provide this program.

I am committed to being an advocate for my students, self, and profession. I am an advocate for social justice and equality education. Every student should have the opportunity to obtain a rigorous academic education. I believe that students are able to learn the same concepts at different levels through tiered learning. I am committed to providing systemic change in the school I work.

Example of School Counseling Belief and Role:

School Counseling Belief Statements

- I believe all students have the ability to achieve their goals through utilizing their strengths.
- I believe all students regardless of developmental stage or academic ability can perform and achieve in the classroom.
- I believe our role is to help students reach their goals inside and outside of the classroom while meeting them where they are and building relationships.
- I believe all decisions should be data-driven in order to meet the needs of all students.
- I believe the ethical decision-making model should be implemented when faced with moral dilemmas and counselors should adhere to the ASCA ethical standards.
- I believe all students have the right to have access to a licensed school counselor.

Role of the School Counselor

- To provide academic, personal/social, and career resources to students,
- To be an advocate on the behalf of students,
- To foster academic, personal/social, and career development, and
- To help students reach their goals inside and outside of the classroom while meeting them where they are and building relationships.

Wrap Up

This chapter is meant to help you to start thinking about how you view your role as a school counselor. Ask yourself, what do I want to achieve in my program? What do I believe about students? What do I believe my role is within the school? Why did I choose to become a school counselor? How do I navigate being assigned responsibilities that are outside the school counselor role? You might be able to answer these questions but continue to develop your identity as a school counselor. As you gain more years of experience, it might evolve or be more concrete. In the next chapter, we will discuss understanding your identity outside of the school.

Note

1 This is a paid permission for the article from The American School Counselor Association.

References

Counseling@NYU (2017, January 9). *The Evolution from "Guidance Counselor" to "School Counselor"*. Retrieved from Counseling@NYU: https://counseling.steinhardt.nyu.edu/blog/difference-between-guidance-counselor-school-counselor/

Rosales, J. (2015, February 1). *neaToday*. Retrieved from With New Roles, School Counselors Are More Indispensable Than Ever: http://neatoday.org/2015/02/01/school-counselors-are-more-indispensable-than-ever/

14 Minimizing Burnout

Professors lecture about maintaining your own mental health, but they never mention how exhausting it is! However, it is really important to do things for yourself in order to do the best at work. What does maintaining your health mean? It can vary from exercising to volunteering. No matter what the activity, it is important to do things that bring fulfillment. Counseling is a career that is very taxing on your own mental health, because you are constantly giving of yourself. A school counselor will hear the complaints of everyone in the school building, but they don't always have someone to vent to. Taking time to define who you are outside of the school is important to help you maintain your own mental health.

Burnout

The reason why self-care is so important is because of burnout. What is burnout? According to the article "The Tell Tale Signs of Burnout ... Do you have them?",

Burnout is a state of chronic stress that leads to:

- physical and emotional exhaustion
- cynicism and detachment
- feelings of ineffectiveness and lack of accomplishment

When in the throes of full-fledged burnout, you are no longer able to function effectively on a personal or professional level.

(Carter, 2013)

The symptoms of burnout can sometimes be obvious. How a person talks about their job and the people they work with can show signs of burnout. Just like with signs and symptoms of any mental health disorder, burnout is something we can look out for.

Symptoms of an impaired counselor have often included anger, cynicism, depression, drug and alcohol abuse, stress, temporary emotional imbalance due to a personal loss or trauma, paranoia, denial of feelings, and over involvement with clients. Other symptoms of impairment have included inappropriate behaviors such as showing up late, missing or canceling appointments, and not responding to client's needs. Skorupa and Agresi suggested that burnout may show up in a counseling session as loss of empathy, respect, and positive feelings for the client. Depersonalization may also occur when a counselor behaviorally acts out, responding to the client in a derogatory way or by negating the client as a person. Reamer described two categories of stress that can lead to impairment: environmental stress and personal stress. Environmental stress is a function of working conditions or professional training. Personal stress can be caused by a number of reasons including marital and relationship problems, emotional and physical ill health, and financial difficulties.

(Nobles, 2011)

What Causes Burnout?

As school counselors, we deal with a lot of emotional circumstances. There are stressors about job ambiguity, high caseloads, limited resources for coping, and limited clinical supervision. I can relate first-hand that job ambiguity and lack of supervision is stressful. As the only school counselor in the building during the first year, it was hard to figure things out on my own. Even though I met with a school counselor outside of my job, it wasn't the same because that person wasn't able to give me direct feedback on what was happening in my building.

There are a number of studies that have been conducted on the relationship between school counselor perceived stress, burnout, and job satisfaction. One study conducted by Patrick R. Mullen, Ashley J. Blount, Glenn W. Lambie, and Nancy Chae found that there was a strong positive correlation between school counselor perceived stress and burnout. Another finding was that the perceived stress and burnout produced a negative relationship with job satisfaction. Another interesting finding was that younger and less experienced school counselors had higher levels of perceived stress and burnout due to how they handled difficulties or face frequent challenges. "School counselors who experienced greater perceived stress also reported more demands at work compared to school counselors who perceived less stress, such as additional paperwork, larger caseloads, and coordination of school-wide testing" (Mullen, Blount, Lambie, & Chae, 2018). It can be inferred that school counselors who are performing duties outside of their role as defined by ASCA have high levels of perceived stress.

School counselors can face multiple and competing demands, leading to symptoms of stress, empathy fatigue, emotional exhaustion, counselor impairment, and eventual departure or resignation from their jobs. School counseling consistently requires empathy and compassion for students in emotionally challenging situations. Simultaneously, school counselors are expected to deliver career education modules in the classroom, consult with parents and teachers, and attend to administrative tasks such as lunch duty. School counselors may become stressed, exhausted, and eventually burned out by attempting to balance their various professional requirements. Authors have noted that the experiences of burnout can lead to a severe diminishment of school counselors' abilities to deliver adequate services to students and their families.

(Mullen, Blount, Lambie, & Chae, 2018)

In addition, the Mayo Clinic identifies the following causes (Mayo Clinic, 2015):

- **Lack of control.** An inability to influence decisions that affect your job—such as your schedule, assignments or workload—could lead to job burnout. So could a lack of the resources you need to do your work.
- **Unclear job expectations.** If you're unclear about the degree of authority you have or what your supervisor or others expect from you, you're not likely to feel comfortable at work.
- **Dysfunctional workplace dynamics.** Perhaps you work with an office bully, or you feel undermined by colleagues or your boss micromanages your work. This can contribute to job stress.
- **Mismatch in values.** If your values differ from the way your employer does business or handles grievances, the mismatch can eventually take a toll.
- **Poor job fit.** If your job doesn't fit your interests and skills, it might become increasingly stressful over time.
- **Extremes of activity.** When a job is monotonous or chaotic, you need constant energy to remain focused—which can lead to fatigue and job burnout.
- **Lack of social support.** If you feel isolated at work and in your personal life, you might feel more stressed.
- **Work–life imbalance.** If your work takes up so much of your time and effort that you don't have the energy to spend time with your family and friends, you might burn out quickly.

School Counselor Implications

When a school counselor is burnt out, it can affect your work with students. A study conducted by Patrick Mullen and Daniel Gutierrez, looked at the influence that perceived stress and burnout had on student direct services. A summary of their findings is as follows:

> The burnout and stress experienced by school counselors is likely to have a negative influence on the services they provide to students, but there is little research exploring the relationship among these variables. Therefore, we report findings from our study that examined the relationship between practicing school counselors' ($N = 926$) reported levels of burnout, perceived stress and their facilitation of direct student services. The findings indicated that school counselor participants' burnout had a negative contribution to the direct student services they facilitated. In addition, school counselors' perceived stress demonstrated a statistically significant correlation with burnout but did not contribute to their facilitation of direct student services. We believe these findings bring attention to school counselors' need to assess and manage their stress and burnout that if left unchecked may lead to fewer services for students. We recommend that future research further explore the relationship between stress, burnout and programmatic service delivery to support and expand upon the findings in this investigation.
>
> (Mullen & Gutierrez, Burnout, Stress and Direct Student
> Services Among School Counselors, 2018)

Tips to Avoid Burnout

There are ways to mitigate burnout. The most important prevention is to practice self-care. Before we get into self-care, I would like to end discussing burnout by going over a few preventions that you can start immediately.

Leave the Job Behind at the End of the Day

This is easier said than done! We work with students who are dealing with stressors from all aspects of their lives. They come to us for guidance and help with those problems. It is hard to leave the problems that students bring to us at work and not take them home. However, if we don't leave them at work then we will become emotionally drained. We won't be able to effectively help our students. Also, don't check your email at home unless it's an emergency. This is mentioned in an earlier chapter, but it is worth repeating and is relevant. Take time to 'clock out' when you're off work.

Spend Time with Loved Ones

Some of the best ways to relax and renew is by being surrounded by people who love you. I cherish the support I get from my family and lean on them in times of stress. Being a school counselor is stressful and there are times when I need affirmation. There are times when I just need time to spend with my family doing things we enjoy. Whether it's going shopping with my mom or attending a football game with dad, I relish those moments that I can escape from the stresses of work.

Speak to a Professional

As school counselors, we refer our students to professional mental health counselors for a variety of issues. We should not be ashamed to see a counselor ourselves. The things that our students come to us with can be heavy. We need to take time to focus on our own mental health as well. As there are many benefits to our students seeing a metal health counselor; those benefits are the same for us.

Get Physical

This reminds me of the Olivia Newton-John song "Physical", but follow the lyrics' advice and get active! Find an exercise that you enjoy and hit the gym. I've tried a few different types of exercise programs, because I like to switch it up. Exercise naturally produces endorphins. According to *The Primary Care Companion,*

> Aerobic exercises, including jogging, swimming, cycling, walking, gardening, and dancing, have been proved to reduce anxiety and depression. These improvements in mood are proposed to be caused by exercise-induced increase in blood circulation to the brain and by an influence on the hypothalamic-pituitary-adrenal (HPA) axis and, thus, on the physiologic reactivity to stress.
>
> (Sharma, Madaan, & Petty, 2006)

Reduce Your Work Load

As the only school counselor in the building, it was hard to reduce my work load. I ran all of the school counselor programming. After my first year, I started relying more on others for help to take the pressure off. For example, my college and career program utilized teachers as coaches to work with the students in small groups. I came up with the lesson plan, but the teachers implemented it. This helped me focus on the program as a whole versus teaching a lesson. It helps to say no to overseeing additional activities, if you can. If you're too busy to oversee a student club, then don't let the students harass you to do it. You might not be able to reduce your work load in terms of your everyday responsibilities, but not saying yes to additional work will help.

Self-Assessment

As you might be going into your first-year school counseling job, you shouldn't be at burnout. However, as you evaluate your first-year experience, here is a quick self-assessment to evaluate your thoughts and feelings on your year. These 15 questions are ranked on a Likert scale of 1–5, with 1 being 'Not at All' and 5 being 'Very Often' (MindTools, 2018).

1. I feel run down and drained of energy most of the day.
2. I have negative thoughts about my job.
3. I am harder and less sympathetic with people than perhaps they deserve.
4. I am easily irritated by small problems, or by my co-workers and team.
5. I feel misunderstood or unappreciated by my co-workers.
6. I feel that I have no one to talk to.
7. I feel that I am achieving less than I should.
8. I feel under an unpleasant level of pressure to succeed.
9. I feel that I am not getting what I want out of my job.
10. I feel that I am in the wrong organization or the wrong profession.
11. I am frustrated with parts of my job.
12. I feel that organizational politics or bureaucracy frustrate my ability to do a good job.
13. I feel that there is more work to do than I practically have the ability to do.
14. I feel that I do not have time to do many of the things that are important to doing a good quality job.
15. I find that I do not have time to plan as much as I would like to.

Your score from 1–5 on each of these answers will help you know where you are in terms of burnout. Obviously, the higher your score the more at risk you are of burnout or you are already at burnout. This self-assessment is meant to help you in knowing what you should do and not become complacent.

Self-Care

Self-care is the best prevention to burnout and maintaining your own well-being. It shouldn't just be something we encourage our students to do, but something we practice in our own lives. There are things you enjoy doing other than being a school counselor. Make sure you continue to do those after you start working full-time. Outside of the school, I really enjoy traveling and attending art events within my city. It can be hard to travel during the academic year, but I try to take a weekend trip once a semester. I try to attend two or three art events a semester. These activities don't take up a lot of time on a daily basis. There are activities that I do regularly to help maintain my mental health. Not everyone's wellness plan looks the same. Find things that you enjoy and help you destress.

You are able to do self-care at work! This may come as a revelation, but there are ways to help you at while you're at school. From "Your Self-Care Matters", here are some ways you can maintain your mental health while at work (Hansen, 2018).

1. **Consultation:** Have someone that you can confide in when things are stressful. This person may not be directly in the building but have another school counselor that you can talk to.
2. **Ask for support:** You're not always going to have all the answers. There are going to be times when you feel overwhelmed and need help. Know the people in your department and school who can help you.
3. **Take your lunch break:** Take enough time for a healthy lunch EVERY DAY. If you're feeling closed in, eat in the staff lunch room or whatever is provided for you so you can socialize. If you'd rather have some time alone, find a quiet place to eat, or go off campus if you can. If you eat in your office, DON'T do work-related paperwork while you eat. Turn on some music, close the door, relax, and recharge.
4. **Choose your self-talk:** Have something (or a list of things) you can tell yourself when things don't go well, so you can keep your perspective. For example, if you see a student heading in a negative direction despite some great ideas you've offered, you may tell yourself, "Even if she doesn't listen now, I may have planted some seeds that will bloom sometime in the future." Or if a student tells you something difficult he's dealing with that you can't do anything about, you can tell yourself, "Well, I was present for him, I really listened, and I know he felt heard and validated. If nothing else, I know there's real value in that."
5. **Stay out of 'chronic complaint mode':** When you're with colleagues, leave or stay out of conversations that turn into chronic complaint sessions about students, parents, colleagues, or administration. Venting is one thing, and is a healthy part of self-care, but getting sucked into a whirlpool of negative conversation will sap your energy and not resolve a thing. The same goes for gossip and any kind of communication triangle. Direct, assertive conversation is more professional and more effective.
6. **Take pro-active steps:** If you do need to have a conversation with your department head or administrator to speak up about something frustrating, make a list ahead of time of your frustrations, and for each one, make a specific request about what you'd like to be different, or suggest a solution if you have one. Your meeting will be much more productive, and you'll present yourself as pro-active instead of negative.

There are also yoga activities that you can find online to do while you're at school. I have done 'yoga in a chair' and that has helped on the days that I'm in my office. On your lunch, take a walk around the gym or outside. If you're school allows you, take 5 minutes to walk to the building in the mid-afternoon. The after-lunch blues are real!

Activities to do Outside of School

There are a host of activities you can do as mentioned in Chapter 1. The most important thing you can do is something you enjoy and take for yourself.

If you're unsure of what to do here are more ideas (California Association of School Counselors, 2018):

- Create an informal support group with other counselors.
- Exercise—run, walk, play your favorite sport, etc.
- Breathe—use the same strategies you teach your students!
- Yoga.
- Spend time with your family.
- Make time for you!
- Dance.
- Listen to calming music.
- Take a hot bath.
- Watch the sunset.
- Keep a journal.
- Separate work from your personal life.
- Go to a movie.
- Get a professional massage.
- Create an anti-stress mantra.
- Remember to control your irrational thinking and remember the power of positive thinking.
- Eat your lunch.
- Create a relaxing environment in your office.

Wrap Up

Don't neglect the importance of self-care and the benefits of maintaining your mental health. You don't want to start to feel burnout after your first year of counseling. It can be easy to get caught up in the overwhelming emotions of your first year. When you take care of yourself and seek out consultation, it will help put the first year into perspective. Below are a few last tips for maintaining self-care for your first year and future years of school counseling.

10 Self-Care Tips for School Counselors *(Hamilton, 2017)*

1. **Remember Your WHY**
   Why did you originally want to become a school counselor? Did you have an impactful school counselor as a child? Think back to why you chose this profession.
2. **Write a Gratitude Letter**
   Send a letter to someone who you are grateful for and tell them why. This can be a close friend, mentor, a parent, anyone who comes to mind!
3. **Take a Break**
   Take your lunch break, that bathroom break, and any well-deserved break. To put it simply, you deserve a break. Allow yourself to rest.

4. **Walk Away from the Teachers' Lounge**
I'm going to guess if you are feeling stressed, the teachers might be feeling similar. Allow yourself to have some physical distance from any complaining or gossiping.

5. **Listen to Music**
Find a good playlist on Pandora or Spotify and jam out. Maybe dance along, too.

6. **Go on a Walk**
Sneak out a side door and take a quick walk in the sunshine. Consider having a group session outside if it's a nice day. A little Vitamin D can go a long way for you and your students.

7. **Read Old Thank You Letters**
Over the years, save thank you letters you receive from your students, their parents, and teachers. Create a 'warm and fuzzy drawer' and read them to remember how important your work is for the community.

8. **Allow Yourself to Feel Upset**
As you know, when we bottle up our emotions they tend to magnify and grow over time. If you can find a minute or two, close your door and cry or scream into a pillow, the release will help diminish the magnitude of the emotion.

9. **Talk with a Supportive Co-Worker**
While the work you do is different from teachers and administrative employees, having someone listen to you for a few minutes can help you feel more connected and appreciated.

10. **Consider Seeing a Counselor**
If this rough day is part of a rough week or a rough month, consider seeing a counselor. As you know, counselors need counselors just like doctors need doctors! Asking for help is the bravest thing anyone can do and having a nonbiased and supportive person on your team can help diminish overwhelming anxiety and sadness.

References

California Association of School Counselors (2018, October 23). *Self-Care*. Retrieved from CASC: www.schoolcounselor-ca.org/files/Advocacy/Self%20Care%20Ideas%20for%20Counselors.pdf

Carter, S.B. (2013, November 26). *The Tell Tale Signs of Burnout... Do You Have Them?* Retrieved from Psychology Today: www.psychologytoday.com/us/blog/high-octane-women/201311/the-tell-tale-signs-burnout-do-you-have-them

Hamilton, L. (2017, July 27). *10 Self-Care Tips for School Counselors*. Retrieved from PsychBytes: www.psychbytes.com/self-care-tips-for-school-counselors/

Hansen, S. (2018, October 22). *Your Self-Care Matters*. Retrieved from School-Counseling-Zone: www.school-counseling-zone.com/self-care.html

Mayo Clinic (2015, September 17). *Job Burnout: How to Spot it and Take Action*. Retrieved from Mayo Clinic: www.mayoclinic.org/healthy-lifestyle/adult-health/in-depth/burnout/art-20046642

MindTools (2018, October 22). *Burnout Self-Test Checking Yourself for Burnout.* Retrieved from MindTools: www.mindtools.com/pages/article/newTCS_08.htm

Mullen, P.R., & Gutierrez, D. (2018, October 17). *Burnout, Stress and Direct Student Services Among School Counselors.* Retrieved from TPC The Professional Counselor: http://tpc journal.nbcc.org/burnout-stress-and-direct-student-services-among-school-counselors/

Mullen, P.R., Blount, A.J., Lambie, G.W., & Chae, N. (2018, June 11). *School Counselors' Perceived Stress, Burnout, and Job Satisfaction.* Retrieved from SAGE journals: http://jou rnals.sagepub.com/doi/10.1177/2156759X18782468

Nobles, M. (2011). *Factors That Influence School Counselor Burnout.* Retrieved from Digital Commons @Brockport: https://digitalcommons.brockport.edu/cgi/viewcontent.cg i?article=1145&context=edc_theses

Sharma, A., Madaan, V., & Petty, F.D. (2006). Exercise for mental health. *The Primary Care Companion to the Journal of Clinical Psychology.* 8(2): 106.

Part VI

Establishing Your Role and Program

15 Applying Your Graduate Knowledge

Now that you are hired, there is a lot to do. Textbook knowledge goes a long way and it's exciting to put it into practice. However, it doesn't happen just like the textbook. We don't know what scenarios students are going to present us with and sometimes they just need an answer to a question. In graduate school, I always struggled with saying the right phrases at the right time when counseling. It would come across as forced and unnatural, but the techniques I learned I use. You learn to use them in ways that fit your personality. Applying the skills that you learn in graduate school isn't always as easy as it was during the role plays.

Theoretical Orientation

As a school counselor it's not as important to choose a theoretical orientation as compared to a mental health counselor. What is important is knowing the theories and which ones work effectively in a school. Many school counselors are eclectic and pull from theories that work best for the situation they are presented with. Due to the nature of our profession, we do brief therapy when counseling. There are a couple of theories that work better for short-term, brief therapy than others.

Michelle Mota states in her portfolio that,

> As a Professional School Counselor, it is important to align oneself with a theoretical orientation that upholds the same philosophical beliefs and values that he or she holds. Throughout my extensive studies in the fields of psychology and counseling, in preparation for my future career as a Professional School Counselor, I have come to align myself with the person-centered approach.
>
> (Moto, 2018)

The reason theoretical orientation is helpful is the foundation it provides for working with students. As school counselors, we can't provide ongoing therapy, but we can help students with their immediate concerns. Those immediate concerns range from college applications to meltdowns. Knowing what to do in those situations is important and using an empirically based theory will better help the student. Applying these theories in a school can be difficult when you come straight out of graduate school. In the following sections, I have provided information and resources on a few common theories that work well in a school environment.

Cognitive Behavioral Therapy

Cognitive Behavioral Therapy (CBT) was developed by Dr. Aaron Beck in the 1960s. It is a psychotherapy that focuses on the cognitive model that how a person perceives a situation will determine how they react to it. CBT doesn't use one particular set of techniques to help clients, but pulls from a variety. Reframing is a common technique used to help clients change their perception about a situation and in turn change their emotions and behaviors. They borrow techniques from

> psychotherapeutic modalities, including dialectical behavior therapy, acceptance and commitment therapy, Gestalt therapy, compassion focused therapy, mindfulness, solution focused therapy, motivational interviewing, positive psychology, interpersonal psychotherapy, and when it comes to personality disorders, psychodynamic psychotherapy.
> (Beck Institute for Cognitive Behavioral Therapy, 2018)

One of the foundations of CBT is understanding and helping clients with Cognitive Distortions. These can be the cause of anxiety, stress, and depression to name a few. All cognitive distortions are (Ackerman, 2017):

- Tendencies or patterns of thinking or believing...
- That are false or inaccurate...
- And have the potential to cause psychological damage.

A few common Cognitive Distortions are (Ackerman, 2017):

- All-or-Nothing Thinking / Polarized Thinking
- Overgeneralization
- Mental Filter
- Disqualifying the Positive
- Jumping to Conclusions—Mind Reading
- Jumping to Conclusions—Fortune Telling
- Magnification (Catastrophizing) or Minimization
- Emotional Reasoning
- Should Statements
- Labeling and Mislabeling

- Personalization
- Control Fallacies
- Fallacy of Fairness
- Fallacy of Change
- Always Being Right
- Heaven's Reward Fallacy

As school counselors, we can apply CBT techniques at all grade levels. At the elementary level, here are few ways to implement CBT (Driscoll, 2018):

- **String test activity:** Hold a string with a small weight tied to it. Tell the student you can move the string by simply imagining that it will move. Allow the child to do the same. This introduces the concept of thoughts controlling our actions. This is a pre-requirement for students to understand that they can 'talk back' to their negative thoughts.
- **Thought paths:** Write down an event that could be perceived negatively or positively. Write down a positive thought you could have and a negative thought you could have. Follow the path from each thought so that a negative thought corresponds to a negative feeling and a negative action, while a positive thought leads to a positive feeling and action.
- **Use books:** One of the best ways to discuss emotions is through books. While reading books, remark on how a character is feeling and how you know that. Do they look a certain way? Did something happen? Did they say something that told you how they felt? Teach students to observe to figure out how someone feels.
- **Feelings inspectors:** When we teach students to observe others to determine how they feel, we talk about how they look. What does their body language tell you? What does their face tell you? How about their voice?
- **Identify a thought a character has in a story.**
- **Identify a thought they had in a neutral situation**
- **Identify a thought they had when upset.**
- **Identify a negative thought that led to a negative feeling or action.**
- **Change a negative thought to a positive thought.**
- **Use positive self-talk to combat negative thinking.**

For adolescents, there are a couple of textbooks for school personnel to use. These provide step-by-step instructions and include all the materials you need for implementation. Below I have listed the titles and descriptions of three books that I found to be reliable and valid.

Cognitive Therapy for Adolescents in School Settings by Torrey A. Creed, Jarrod Reisweber, and Aaron T. Beck (Guilford Press, 2018):

This first concise guide to conducting cognitive therapy (CT) with adolescents in school settings features in-depth case examples and hands-on clinical tools. The authors—who include renowned CT originator Aaron T. Beck—provide an accessible introduction to the cognitive model and demonstrate specific therapeutic techniques. Strategies are illustrated for engaging adolescents in therapy, rapidly creating an effective case conceptualization, and addressing a range of clinical issues and stressors frequently experienced in grades 6–12. The challenges and rewards of school-based CT are discussed in detail. In a convenient large-size format with lay-flat binding for easy photocopying, the book contains 16 reproducible handouts, worksheets, and forms. Purchasers also get access to a Web page where they can download and print the reproducible materials.

Cognitive Behavioral Therapy in K–12 School Settings: A Practitioner's Toolkit by Diana Joyce-Beaulieu, Michael L. Sulkowski (2018):

> Twenty percent of school-age children in the United States experience mental health issues each year and cognitive behavioral therapy (CBT) is one of the most effective and empirically supported interventions to address these needs. This practical, quick-reference handbook is for mental health professionals in the K–12 school setting who are seeking a hands-on guide for practicing CBT. Based on a wealth of research supporting the efficacy of CBT for school-age children, it features specific interventions that can be applied immediately and is tailored to the needs of busy school psychologists, counselors, and social workers. Importantly, this book describes how to use CBT within contemporary school-based service delivery frameworks such as multitiered systems of support (MTSS) and response to intervention (RtI).

Examining the core components of CBT in the context of school-based therapy, this book offers developmentally appropriate treatment plans targeted for specific issues based on the new *DSM-5* criteria, as well as tools for measuring progress and outcomes. Case conceptualization examples are provided in addition to contraindications for counseling therapy. The book also explains how to adapt treatment in light of developmental issues and cultural considerations. Case examples, sample reports, and a great variety of reproducible handouts (also available in digital download format) are provided to help school mental health professionals use CBT as part of their regular practice.

Key Features:

- Presents content that is highly practical and immediately applicable for professionals and trainees
- Designed to work within and meet the needs of the specific service delivery environment of schools, including MTSS and RtI

- Reflects *DSM-5* criteria and the Patient Protection and Affordable Care Act
- Includes case studies and hands-on session outlines, report templates, and student activities (also available in digital download format)

Cognitive-Behavioral Therapy in Schools: A Tiered Approach to Youth Mental Health Services by Linda Raffaele Mendez (ResearchGate, 2018):

> In recent years, many U.S. schools have implemented tiered models of support to address a range of student needs, both academic and behavioral, while cognitive behavioral therapy (CBT) has simultaneously gained popularity as an effective means of supporting the mental health needs of students. Cognitive Behavioral Therapy in Schools provides school-based practitioners with the necessary skills to determine students' mental health needs; establish a tiered, CBT-based system of supports; select appropriate programs at Tiers 1, 2, and 3; deliver CBT using various formats to students who are at risk or demonstrating problems; progress monitor multiple tiers of service; and work collaboratively with teachers, administrators, and families.

Solution Focused

Solution-Focused Brief Therapy was developed by Steve Shazer and Insoo Kim Berg in the 1970s. It is future focused and solution oriented.

> Described as a practical, goal-driven model, a hallmark of SFBT is its emphasis on clear, concise, realistic goal negotiations. The SFBT approach assumes that all clients have some knowledge of what would make their life better, even though they may need some (at times, considerable) help describing the details of their better life and that everyone who seeks help already possesses at least the minimal skills necessary to create solutions.
>
> (Institute for Solution-Focused Therapy, 2018)

Techniques for Solution-Focused Therapy

Major tenets of SFBT (Franklin & Belciug, 2015):

- Clients are encouraged to increase the frequency of current useful behaviors.
- Social workers help clients find alternatives to current undesired patterns of behavior.
- Small increments of change lead to larger increments of change, which may lead to a permanent solution.

- Clients' solutions are not necessarily *directly* related to any problem, but are created through goal-setting and deciding on specific ways to achieve those goals.

The major techniques of SFBT are (Franklin & Belciug, 2015):

- **The search for strengths or solutions.** Methods such as purposefully using the client's language, grounding understanding in communication exchanges, and the awareness that questions and language are not neutral but shape perceptions and outcomes have been explored in process studies and determined to be important to SFBT change strategies.
- **The use of the miracle question.** The Miracle Question helps to: set goals, start talking about situations after solution, avoid differing problem definitions, develop solutions separate from the problem, explore new possibilities, reduce blame about the problems, broaden the context, and in fact may solve more than one problem.
  - "Imagine tonight while you are sleeping a miracle occurs. The miracle is the difficulties and problems that have brought you here (to counseling) have somehow been resolved while you were sleeping."
  - "What is the first small thing that tells you this miracle has happened (and what else, etc., etc.)" "What would you be doing or what would you notice that is different to tell you the miracle has occurred?"
  - "What would other people notice you were doing?" Make sure to focus on details.
- **The use of scaling questions.** Scaling questions provide clients with the opportunity to examine or evaluate progress toward identified goals and also serves as a method for envisioning the next steps needed to build a solution. This process allows both the client and practitioner to quantify client progress and to identify the next steps to change by using a numeric rating scale (usually ranging from 0 or 1–10 with 0 or 1 as the lowest and 10 as the highest).
- **The goal-setting.** Goal setting is a fundamental element of the Solution-Focused process. In order to set an appropriate goal, the social worker has a conversation with a client about how they want their life to be different. Questions include: what has to happen for it to be worth your time to come here today? Suppose after we talk today that your life would be different—what would have to happen? What do you want to happen instead? This conversation may also involve ways that others want the client to change even if the client does not agree with those changes.
- **The search for the exceptions to the problem.** Exception questions are questions that allow the practitioner and client to explore points in the client's life where an identified problem could have occurred, but did not.
  - Tell me a time when this problem does not occur?
  - What was different then?
  - What's been better?
  - What has changed?

- **The consulting break and set of compliments offered to the client.** Breaks are often taken near the end of a session. This gives the social worker a moment to collect thoughts and develop compliments and to also think of the next steps, tasks, or experiments to propose to the client.
- **The homework tasks.**

Solution-Focused Therapy works well in terms of keeping track of student progress, building rapport, outlining a pathway to change, clarifying and defining a problem, and creating goals (Bolling, 2017). The techniques mentioned are ones that a school counselor can use without additional certification. Seeking additional training and resources is encouraged, but you don't have to earn a certificate as with some theoretical orientations. The tenets are foundational counseling skills that all school counselors and mental health counselors are taught in their graduate coursework.

Reality Therapy

A common theory that school counselors use is Reality Therapy.

> Reality Therapy can successfully be used in a school setting by school counselors. It helps students redirect their feelings, thoughts, and actions to achieve their goals in a positive, forward-thinking way. Reality Therapy is compatible with setting goals in the domains of Academic, Social/ Personal, and Career Development that are promoted by ASCA. This method is efficient in that results can be seen in a relatively short amount of time. Reality Therapy can be an excellent tool for school counselors in helping students set realistic goals to improve their academic performance.
> (Graham Smith, 2018)

An article from Dr. Yvette Stupart in *Owlcation* discusses Reality Therapy and its methods (Stupart, 2018):

What is Reality Therapy?

William Glasser, a psychiatrist, developed a method of counseling called Reality Therapy. This therapy is based on Choice Theory which assumes that behaviors are based on choice, and humans are motivated to satisfy five basic needs. Survival, love and belonging, power, freedom, and fun are the five needs.

Reality Therapy and Choice Theory

Reality Therapy, based on Choice Theory, is formulated to make it useful to therapists, school counselors, teachers, and others. According to Glasser and Wubbolding, this therapy, "helps people to examine their wants, and needs, evaluate their behavior and make plans for fulfilling needs" (Glasser & Wubbolding, 1995).

An important ingredient to Reality Therapy is the concept of choice. So, Reality Therapy rejects the idea that people are victims of their behaviors and circumstances. Instead, they choose the kinds of behavior they produce. In other words, people choose how to behave. Reality Therapy, then, provides the structure to help people satisfy their needs for survival, love and belonging, achievement, fun, and freedom or independence. People's behavior is the vehicle that is used to meet their needs.

WDEP System

According to Glasser, personal history is only important to the degree that it influences present choices, and so the emphasis is on current and recent lifestyle behaviors. Reality Therapy uses interventions that lead individuals to evaluate their lives and make decisions to move in more productive directions.

Each letter in WDEP, formulated by Robert E, Wubbolding, represents skills and techniques to assist people in taking control of their lives and fulfilling their needs.

W: Ask clients what they want. This helps clients to clarify and prioritize their desires. This line of questioning helps them to describe what they want from themselves and others, including their parents, teachers, and peers.

D: Ask clients what they are doing. This question helps clients to be more aware of their choices, and where these choices might take them.

E: Ask clients to conduct self-evaluation. Self-evaluation is a key element in Reality Therapy. This is the most important question, which in essence asks clients, "Is what you are doing getting you what you want?"

P: Ask clients to make plans to effectively fulfill their needs. This asks clients for detailed strategies for change that will help them to take charge of the direction in which their lives are going.

Reality Therapy can be effective for high school counselors using the approach mentioned in the article. However, it can also work well with elementary schools. A qualitative research study done by Eric S. Davis from Argosy University and Mary Ann Clark from University of Florida, shows that there are benefits for using Reality Play Counseling (Davis & Clark, 2018):

Reality Play Counseling

Throughout the years of research and evidence of the effectiveness of both Play Counseling and Reality Therapy, there is no evidence that an attempt to combine the two has ever been undertaken. Reality Play Counseling can be a potentially powerful tool for elementary school counselors. Most children below the age of 11 lack a fully developed capacity for abstract thought needed for verbal expression or understanding of complex issues and feelings. Using creative techniques to connect with clients across ages and development further enhances the potential usefulness of Reality Play Therapy.

Both counseling approaches have been considered to be well-suited for short-term counseling while helping students discover how to make choices regarding behavior, taking responsibility, and using the techniques throughout life to meet needs. Once such needs are addressed or fulfilled, it is postulated that students can become more enthusiastic about learning, thus leading to improved academic performance. Therefore, the primary purpose of this study was to investigate elementary school counselors' perceptions of the usefulness of Reality Play Counseling with elementary school students in relationship building and problem-solving skills.

Considering the number of students a school counselor must see within the academic year and throughout the day, it is important to use a theoretical approach that is concise and effective. Reality Therapy can be used in all grade levels for most situations. It can be a good approach for helping students who have disciplinary problems. A quote from the *Middle School Journal* states (Walter, Lambie, & Ngazimbi, 2008),

The middle level educator's role with students who have disciplinary problems

The developmental needs of young adolescents have implications for the programs and services middle school teachers and counselors deliver, and these needs, specifically the need for belonging, should be a primary focus of middle school counseling programs and other educational interventions. With their practices, educators may seek to maximize school connectedness by working to provide a social environment that meets middle school students' core developmental need for belonging. Beck and Malley underscored the need for the school's involvement in meeting an individual's belonging needs. Other significant developmental needs of these students include (a) opportunities to demonstrate competence, (b) acceptance by peers, and (c) opportunities for autonomy. Because peers become much more influential during this time in their development, counseling and teaching young adolescents in groups are strategies well suited to promoting student belonging through positive peer interaction. When group participants are carefully and purposefully selected, group counseling and learning activities may provide students who lack appropriate behavioral skills the opportunity to learn from students who are perceived as having these skills. Dalbech suggested that middle school students are more likely to be receptive to comments about how to establish responsible behavior from peers than from adults.

Wrap Up

When you're a first-year school counselor, rely on the foundations of what you were taught in your graduate program. You don't need to know the tenets and techniques of every theory, but spend your time focusing on what works for school counselors. By developing your understanding further on specific theories, you will be better equipped to do brief counseling. The counseling theories mentioned in this chapter have been researched and studied by professionals who understand the school environment. It will take practice to feel comfortable using these techniques and skills, but eventually they will become second nature. Although we are not able to diagnose students with mental health disorders, we know the signs and are able to give some assessments. These are ways we help our students know to seek outside professional help. Our foundation in mental health enables us to be 'general practitioners' in the field. We aren't experts in mental health disorders, but we do have a broad understanding. That is why continuing education is crucial to helping our students. Seek advice and consult with professionals. Whether you decide to use Solution Focused, Reality, Cognitive Behavioral, or another theory entirely, be sure to evaluate if you're getting results with your students. Don't be discouraged if this doesn't happen the first year! You are still developing as a school counselor and will continue to do so.

References

Ackerman, C. (2017, September 29). *Cognitive Distortions: When Your Brain Lies to You (+ PDF Worksheets)*. Retrieved from Positive Psychology Program: https://positivepsychologyprogram.com/cognitive-distortions/#what-cognitive-distortions

Beck Institute for Cognitive Behavioral Therapy (2018, October 31). *What Is Cognitive Behavior Therapy (CBT)?* Retrieved from Beck Institute for Cognitive Behavioral Therapy: https://beckinstitute.org/get-informed/what-is-cognitive-therapy/

Bolling, S.H. (2017, September 26). *Solution-Focused Counseling in Middle and High Schools*. Retrieved from Classroom: https://classroom.synonym.com/solutionfocused-counseling-middle-high-schools-18183.html

Buchholz Holland, C.E. (2018, October 30). *Solution-Focused Applications for School Settings*. Retrieved from Kansas State University: https://coe.k-state.edu/events/school-counsel-camp/docs/Buchholz-Holland-SF-Schools.pdf

Davis, E.S., & Clark, M. (2018, October 29). Elementary school counselors' perceptions of reality play counseling in students' relationship building and problem-solving skills. *Journal of School Counseling*. Retrieved from: http://jsc.montana.edu/articles/v10n11.pdf

Driscoll, L. (2018, October 31). *Using Cognitive Behavioral Therapy with Younger Students*. Retrieved from Social Emotional Workshop: https://socialemotionalworkshop.com/2018/01/cognitive-behavioral-therapy-with-younger-students/

Franklin, C., & Belciug, C. (2015, March). *Solution-Focused Brief Therapy in Schools*. Retrieved from Encyclopedia of Social Work: http://socialwork.oxfordre.com/view/10.1093/acrefore/9780199975839.001.0001/acrefore-9780199975839-e-1040?print=pdf

Graham Smith (2018, October 29). *Reality Therapy and School Counseling*. Retrieved from Graham Smith School Counseling: http://grahamsmithschoolcounseling.weebly.com/uploads/2/6/9/3/26939509/realitytherapy.pdf

Guilford Press (2018, October 31). *Cognitive Therapy for Adolescents in School Settings*. Retrieved from Guilford Press: www.guilford.com/books/Cognitive-Therapy-for-Adolescents-in-School-Settings/Creed-Reisweber-Beck/9781609181338/summary

Institute for Solution-Focused Therapy (2018, October 29). *What is Solution-Focused Therapy?* Retrieved from Institute for Solution-Focused Therapy: https://solutionfocused.net/what-is-solution-focused-therapy/

Joyce-Beaulieu D., & Sulkowski, M. (2018, October 31). *Cognitive Behavioral Therapy in K-12 School Settings.* Retrieved from Springer Publishing Company: www.springerpub.com/cognitive-behavioral-therapy-in-k-12-school-settings-9780826196385.html

Moto, M. (2018, October 25). *Portfolio.* Retrieved from Theoretical Orientation: http://michellemota.weebly.com

ResearchGate (2018, October 31). *Cognitive-Behavioral Therapy in Schools: A Tiered Approach to Youth Mental Health Services.* Retrieved from ResearchGate: www.researchgate.net/publication/313510677_Cognitive-Behavioral_Therapy_in_Schools_A_Tiered_Approach_to_Youth_Mental_Health_Services

Stupart, Y. (2018, April 15). *How to Promote Teen School Engagement with Reality Therapy.* Retrieved from Owlcation: https://owlcation.com/academia/UsingRealityTherapytoPromoteTeenSchoolAchievement

Walter, S.M., Lambie, G.W., & Ngazimbi, E.E. (2008). A choice theory counseling group succeeds with middle school students who displayed disciplinary problems. *Middle School Journal,* 40: 4–12.

16 Working with Administrators

As the only school counselor at my school, I am considered part of the administration. Normally, this would be put on the head school counselor rather than the first-year. There is a lot to be learned from being on the administrative team. This experience forces a school counselor to be an advocate for themselves, the profession, and the students. Working with the administration is key to implementing a successful counseling program. This chapter will discuss what it means to be on an administrative team and the importance of advocacy in the profession.

Advocacy

In order to work with administration about your counseling program, you first have to be an advocate for it. I found this to be the most important aspect of collaborating with administration. There are administrators who are not aware of what the school counselor does or what the role should look like. We need to be able to effectively advocate for ourselves and the profession to our administrators. Do not get discouraged if your advocacy doesn't make change immediately. It can take time to change a mindset that has been in place for years.

Mindy Hall discusses how to be an advocate for your counseling program in her article, "Advocating for Your School Counseling Program Using ASCA Resources". She states:

> Advocacy ensures that stakeholders understand the role of the school counselor and the importance to students of implementing a comprehensive school counseling program. Advocacy means communicating to stakeholders what the comprehensive school counseling program is, how it makes a difference, and how it affects the success of all students. The ASCA position statement on comprehensive school counseling programs provides a concise rationale for counselors to use.
>
> Think about your school counseling program. Make connections between what your stakeholders want and need and the services and

supports that your school counseling program can provide. Who are your stakeholders (internal and external)? Realizing that some stakeholders still cling to the old role description of guidance counselors (career/vocational), it is important for today's counselors to correct those misconceptions and provide stakeholders with an updated picture of the benefits of standards-driven comprehensive school counseling programs. Presenting ASCA Mindsets and Behaviors will help define a school counselor's role in supporting K–12 college and career readiness for all students.

(Hall, December Newsletter, 2017)

It is vital that we are using the ASCA model and resources to measure and evaluate our school counseling program. By doing this, we are able to effectively inform stakeholders of the impact of our programming. It's not a question of whether we impact students' lives, but how we impact them. We live in the era of data and we use data to our benefit. Chapter 17 goes into more depth about implementing the ASCA National Model.

A couple of quotes from school counselors on advocacy taken from the *Confident Counselors* blog are as follows (Confident Counselors, 2017):

Developing a positive relationship with admin is vital in advocating for the role of counselor. Seek ways to partner with admin to reach school wide goals and work to align at least one of the counseling goals to the school improvement plan. Share a results report that reflects all of your amazing program accomplishments including activities and data. Volunteer to chair one of the faculty teams. Publicize your schedule and website, send counseling department info through your PTA/PTO, develop a school counseling handbook for faculty, and strive to demonstrate how your role as counselor benefits all students.

There's a difference between education and advocating. Sometimes you need to figure out which one in your school building you need to be doing first. Most of the time it will be educating stakeholders about what your role as a school counselor is. Once they are aware, then you need to advocate for time, space, and responsibilities you should be doing based on what you told them you are supposed to do. Promote your program, use data, and keep records—these are the surest ways to educate and advocate.

In this day and age, advocacy is a big part of our job as school counselors. And it's like going to the gym or flossing—no one has time for it, but you MUST make time for it, carving 15 minutes or more into your daily schedule to work on it. Most administrators and educators have no idea what our SC job roles/duties are according to ASCA. Therefore, we must tell them—professionally, politely, and in increments. If you are at a school with no comprehensive school counseling program (CSCP), give yourself 3–5 years to work with your admin (adding new components every month and showing data to support how these components help students) to create your CSCP.

Advocacy is integrated into our school counseling program. If you are aligning your program with the ASCA National Model, then the two can't be separated. Everything you do that aligns with ASCA will benefit your program when advocating for it. Another component of advocating for your school counseling program is knowing your state standards and evaluation. If your school is not evaluating you based on their state's requirements, then that needs to be addressed.

State Standards

Each state should have their own standards for school counselors. Standards, like those in the classroom, determine what a counselor should be doing in regard to the role and responsibility. An example of state standards is from the Ohio Department of Education (Ohio Department of Education, 2018):

The Standards in the Context of Ohio's Standards-Based Reforms:

The Ohio Standards for School Counselors are an extension of the standards-based reforms that have taken place in Ohio over the past decade. The state has detailed student academic learning standards for P-12 (http://education.ohio. gov/Topics/Ohio-s-New-Learning-Standards/Ohios-New-Learning-Standards), as well as the Ohio Standards for the Teaching Profession, the Ohio Standards for Principals, the Ohio Standards for Superintendents, the Ohio Standards for Professional Development, and the Ohio Standards for School Treasurers and School Business Managers. Together, these standards show what is known about the practices of effective district leaders, school leaders, teachers and professional development systems. Copies of these standards are available on the Ohio Department of Education website: http://education.ohio.gov/Topics/Teaching/Educator-Equity/Ohio-s-Educator-Standards

Common themes cross all of these sets of standards. These shared foundations include an emphasis on:

- Student learning and achievement;
- Shared leadership;
- Data-based decision-making;
- Communication and collaboration; and
- Ongoing professional learning.

Some states have standards that are specific for each grade level. The Virginia Department of Education outlines their standards for school counselors based upon topic and grade level.

Table 16.1 Ohio Standards for School Counselors

Section ii. Ohio Standards for School Counselors	
standard 1: Comprehensive School Counseling Program Plan	School counselors collaboratively envision a plan for a comprehensive school counseling program that is developmental, preventative and responsive, and in alignment with the school's goals and mission.

standard 2:
Direct Services for
  Academic, Career
  and Social/Emotional
  Development
	School counselors develop a curriculum, offer individual student planning and deliver responsive services in order to assist students in developing and applying knowledge, skills and mindsets for academic, career and social/emotional development.

standard 3: Indirect Services: Partnerships and Referrals	School counselors collaborate and consult with school personnel, parents/guardians, community partners and agencies/organizations to coordinate support for all students.
standard 4: Evaluation and Data	School counselors collaboratively engage in a cycle of continuous improvement using data to identify needs, plan and implement programs, evaluate impact and adjust accordingly.
standard 5: Leadership and Advocacy	School counselors lead school efforts and advocate for policies and practices that support an equitable, safe, inclusive and positive learning environment for all students.
standard 6: Professional Responsibility, Knowledge and Growth	School counselors adhere to the ethical standards of the profession, engage in ongoing professional learning and refine their work through reflection.

For example, (Virginia Department of Education, 2018):

The Standards for School Counseling Programs in Virginia Public Schools are organized by grade level under the following goals:

Academic Development

Students will acquire the academic preparation essential to choose from a variety of educational, training, and employment options upon completion of secondary school.

Career Development

Students will investigate the world of work in order to make informed career decisions.

Personal/Social Development

Students will acquire an understanding of, and respect for, self and others, and the skills to be responsible citizens.

Although the "Standards for School Counseling Programs in Virginia Public Schools" are defined at certain grade levels, school counseling programs should reinforce previously acquired knowledge and skills as defined by these standards throughout the course of a student's subsequent educational experience.

Then, they breakdown each of their standards per grade level:

Academic Development

Goal

Grades K–3: Students will:

1. EA1. Understand the expectations of the educational environment,
2. EA2. Understand the importance of individual effort, hard work, and persistence,
3. EA3. Understand the relationship of academic achievement to current and future success in school,
4. EA4. Understand that mistakes are essential to the learning process,
5. EA5. Demonstrate individual initiative and a positive interest in learning,
6. EA6. Use appropriate communication skills to ask for help when needed,
7. EA7. Work independently to achieve academic success,
8. EA8. Work cooperatively in small and large groups towards a common goal, and
9. EA9. Use study skills and test-taking strategies.

Grades 4–5: Students will:

10. EA10. Recognize personal strengths and weaknesses related to learning,
11. EA11. Demonstrate time management and organizational skills,
12. EA12. Apply study skills necessary for academic achievement,
13. EA13. Use critical thinking skills and test-taking strategies, and
14. EA14. Understand the choices, options, and requirements of the middle school environment.

Grades 6–8: Students will:

1. MA1. Understand the relationship of personal abilities, goals, skills, interests, and motivation to academic achievement,
2. MA2. Understand the relationship of dependability, productivity, and initiative to academic success,
3. MA3. Understand the importance of high school course and/or program selection in relation to future academic and career options,
4. MA4. Understand high school graduation requirements,
5. MA5. Understand individual assessment results in relation to educational progress,

6. MA6. Demonstrate the skills needed to develop a high school educational plan based on ability, interest, and achievement, and Students will acquire the academic preparation essential to choose from a variety of educational, training, and employment options upon completion of secondary school.

State Evaluations

Depending upon your state, you will have an evaluation process just like teachers do. Not every state has standards and evaluations but having these helps with advocating for your roles and responsibilities. If you do have an evaluation, then it will be based on the state standards for school counselors. Since I used an example of Ohio's state standards for school counselors, I included a portion of their evaluation.

Ohio Department of Education (Ohio Department of Education, 2016):

Evaluation Framework for School Counselors

Ohio is serious about its commitment to quality schools. In 2015, the State Board of Education adopted standards for school counselors. With the adoption of the Ohio Standards for School Counselors, Ohio has clearly defined the knowledge, skills and competencies of effective school counselors. These standards promote the most effective school counseling practices and offer a core set of expectations for Ohio school counselors. Professional school counselors offer students access to high-quality services, which support students' academic, career and social/emotional development.

Each school counselor will be evaluated according to Ohio Revised Code and the Evaluation Framework which is aligned to the Ohio Standards for School Counselors. The Ohio School Counselor Evaluation System (OSCES) was designed to be transparent, fair and adaptable to the specific contexts of Ohio's districts.

OSCES is a standards-based integrated model that is designed to foster the professional growth of school counselors in knowledge, skills and practice. In OSCES, each school counselor is evaluated based upon multiple factors including performance on all areas identified by the standards and the ability to produce positive student outcomes using metrics in order to determine the holistic final summative rating of effectiveness according to ODE requirements. The choice of metrics for student outcomes will be determined locally.

Ohio also includes a rubric for each of these rating categories and standards. This has helped me in my own advocacy work.

The Iowa School Counselor Association gives great information on a multitiered structure on advocacy (Iowa School Counselor Association, 2018) in Table 16.2.

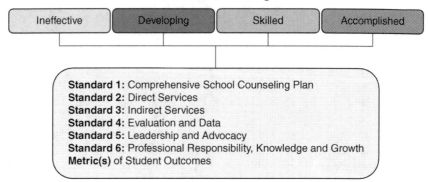

Figure 16.1 Ohio Standards for School Counselors.

School Board and Administration

Because I understand what the state policies and laws are, I have been able to advocate for school counselors at the local level. I have worked with local school counselors to write resolutions to local district policy on school counselors' roles and responsibilities to align with the policy on school counselor evaluations. This is the best way to make sure your roles and responsibilities are clearly defined for your school administrators. I recently wrote a resolution to a school board policy to align with their state's standards and evaluation policy. I met with a former school board member to help me with the 'how to' and what to include in the policy. Then, I met with the lead school counselor in the district to have her present with me. I thought it was important to have a current school counselor share their insights. We presented this during a committee meeting. It was well received and will most likely be voted on to become a formal resolution to the policy on school counselors. Building coalitions with the folks in administration and the school board has really helped me be an effective advocate for the school counseling profession. It has also helped me understand how schools function on a district level. This is only one example of a plethora of ways you can be an advocate.

There a number of ways you can advocate at the district level (Washington School Counselor Association, 2018).

1. Publicize your successes/achievements at parent, administrative, and school board meetings, and in building, district and community newsletters.
2. Use a needs assessment to determine interventions & then report results (use data to illustrate).
3. Develop a strategic plan with long- and short-term goals (tie it to your building and/or district plan!).

Table 16.2 Ohio Standards for School Counselors

Level 1	Level 2	Level 3
• Be physically visible	• Yearly goal setting aligned with district goals using data	• Yearly goal setting aligned with district goals using data
• Introduce yourself and use School Counselor terminology and signage everywhere	• Develop PLC (Professional Learning Committee)	• Develop PLC (Professional Learning Committee)
• Develop a program brochure	• Management agreement	• Management agreement
• Implement ASCA Model and Iowa School Counseling Framework—Use data!	• Time Analysis	• Time Analysis
• Print business cards	• Develop and share calendar	• Develop and share calendar
• Celebrate National School Counselor Week	• Presentation on program results with staff, admin, school board, and PTA	• Presentation on program results with staff, admin, school board, and PTA
• Use social media to communicate	• Use School Counselor Evaluation Tool	• Use School Counselor Evaluation Tool
• Bulletin boards	• Member of building leadership committees	• Member of building leadership committees
• Know how you are funded	• Connections with community	• Connections with community
• Consistent communication and conversations with administrators and staff	• Active in SCA	• Active in SCA
• Advisory committee	• Present at SCA conference	• Present at SCA conference
• Join professional organizations	• Be informed about state legislative issues.	• Be informed about state legislative issues.
• Join SCA and ASCA and attend conferences	• Contact legislators and attend forums	• Contact legislators and attend forums
• Display SCA membership certificate, clothing, mug, water bottle etc.	• Attend Visit the Hill Day	• Attend Visit the Hill Day
• Nominations for grants		

4. Ask your school board to develop a policy statement that supports school counseling.
5. Make sure counselors are part of District Strategic Plans (get on those committees!).
6. Encourage your fellow counselors to become involved in the local and state educator's union.
7. Find a champion (parent, student, teacher, admin, district staff, and/or board member) to help you with 'marketing'.

Meet with your school board members and get to know them. That is one of the best ways to advocate for your profession. There are school board members who don't know what a school counselor does and if it's different than a social worker. Make an effort to talk to them one-on-one and share what you do. Advocacy doesn't have to start with a presentation at a board meeting.

When you're advocating your position and counseling program to administration, it can be intimidating to speak up. After all, this is your full-time job and the administrators decide who gets a contract renewal. Our approach to advocacy should be done with understanding why we are advocating. We should be advocating for our role, because we are better able to serve our students. We shouldn't have an 'us versus them' mentality. Even if it seems like it, we should maintain perspective and make sure our hearts are in the right place.

As a first-year school counselor, I was thrust into the role of the administration team. I had to attend weekly administration meetings and close the building on a number of days per month. There were times when I had to act as administration if there wasn't another administrator in the building. This isn't the case at every school and when I had a change of principals it wasn't the case. I will say that being a part of the administration meetings gave me ample opportunity to advocate for my school counseling program. There were times when distribution of duties was talked about so that I could let the administration know what would not be beneficial. For example, giving an ACT review class would not benefit the students. Number one, I have not mastered the college standardized tests and do not teach any subjects on those tests. Therefore, I am the least qualified person to give an ACT review class. In that regard, there were benefits to be on the administration team. With the change in principal, I was no longer considered administration. He/she felt that the duties of administrator were not those of the school counselor. That is also true. My point is, you're not going to get to decide some of your roles as a new school counselor. Take the opportunities you are given, even if they're not a part of the role per ASCA and learn from them. Find ways to make it an opportunity to better serve your students.

Tips for Advocacy

The Arizona School Counselor Association uses the alphabet to identify ways to advocate. Starting with A, awards, and ending in Z, zoom into the zone (Arizona School Counselors Association, 2018). They state, "Advocacy is a key component to being an effective school counselor. Not only is it critical for school counselors to serve as advocates to their students, it is also important that school counselors advocate for their own profession".

An article by Mindy Hall highlights the following areas of advocacy and is great material to reference (Hall, American School Counselor Association , 2017):

Advocacy in Defining the Role of the School Counselor: The school counselor's role remains unclear in many school districts. School counselors' tasks, expectations and demands vary from district to district and school to school. In many cases, the definition of the school counselor's role is left to the administrator's discretion. When faced with questions about their roles and responsibilities, school counselors can refer to One Vision, One Voice resources. Developed by the American School Counselor Association (ASCA) in conjunction with representatives from 51 state school counseling associations, these resources promote the mission and work of school counselors.

Advocacy for Your School Counseling Program: Advocacy ensures that stakeholders understand the role of the school counselor and the importance to students of implementing a comprehensive school counseling program. Advocacy means communicating to stakeholders what the comprehensive school counseling program is, how it makes a difference, and how it affects the success of all students.

Advocacy Everyday: Promote your role in the school by being visible. Introduce yourself with the use of school counselor terminology and signage everywhere.

Advocacy within the District and State: Set yearly goals aligned with district and ASCA goals using data. Maintain usage of time agreements. Analyze your daily/weekly schedules. Present program results to staff, administrators, school board, home and school. Participate in official NJSCA/NJPSA school counselor mentor training each year.

Take Action: It is your responsibility to advocate for what school counselors in your local district should be doing. ASCA and NJSCA are continually working to share position statements, model programs, and research to support the effectiveness of school counselors.

References

Arizona School Counselors Association (2018, November 17). *Arizona School Counselors Association.* Retrieved from Advocacy Toolkit: A Practical Approach to Advocacy: www.azsca.org/files/advocacy/advocacytoolkit.pdf

Confident Counselors (2017, February 5). *School Counselor: Advocating for Your Role.* Retrieved from Confident Counselors: https://confidentcounselors.com/2017/02/05/school-counselor-advocacy/

Hall, M. (2017, December). *American School Counselor Association.* Retrieved from Advocating for Your School Counseling Program Using ASCA Resources: www.s

choolcounselor.org/newsletters/december-2017/advocating-for-your-school-counseli
ng-program-usin?st=nj

Hall, M. (2017, December). *December Newsletter*. Retrieved from School Counselor: www.
schoolcounselor.org/newsletters/december-2017/advocating-for-your-school-counseli
ng-program-usin?st=nj

Iowa School Counselor Association (2018, November 12). *Iowa School Counselor Association*.
Retrieved from Advocacy: www.iowaschoolcounselors.org/Advocacy

Ohio Department of Education (2016, April 12). *Ohio Department of Education*. Retrieved
from Evaluation Framework for School Counselors: http://education.ohio.gov/geta
ttachment/Topics/Career-Tech/Career-Connections/School-Counselors/School-Co
unselor-Standards-and-Evaluation/School-Counselor-Evaluation-Framework-04-1
5-2016.pdf.aspx

Ohio Department of Education (2018, November 6). *Ohio Standards for School Counselors*.
Retrieved from Ohio Department of Education: http://education.ohio.gov/getattach
ment/Topics/Career-Tech/Career-Connections/School-Counselors/School-Counsel
or-Standards-and-Evaluation/SchoolCounselorStandards.pdf.aspx

Virginia Department of Education (2018, November 7). *School Counseling & Advisement*.
Retrieved from Virginia Department of Education: www.doe.virginia.gov/support/s
chool_counseling/index.shtml

Washington School Counselor Association (2018, November 12). *Let Me Show You What
I Do: Advocacy in Action*. Retrieved from www.wa-schoolcounselor.org/Files/Advocac
ypresent4WSCAConf2014.ppt

17 Implementing the ASCA National Model

There are many lessons learned from the first year of counseling. One of the lessons I learned right away was how hard it was to implement a counseling program that was ASCA approved. The goal for every school counselor is to be a Recognized ASCA (American School Counselor Association) Model Program 'RAMP'. This doesn't happen overnight or even in the first year. Creating a program that represents the ASCA National Model takes time to build.

The first step in creating a comprehensive program that is in line with the ASCA National Model is to start with the foundation. You might start at a school that already has this in place, which is awesome! However, if not this is where you will want to start. It is the one aspect of a comprehensive program that won't need approval from the administration, unless you publish it on the school's website. Just like every house has a foundation, so should your counseling program.

Foundation

The ASCA National Model states, "School counselors create comprehensive school counseling programs that focus on student outcomes, teach student competencies and are delivered with identified professional competencies" (American School Counselor Association, 2018). They provide an in-depth overview of what a school counseling program should look like. The following information is taken from their website (American School Counselor Association, 2018):

Program Focus: To establish program focus, school counselors identify personal beliefs that address how all students benefit from the school counseling program. Building on these beliefs, school counselors create a vision statement defining what the future will look like in terms of student outcomes. In addition, school counselors create a mission statement aligned with their school's mission and develop program goals defining how the vision and mission will be measured.

Student Standards: Enhancing the learning process for all students, the "ASCA Mindsets & Behaviors for Student Success: College- and Career-Readiness Standards for Every Student" guide the development of effective school counseling programs around three domains: academic, career and social/emotional development. View the ASCA Mindsets & Behaviors Planning Tool. School counselors also consider how other student standards important to state and district initiatives complement and inform their school counseling program.

Professional Competencies: The ASCA School Counselor Competencies outline the knowledge, attitudes and skills that ensure school counselors are equipped to meet the rigorous demands of the profession. The ASCA Ethical Standards for School Counselors specify the principles of ethical behavior necessary to maintain the highest standard of integrity, leadership and professionalism. They guide school counselors' decision-making and help to standardize professional practice to protect both students and school counselors.

School Counselor Standards and Competencies

It is important as you're following the ASCA National Model to build your program from the standards and competencies. You have to know these in order to write your mission, vision, and belief statements. According to ASCA,

> The ASCA School Counselor Competencies outline the knowledge, abilities, skills and attitudes that ensure school counselors are equipped to meet the rigorous demands of the profession and the needs of pre-K–12 students. These competencies help ensure new and experienced school counselors are equipped to establish, maintain and enhance a comprehensive school counseling program addressing academic achievement, career planning and personal/social development.
>
> (American School Counselor Association, 2018)

You can find a full list of the competencies on their website and in my references. These will address every domain in depth about what school counselors should know.

In addition, ASCA outlines the standards for school counselors in their article on mindsets and behaviors (American School Counselor Association, 2014):

> The ASCA Mindsets & Behaviors for Student Success: K–12 College- and Career Readiness for Every Student describe the knowledge, skills and attitudes students need to achieve academic success, college and career readiness and social/emotional development. The standards are based on a survey of research and best practices in student achievement from a wide array of educational standards and efforts. These standards are the next generation of the ASCA National Standards for Students, which were first published in 1997.
>
> The 35 mindset and behavior standards identify and prioritize the specific attitudes, knowledge and skills students should be able to demonstrate as a result of a school counseling program. School counselors use the standards to assess student growth and development, guide the development of strategies and activities and create a program that helps students achieve their highest potential. The ASCA Mindsets & Behaviors can be aligned with initiatives at the district, state and national to reflect the district's local priorities.

To operationalize the standards, school counselors select competencies that align with the specific standards and become the foundation for classroom lessons, small groups and activities addressing student developmental needs. The competencies directly reflect the vision, mission and goals of the comprehensive school counseling program and align with the school's academic mission.

One of the first things you will do when you're establishing your school counseling program is create your mission, vision, and belief statements. I include these under the Foundation section, because ASCA includes it in their foundation. This was the first thing I did my first year. I decided to update the school counseling page on the school's website and when I did, I included my mission, vision, and belief statements on there. I have included the ones I wrote for the school I worked for (Couch, 2018):

Mission Statement

Through a comprehensive school counseling program, the CLS Counseling Department will form Christian leaders, evoke self-exploration, develop confidence to think critically and analytically, and facilitate academic and career development growth in every student by utilizing evidence-based practices.

Vision Statement

It is the vision of the Covington Latin School Counseling Department that all students find their passion as they become emerging Christian leaders in the community, achieve their full academic potential, and recognize their purpose through high school and beyond.

Belief Statement

- We believe all students have the ability to achieve their goals through utilizing their strengths.
- We believe all students regardless of developmental stage or academic ability can perform and achieve in the classroom.
- We believe our role is to help students reach their goals inside and outside of the classroom while meeting them where they are and building relationships.
- We believe all decisions should be data-driven in order to meet the needs of all students.
- We believe the ethical decision-making model should be implemented when faced with moral dilemmas and counselors should adhere to the ASCA ethical standards.
- We believe all students have the right to have access to a licensed school counselor.

Delivery

The delivery aspect of school counseling is my favorite part of being a school counselor. The reason why I'm a school counselor is the students and building relationships. So, I jump at every chance to work with them directly. I enjoy being over programs that serve students, but there is nothing like working with them directly. Since ASCA is thorough about what direct and indirect services are, I have included their information as follows.

Direct Student Services

Direct services are in-person interactions between school counselors and students and include the following (American School Counselor Association, 2018):

School counseling core curriculum: This curriculum consists of structured lessons designed to help students attain the desired competencies and to provide all students with the knowledge, attitudes and skills appropriate for their developmental level. The school counseling core curriculum is delivered throughout the school's overall curriculum and is systematically presented by school counselors in collaboration with other professional educators in K-12 classroom and group activities.

Individual student planning: School counselors coordinate ongoing systemic activities designed to assist students in establishing personal goals and developing future plans.

Responsive services: Responsive services are activities designed to meet students' immediate needs and concerns. Responsive services may include counseling in individual or small-group settings or crisis response.

Indirect Student Services

Indirect services are provided on behalf of students as a result of the school counselors' interactions with others including referrals for additional assistance, consultation and collaboration with parents, teachers, other educators and community organizations.

In Chapters 9 and 10, there is more information and resources on direct service programming for your students.

Management

The ASCA website has templates for lesson plans, calendar, monthly checklists, use of time assessments, action plans, school data profile, curriculum action plan, and more. The ASCA website will become your best friend as you're establishing your school counseling program. Their books are a worthwhile investment as well because of the templates and resources in them. ASCA describes management as the following (American School Counselor Association, 2018):

> School counselors incorporate organizational assessments and tools that are concrete, clearly delineated and reflective of the school's needs. Assessments and tools include:
> **School counselor competency and school counseling program assessments** to self-evaluate areas of strength and improvement for individual skills and program activities.

I have used other school counselors' assessments and I've created my own. I'm a firm believer in not reinventing the wheel if you don't have to. I will modify what others have done to fit my school. Using Google Forms is an easy, paperless option that will give data quickly. If your students have their own tablets or you have access to a computer lab, I have found that it saves time. Here are a few sample questions that I use on my school counseling program assessment survey:

Please circle the appropriate number after each statement that best reflects your opinion.

1 = Strongly Disagree **2 = Disagree** **3 = Neither agree nor Disagree** **4 = Agree** **5 = Strongly Agree**

I feel comfortable meeting with my school counselor. 1 2 3 4 5

The school counselor actively listens to and responds to what I say. 1 2 3 4 5

My school counselor has helped me with personal and/or school problems. 1 2 3 4 5

My school counselor has helped me to think about my goals after graduation from high school. 1 2 3 4 5

My school counselor has provided me with information about careers and college. 1 2 3 4 5

My school counselor has helped me with future educational planning, college selection, and placement. 1 2 3 4 5

I have participated in classroom or small group programs covering topics such as social emotional learning, peer pressure, bullying, and healthy relationships. 1 2 3 4 5

My school counselor has provided services that have been helpful to me. 1 2 3 4 5

Use-of-time assessment to determine the amount of time spent toward the recommended 80 percent or more of the school counselor's time to direct and indirect services with students.

Annual agreements developed with and approved by administrators at the beginning of the school year addressing how the school counseling program is organized and what goals will be accomplished.

An example of an Annual Agreement from the Recognized ASCA Model Program (RAMP) Application outlines how Ferguson Elementary school counselors developed their annual agreement with their administration (Ferguson Elementary, 2018):

> The Annual Agreement of the Ferguson Elementary Counseling Department was developed during July and August of 2016. First, the counseling department held a meeting during summer leadership where input from teachers, staff and administrators was gathered from all grade levels. Academics, demographics, attendance, and behavioral data was analyzed and used to drive the discussion for counseling department programs. Program selection was also based on the needs of our largely economically disadvantaged population and our largely limited English-proficient student population.
>
> During the July meeting the counselors decided how to delegate duties based on counselor interest and expertise.
>
> A plan for how to address the three program goals for the 2016-2017 school year was also developed in August through Counseling Department meetings. Program goal one focuses on attendance and will be monitored by both counselors through morning check-ins, weekly meetings with our social worker, SARC (Student Attendance Review Committee) meetings, and core curriculum lessons. Program goal two focuses on behavior, therefore both counselors will work on this goal through individual counseling, small group counseling, and core curriculum lessons. Program goal three addresses 4th and 5th grade academics.
>
> The second step in developing the annual agreement was to analyze the counselor portal data. Gwinnett County Public Schools requires all professional school counselors to account for their time on a daily basis using the counselor's portal.
>
> The third step in developing the annual agreement was a meeting with the school principal which took place in August. During this meeting school wide data and portal data were shared with the principal...
>
> **Advisory councils** made up of students, parents, teachers, school counselors, administrators and community members to review and make recommendations about school counseling program activities and results.

This year I personally formed an advisory council that consisted of faculty and stakeholders. Here is an example of my advisory council layout:

ABC Counseling Advisory Council

ABC School Counseling Department seeks to align with the American School Counselor Association (ASCA) National Model. To help enhance the effectiveness of the counseling program, the ABC School Counseling Advisory

Council will conduct reviews and make recommendations about the school counseling program activities and results. The council will help to set and monitor the school counseling program goals. The council will consist of school counselors, administrators, parents, students, teachers, and community members.

There will be at least 5 members of the ABC School Counseling Advisory Council for the first year of implementation, 2018–2019. The Chairperson(s) of the council will be Professional School Counselor, Heather Couch who has been trained in the ASCA National Model. The Council meets twice a semester at the high school during the allotted department meeting times on Thursdays at 8:40 am. Any parent or staff member wishing to serve on the School Counseling Advisory Council should contact Heather Couch.

The Advisory Council includes:

Counselors (1): The counselors will be on the advisory council throughout their employment at the high school. They will provide insight on the needs of the student body and information about the counseling program and ASCA National Model.

Students (2): As the primary stakeholders of the school counseling department, two students will serve on the advisory council. At its inception, a 9th grade student and an 11th grade student will start on the council; thereafter, there will continue to be two students on the advisory council at all times, appointed as 9th graders. When one student graduates, an upcoming 9th grader will join the following year. Students will serve on the council from appointment until graduation, unless they ask to leave the council or if they transfer. By spacing student grade, the students should bring a perspective of developmental and specific grade level needs to the council.

Teachers (3): Chemistry Teacher, Science Teacher, and Religion Teacher. These teachers will bring a diverse background of content and grade level in order to provide the council with a wide range of teacher and student perspective and needs. Teacher terms on council will be for three years and then rotated by discipline and grade level to represent other subjects and grades. A special education coordinator or intervention specialist will always serve on the council in order to provide specific insight into this underserved population.

Parents (2 total: 1 explained in other sections—teacher and 1 parent with no other affiliation): _____. As collaborators and stakeholders of the school counseling department, the parents will provide the council with their unique perspective as individuals who want the best education and experiences for their child(ren). The parents will share their ideas as well as concerns they have about the students. There will be one parent represented who is a teacher and one parent who is a board member. There will be one additional parent member who is a parent with no other affiliation. This no affiliation position will be a two-year term on the advisory council. The parent/teacher member and parent/board member will remain on the council until their student graduates. These two positions will be replaced by new members who fit the parent/teacher and parent/board member roles.

Administrator (1): The ABC School Counselor is a member of the administrative team and attends weekly meetings. Therefore, another administrator will not be present, but the counselor is required to share meeting notes with the administration.

Board Member (1): _____. This position will serve as a liaison between the school counseling department and the school board. This person will bring board member needs and ideas to the council. To meet accountability standards, this member will relay important information about the school counseling department, such as what is working and what needs improvement, to the school board. This board member is also a teacher.

Community Member (1): The community member selected for the advisory council is _____. This member will provide the council with information about the needs of our students within the community and information about what goes on with our students in our community outside of the school day. The term for this position will be a permanent one, but additional community members can be added for one-year terms at the beginning of the school year if there is a perceived need.

Use of data to measure the results of the program as well as to promote systemic change within the school system so every student graduates college- and career-ready.

We live in a data-driven society and school counselors can use that to their advantage. There three types of data: process, perception, and outcome. We are able to use all three to help support our program. Process data is the information about who was impacted and the process you went through. Perception data answers the question 'What do people think they can do?' Gathering this type of information is done by needs assessments, pre-post tests, and school-wide initiatives. Outcome data is the impact that was made on the students. It could be the data received from a yearlong initiative.

(Simply Imperfect Counselor, 2017)

Data is so important in our field and it can be overwhelming if you have to gather it on your own. Here are some great books to help with ensuring you're using data in your school counseling program.

The Use of Data in School Counseling: Hatching Results for Students, Programs, and the Profession by Trish Hatch. Data does make the difference for today's embattled school counseling programs. This insightful book shows school counselors and administrators how to collect, manage, and use data to implement, evaluate and improve their programs for students. Aligned with current research in evidence-based practice and the ASCA standards, this essential 'must have' resource includes a complete set of user-friendly tools and templates for data collection, analysis, action planning, and reporting (Hatching Results, 2018).

Readers will learn how to:

- Develop a school counseling program that aligns with the Common Core Standards
- Replace 'random acts of guidance' with intentional, data-driven interventions
- Measure process, perception (pre-post) and outcome data
- Design systems change action plans
- Use their time efficiently and effectively
- Create and deliver compelling results reports that demonstrate your program's impact

Facilitating Evidence-Based, Data-Driven School Counseling by Brett Zyromski and Melissa A. Mariani. As students' needs change, dedicated school counselors have been evolving their practice. You see the results every day, on the faces of the at-risk students you serve. To meet accountability standards, though, you need more than faces: you need data the number-crunchers can understand. With this user-friendly manual, make the shift to evidence-based practices and interventions in a data-driven, comprehensive school counseling program based on ASCA's national model—while keeping the personal nature of your work intact. The book includes:

- Visual guides and checklists for every step of the process
- Examples of successful counseling program evolution
- Guidance on developing and submitting a successful Recognized ASCA Model Program (RAMP) application
- Supporting documents in an online resource center
- Ensure that school counseling is recognized as an essential part of school improvement and students' academic success by using this unique and innovative model.

(SAGE Publications, 2018b)

Evidence-Based School Counseling, Making a Difference With Data-Driven Practices by Trish Hatch, John C. Carey, and edited by Carey Dimmitt. Today's school counselors are under enormous pressure to document their effectiveness by using data and producing quantitative accountability reports—whether or not they've had the appropriate training. This authoritative guide from highly respected counselor educators and trainers gives pre-service and in-service school counselors the tools to knowledgeably identify evidence-based practices in their field and to use data in designing, implementing, and evaluating programs and interventions (SAGE Publications, 2018b).

Evidence-Based School Counseling provides a practical process for using evidence to determine three critical issues: what needs to be done, which interventions should be implemented, and whether or not the interventions are effective. Aligned with the American School Counselor Association's National Model, this resource offers counselors skill-building guidelines for:

- Selecting, collecting, and analyzing data for informed planning
- Carrying out action research and building collaborative partnerships
- Measuring student learning and behavior change
- Communicating results to stakeholders, and more

As counselors successfully incorporate data-based decision-making and program planning into their work, they will witness positive academic and personal changes in the lives of their students (SAGE Publications, 2018b).

Transforming the School Counseling Profession (5th Edition) by Bradley T. Erford. *Transforming the School Counseling Profession* demonstrates how to effectively implement systemic, data-driven school counseling programs. This clearly written text presents the profession in easy-to-understand language, and is illustrated with numerous applied examples, case studies, and vignettes. The 5th Edition has been updated to include all of the latest CACREP, ASCA, and ACA standards. It also now includes the DSM-5. Coverage of cultural competence has been expanded throughout the book (Pearson, 2018).

Curriculum, small-group and closing-the-gap action plans including developmental, prevention and intervention activities and services that measure the desired student competencies and the impact on achievement, behavior and attendance.

Please see Chapter 10 for resources on curriculum and group activities.

Annual and weekly calendars to keep students, parents, teachers and administrators informed and to encourage active participation in the school counseling program.

Accountability

ASCA states,

> To demonstrate the effectiveness of the school counseling program in measurable terms, school counselors analyze school and school counseling program data to determine how students are different as a result of the school counseling program. School counselors use data to show the impact of the school counseling program on student achievement, attendance and behavior and analyze school counseling program assessments to guide future action and improve future results for all students. The performance

of the school counselor is evaluated on basic standards of practice expected of school counselors implementing a comprehensive school counseling program.

(American School Counselor Association, 2018)

In Chapter 16, I have referenced state standards and evaluations. ASCA also has guides to evaluating your school counseling program. It's important that you're doing this yearly so that you can track progress and know what to change. Work with your administrators to implement school-wide initiatives. Then make assessments at the end of the semester or year.

Wrap Up with RAMP

Being a RAMP school is the gold star that every school counselor wants to have. It is attainable, but it might take a few years to get it. You will need the full support of your administrators. If you don't then you will exhaust yourself with the constant fight. There are some administrators who will not change their mindset on the traditional 'guidance' counselor. If you find yourself in that situation, then evaluate and reflect on whether that school is a good fit for you. There is nothing wrong with you making a personal assessment!

ASCA has updated their RAMP website and included an introduction video. Let ASCA be your number 1 resource for everything related to RAMP. Even if you're not applying for RAMP yet, use their templates and assessments in your program. This will get you started on the path of applying. When you're applying take the application in chunks. Don't try to do it all in one day! It is an extensive application that requires a lot of time. Talk to the schools in your region who have RAMP programs and get their advice. ASCA has coaching available if your school will fund it. There are videos online and books available for purchase. A quick Google search will give you plenty of resources.

For those of you who feel disheartened by not being able to implement the ASCA National Model, keep the faith and do what you can. You are making a difference!

References

American School Counselor Association (2014). *American School Counselor.* Retrieved from ASCA Mindsets & Behaviors for Student Success: K-12 College- and Career-Readiness Standards for Every Student: www.schoolcounselor.org/asca/media/asca/home/MindsetsBehaviors.pdf

American School Counselor Association (2018a, November 29). *Accountability.* Retrieved from School Counselor: www.schoolcounselor.org/school-counselors/asca-national-model/accountability

American School Counselor Association (2018b, November 21). *American School Counselor Association.* Retrieved from ASCA National Model Foundation: www.schoolcounselor.org/school-counselors/asca-national-model/foundation

American School Counselor Association (2018c, November 22). *American School Counselor Association*. Retrieved from ASCA School Counselor Competencies: www.schoolcouns elor.org/asca/media/asca/home/SCCompetencies.pdf

American School Counselor Association (2018d). *American School Counselor Association*. Retrieved from Delivery: www.schoolcounselor.org/school-counselors/asca-national-model/delivery

American School Counselor Association (2018e, November 27). *American School Counselor Association*. Retrieved from Management: www.schoolcounselor.org/school-counselor s/asca-national-model/management

Couch, H. (2018, November 22). *Counseling*. Retrieved from Covington Latin School: www.covingtonlatin.org/view/home/counseling.aspx

Ferguson Elementary (2018, November 27). *Recognized ASCA Model Program*. Retrieved from RAMP Application: https://schoolcounselorawards.org/ramp/example?view=2714

Hatching Results (2018, November 27). *Hatching Results*. Retrieved from Use of Data: www.hatchingresults.com/books/use-of-data/

Pearson (2018, November 27). *Pearson*. Retrieved from Transforming the School Counseling Profession, 5th Edition: www.pearson.com/us/higher-education/program/Erford-Tran sforming-the-School-Counseling-Profession-plus-My-Lab-Counseling-with-Enhan ced-Pearson-e-Text-Access-Card-Package-5th-Edition/PGM1258668.html

SAGE Publications (2018a, November 27). *Corwin*. Retrieved from Evidence Based School Counseling: https://us.corwin.com/en-us/nam/evidence-based-school-counseling/book229372

SAGE Publications (2018b, November 27). *SAGE Publications*. Retrieved from Facilitating Evidence-Based, Data-Driven School Counseling: https://us.corwin.com/en-us/nam/evidence-based-and-data-driven-comprehensive-school-counseling/book247946

Simply Imperfect Counselor (2017, August 26). *Simply Imperfect Counselor*. Retrieved from Beginners Guide to School Counseling Data: https://simplyimperfectcounselor.com/beginners-guide-to-school-counseling-data/

18 Meeting the Needs of the Whole Child

Part of being a school counselor is meeting the needs of the whole child. This is part of creating a holistic program that will allow the school to see that the school counselor does more than coordinate testing. The school counselor can help close achievement gaps, teach social emotional learning skills, guide students in their college and career goals, and assist the school administration in identifying school-wide need. Meeting the needs of the 'whole' child will help prevent crisis.

Whole Child

There are a couple of buzzwords and trending topics in education lately and those happen to be 'whole child' and Social Emotional Learning. What is 'whole child'? In 2007, the ASCD started the 'Whole Child Initiative' to an

> effort to change the conversation about education from a focus on narrowly defined academic achievement to one that promotes the long-term development and success of children. Through the initiative, ASCD helps educators, families, community members, and policymakers move from a vision about educating the whole child to sustainable, collaborative action. ASCD is joined in this effort by Whole Child Partner organizations representing the education, arts, health, policy, and community sectors
>
> (ASCD, 2018)

The whole child is composed of the following tenets (ASCD, 2018):

1. Each student enters school healthy and learns about and practices a healthy lifestyle.
2. Each student learns in an environment that is physically and emotionally safe for students and adults.
3. Each student is actively engaged in learning and is connected to the school and broader community.

4. Each student has access to personalized learning and is supported by qualified, caring adults.
5. Each student is challenged academically and prepared for success in college or further study and for employment and participation in a global
environment.

These tenets are in a hierarchy that is similar to Maslow's Hierarchy of Needs;
the words before the forward-slash are the Whole Child tenets and the words
after are Maslow's (Rulon, 2015).

The Whole Child initiative was their response to a global issue of child
obesity, mental health, school safety, and overall health and wellness. This is
all backed by research that shows students have better academic performances
when their basic needs are met, and they are healthy. Some of the research
ASCD mentions in their article "Marking the Case Educating the Whole
Child" (ASCD, 2012) is as follows:

- Regular physical activity can improve the health and quality of life of people of all ages; however, only 17 percent of high school students currently
meet the recommended daily amount.
- Over the past three decades, childhood obesity rates in the United States
have tripled. Today nearly one-third of U.S. children are overweight and
almost 17 percent of children and adolescents are obese.
- Research shows that one of five children and adolescents experiences symptoms of a mental health illness and as many as 80 percent may go untreated.
Children and adolescents with mental disorders are at much greater risk for
dropping out of school and suffering long-term impairments.

Figure 18.1 Hierarchy of Needs.

- Research shows that programs offering breakfast at no cost to all children, regardless of income, during the first part of the school day dramatically increase student participation in school breakfast. However, only 9.7 million of the 20 million low-income students who are eligible for a school breakfast receive it.

- Improved health can also improve attendance at school. Higher rates of absenteeism have been reported for those students who are overweight; suffer from asthma; or have poor health status, diet, or lack of sleep. Studies have also shown that health-related absenteeism can be reversed by increasing access to services and increasing physical activity.

As school counselors, it is important that we are meeting the students where they are. We already have a Whole Child model built into our philosophy. For us, it's about advocating for the Whole Child model to be implemented in our schools.

School, District, and Statewide Implementations

There are many schools across the nation who have adopted the Whole Child Initiative. I personally helped create and run the Whole Child Initiative at my first-year school counseling job. It was started due to a number of parent and student concerns. We created a new homework policy and incorporated Social Emotional Learning (SEL) into my guidance curriculum. I went into the middle grades twice a month, the sophomores have a class once a week, and the upperclassmen met with me one to two times a month. I saw growth in my students being able to identify and manage their emotions, be able to know and implement coping techniques, and improved school climate and culture.

An example of a thriving school that implements the Whole Child model is Lusher Charter School in New Orleans (ASCD, 2015),

> Lusher Charter School is one of the most sought-after public schools in the city of New Orleans. In addition to its academic success and recognition as an Ashoka ChangeMaker School, Lusher is best known for its positive school culture, built on the school's number one rule: be kind. In addition to doing Responsive Classroom's morning meeting on a daily basis, Lusher encourages its staff, students, and parents to implement ideas that build a culture of kindness. For example, after Hurricane Katrina, teachers collaborated with Tulane University's Department of Psychology to design an arts-based healing curriculum that included activities such as painting ceramic eggs to symbolize rebirth and interviewing students about their visions for New Orleans. Fifth graders also took the opportunity to redesign the school's bathrooms and the school cafeteria, installing a salad bar and round tables in the latter.

You can read about many examples of successful Whole Child model programs on the ASCD's website at wholechildeducation.org.

District

The Cincinnati Public School District has been implementing the initiative since 2015. They focus on areas of (Cincinnati Public School, 2015):

1. Integrated approach for educating the whole child,
2. Ensuring support for heathy living, social-emotional well-being, personalized academic learning and growth, and robust family and community engagement.

This tied into the School Board's mission and vision for the district. This is still part of their vision and goals for the current academic year.

An example of another school district implementing the Whole Child model is Tacoma Public Schools. In an article from Scholastic EDU, the Deputy Superintendent Dr. Josh Garcia talks about the morale of the district and why they initiated the Whole Child model (Garcia, 2016).

> In 2010, Tacoma's graduation rates were 55%. Every comprehensive high school had been labeled a dropout factory. The schools had some of the highest discipline rates in the state. Few kids were entering post-secondary experiences. The city was angry, and board members and superintendents were in flux. There was little trust among stakeholders, and the only thing everyone agreed on was that everyone else was disrespectful and irresponsible, and the kids weren't safe. To say the least, we were facing major challenges on all sides. But we kept our dream for Tacoma's kids top-of-mind.
>
> Looking deeper in the mirror, we found in our school community a rich history of innovation, pride, grit, and underlying belief in supporting the whole child.
>
> This brought focus: we knew we didn't need a person or a program to save us, we needed to agree on what success was going to look like. If we were going to raise a whole child, we had to define and measure our efforts. The way to improve academic achievement and to close the achievement gap is to close the opportunity gap: the opportunity for every child to be safe, healthy, supported, engaged and challenged. And in order to make this a reality, we knew we had to quantify our goals and our results.

State

The Ohio Department of Education just announced its strategic plan for 2019–2024 to include the Whole Child model.

Each Child, Our Future is Ohio's shared plan for ensuring that each student is *challenged, prepared* and *empowered* for his or her future by way of an excellent prekindergarten through grade 12 (pre-K–12) education. The plan's purpose: to lift aspirations, create hope and excitement, guide development of state-level education policies and promote high-quality educational practices across the state.

With 240,000 educators serving in 3,500 schools and educating more than 1.7 million schoolchildren, education in Ohio is a complex business. Partners identified the plan's multifaceted components based on potential impact on student success. The **whole child** is at the center of the plan. The state-level **vision** provides an aspirational guide for students, parents, partners and the education system. **One goal** represents the state's annual target. **Three core principles, four learning domains** and **10 priority strategies** work together to support the whole child and enable the state-level vision and goal.

This is one example of a state making the decision to implement the Whole Child model into their schools. More and schools and districts are embracing the Whole Child. The Kentucky Department of Education published the following statement on meeting the needs of the whole child (Bunge, 2018):

> Establishing healthy behaviors during childhood is easier and more effective than trying to change unhealthy behaviors during adulthood. Schools play a critical role in promoting the health and safety of young people and helping them establish lifelong healthy behavior patterns. Research shows a link between the health outcomes of young people and their academic success. To have the most positive impact on the health outcomes of young people, government agencies, community organizations, schools, and other community members must work together through a collaborative and comprehensive approach.
>
> The Whole School, Whole Community, Whole Child (WSCC) model expands on the eight elements of CDC's coordinated school health (CSH) approach to strengthen a unified and collaborative approach designed to improve learning and health in our nation's schools.
>
> The education, public health, and school health sectors have each called for greater alignment, integration, and collaboration between education and health to improve each child's cognitive, physical, social, and emotional development. Public health and education serve the same children, often in the same settings. The WSCC focuses on the child to align the common goals of both sectors. The expanded model integrates the eight components of a coordinated school health (CSH) program with the tenets of a whole child approach to education.

California is another example of implementing a statewide model of the Whole Child. They have an accountability model, symposiums on serving the whole child, data/statistics, and other resources available. Their platform is (California Department of Education, 2018):

> The California Department of Education (CDE) is committed to aligning a system of supports to better meet the needs of the whole child (from cradle to career) and the Local Control Accountability Planning process. Learn more about resources and initiatives that will assist local educational agencies, schools, and local stakeholders as they plan and implement their LCAP or other improvement planning processes.

When schools and districts implement the Whole Child model, there will be change in school culture and climate. Studies show that students thrive when there is focus on their health and well-being. One of the tenets of the Whole Child that substantiates the benefit of mental health awareness is Social Emotional Learning (SEL).

Social Emotional Learning (SEL)

According to Collaborative for Academic, Social, and Emotional Learning (CASEL), "Social and emotional learning (SEL) enhances students' capacity to integrate skills, attitudes, and behaviors to deal effectively and ethically with daily tasks and challenges. Like many similar frameworks, CASEL's integrated framework promotes intrapersonal, interpersonal, and cognitive competence" (Collaborative for Academic, Social, and Emotional Learning, 2018a). They identify five core competencies of SEL:

1. Self-awareness: the ability to identify one's own emotions, accurate self-perception, recognizing strengths, self-confidence, and self-efficacy.
2. Self-management: the ability to regulate one's emotions, thoughts, and behaviors.
3. Social awareness: the ability to take the perspective and empathize with others, appreciated diversity, and respect others.
4. Relationship skills: the ability to maintain healthy relationships, communicate effectively, resolve conflict, listen, and be a part of a team.
5. Responsible decision making: the ability to make constructive choices, identify problems, analyze a situation, solve problems, evaluate, reflect on the choice they made, and make ethical decisions.

Even if you're not implementing SEL in your school these components might sound familiar. These are referred to as 'soft skills' and other programming addresses them. Dialectical Behavioral Therapy uses these components as well. There is a strong argument for SEL in schools. The data supports teaching these 'soft skills'.

CASEL created the Collaborating Districts Initiative (CDI) in 2016 to help school districts systemically integrate social and emotional learning into everything they did. Their results and findings were as follows (Collaborative for Academic, Social, and Emotional Learning, 2018a):

> The Collaborating Districts Initiative (CDI) was organized in 2016 to help school districts across the country systemically integrate social and emotional learning (SEL) into all their work. To assess the impact of the CDI's efforts, CASEL entered into an ongoing data collection and evaluation partnership with the districts and American Institutes for Research (AIR). Data were collected to measure the implementation and resulting outcomes. Since implementation of the CDI, academic achievement has improved consistently in reading and math. Teachers have become more effective. Attendance and graduation rates are up. Suspensions and expulsions are down. Students feel safer and more connected to school. While the availability of data varied by district, qualitative and quantitative outcomes are promising. External evaluations also showed consistent year-to-year improvements in school culture and climate, as well as student outcomes. The bottom line: even very modest investments in SEL can pay off for individuals, schools, and society.

Improved Academics:

The three districts that use the National Assessment of Educational Progress (NAEP) (Austin, Chicago, and Cleveland) all improved their reading and math scores during the CDI implementation years.

In Anchorage, Austin, Chicago, Cleveland, Oakland, and Nashville, GPAs were higher at the end of the 2015 school year than before the CDI started. The improvements were particularly noticeable in Chicago, going from an average of 2.19 in the three years before the CDI to 2.65 in 2015, an increase of nearly 21%.

Nashville, the only district with consistent standardized tests across the CDI years, showed improvements in both ELA and math achievement.

Improved Behavioral Outcomes:

Chicago's graduation rate increased 15% during the CDI years.

Attendance improved in four of six districts that collected this data.

Suspensions declined in all five of the districts that collected this data.

Districts also reported that students' social and emotional competence improved, based on student and teacher surveys.

Improved School Environment:

School climate, as measured by district surveys in Chicago and Cleveland, improved during the CDI years. In Anchorage climate began an upward trajectory before the CDI and sustained that same significant and positive growth during the CDI years.

You can read more about the CDI on CASEL's website. The bottom line is that the more research being done and data being gathered shows that SEL is an important part of educating students. The National Commission on Social, Emotional, and Academic Development was created in 2016 as a project of the ASPEN Institute. Needless to say, SEL is a big trend. For the past six years, it has been continuously researched and studied within schools. Is it still as relevant in 2018 as it was in 2011? Concordia University states in an article online (The Room 241 Team, 2018),

> Students spend most of their time in school, so to ignore their social-emotional learning needs for the 30+ hours a week they spend in classrooms would be a waste of precious developmental learning time. School is also the place where students encounter the bulk of their social interactions, challenges, and opportunities for personal growth. Certainly, schools and teachers have been providing way more than academic learning for decades. However, research shows that by providing consistent, purposeful, and robust SEL programs, students can benefit in multiple ways.
>
> According to The Pennsylvania State University and Robert Wood Johnson Foundation research brief Social Emotional Learning in Elementary School, 'extensive research shows that SEL programs can promote academic achievement and positive social behavior, and reduce conduct problems, substance abuse, and emotional distress. Benefits of SEL in the elementary years have been documented in reviews by independent research teams and through meta-analyzes which demonstrate the immediate and long-term positive outcomes of well-designed, well-implemented SEL programming.'
>
> An NPR report on SEL notes that 'kids who act up a lot in school and at home—even very young kids—are more likely to have mental health problems and commit crimes years later as adults.' Thus, researchers have set out to create SEL programs that serve as emotional intelligence interventions, discovering that much like we teach academic subjects, emotional intelligence can also be taught.

Counselor Implications

This chapter isn't to sell you on the Whole Child model or SEL. It is to offer you an example of a holistic program that is current in the education profession and empirically based. These programs help us create a school counseling program that is ASCA approved. The schools don't need to hire separate people in the building to just implement these programs, because we have the knowledge and skills to do so. When schools implement these programs it's the perfect opportunity to advocate for our profession. That's not saying we won't welcome additional help!

If you are currently working in a school that has a Whole Child model and/ or implements SEL, you most likely have your own assessment tools. If you're not working in a school who has implemented these initiatives, then I have given you a couple of assessment tools to help you with your programming and advocacy as follows.

ACT Tessera:

The description from ACT's website (ACT, 2018): ACT Tessera™ is a comprehensive next-generation assessment system designed to measure Social and Emotional Learning (SEL) skills. It provides assessments to help K–12 educators measure and evaluate 6–12th grade students' SEL skills, determine their strengths and areas for improvement, and identify interventions to help them succeed.

The school I worked at as a first-year school counselor gave the ACT Tessera assessment to freshmen and sophomores my third year. This assessment's foundation is in SEL and is based on the Big 5 personality traits. There are many SEL assessments that a school and district can give to their students. We used the ACT Tessera, because we were already giving the other ACT tests. This helped us know where students were with their soft skills. It measures resiliency, grit, teamwork, leadership, and curiosity. This was a great tool for me to know where the students were as a class and what their self-perception was. The results reaffirmed to me that there is a need for SEL.

Panorama Social-Emotional Learning—Student Measures:
Information taken from website *Measuring SEL* (Measuring SEL, 2018):

Panorama Social-Emotional Learning—Student Measures is a norm-referenced self-report rating scale that assesses nine student SEL competencies, for children in kindergarten through twelfth grade. The assessment is strength-based, completed by students.

The RAND Assessment Finder's page for this measure has references to studies of the reliability of the measure and/or its validity for particular purposes. The developer also provided additional information on the measure's reliability and validity (see Technical Documentation section).

Data from the Panorama Social-Emotional Learning—Student Measures can be reported at the individual level or can be aggregated and reported at the group level. The measure includes sufficient items to assess and report scores for individual domains of SEL competence, in addition to an overall SEL competence score.

There are many SEL assessments and I encourage you to go to http://measurin gsel.casel.org/assessment-guide/ to compare them and find one that works best for your school. There are assessments that include parent and teacher reports, and there are ones that just focus on a specific area.

In Chapter 10, I have given curriculum resources that are helpful when teaching SEL in guidance lessons. However, below is information from CASEL about selecting a SEL program for your school or district. It is important to make sure you select the right program for your school. You can learn more about selecting a SEL program from the *2015 CASEL Guide Effective Social and Emotional Learning Programs* (CASEL, 2015):

When school and district planning teams oversee the careful selection and effective implementation of evidence-based social and emotional learning programs, the students they serve benefit socially, emotionally, and academically. This page links to guidelines SEL teams can follow to ensure they ultimately adopt the best programs for their particular school community.

To begin, three key principles support the effective selection, implementation, impact, and sustainability of evidence-based SEL programs.

Principle 1: School and district teams—rather than an individual—should engage diverse stakeholders in the program adoption process to identify shared priorities.

Principle 2: Implementing evidence-based SEL programs within systemic, ongoing district and school planning, programming, and evaluation leads to better practice and more positive outcomes for students.

Principle 3: It is critical to consider local contextual factors (e.g., student characteristics, programs already in place) when using the *CASEL Guide* and gathering additional information in order to make the most effective decisions about which programs to implement.

Some schools may prefer to develop their own approach to SEL, rather than adopting one of the evidence-based SELect programs identified in this *Guide*. We believe it is better to start from a foundation that is evidence-based. A SELect program can serve as a base from which to coordinate schoolwide SEL, school-family partnerships, and community programming. The benefits of using programs that embody years of scientific program development, evaluation, and evidence are worth the effort.

Wrap Up

In closing this chapter, I hope you have gained an understanding of the Whole Child model and SEL. These two programs are holistic in design and embrace the philosophy of counseling. There are other programs out there such as growth mindset and mindfulness, but I believe the Whole Child model integrates those important skills in their design. That is why I'm a proponent of the Whole Child model and SEL. I like that it includes the community in its principles. It can be easy to focus solely on the students and neglect the other people in their lives. The Whole Child model can be a great option for your school counseling program and school.

References

ACT (2018, December 6). *Tessera*. Retrieved from ACT: www.act.org/content/act/en/products-and-services/act-tessera.html

ASCD (2012). *Whole Child Education*. Retrieved from Making the Case for Educating the Whole Child: www.wholechildeducation.org/assets/content/WholeChild-MakingThe Case.pdf

ASCD (2015). *The Number One Rule: Be Kind*. Retrieved from Whole Child Education: The Number One Rule: Be Kind.

ASCD. (2018a, December 3). *Whole Child*. Retrieved from ASCD: www.ascd.org/whole-child.aspx

ASCD (2018b, December 4). *Whole School Whole Community Whole Child*. Retrieved from ASCD: www.ascd.org/ASCD/pdf/siteASCD/publications/wholechild/wscc-a-collaborative-approach.pdf

Bunge, S. (2018, July 10). *Whole Child*. Retrieved from Kentucky Department of Education: https://education.ky.gov/curriculum/CSH/wholechild/Pages/default.aspx

California Department of Education (2018, December 5). *California One System Serving the Whole Child*. Retrieved from California Department of Education: www.cde.ca.gov/eo/in/onesystem.asp

CASEL (2015). *2015 CASEL Guide Effective Social and Emotional Learning Programs*. Retrieved from CASEL: http://secondaryguide.casel.org/#Importance

Cincinnati Public School (2015, November 4). *CPS-12*. Retrieved from Cincinnati Board of Education Superintendent's Midterm Report: Cincinnati Board of Education Superintendent's Midterm Report.

Collaborative for Academic, Social, and Emotional Learning (2018a, December 6). *Core Competencies*. Retrieved from CASEL: https://casel.org/core-competencies/

Collaborative for Academic, Social, and Emotional Learning (2018b, December 6). *Key Findings*. Retrieved from CASEL: https://casel.org/key-findings/

Garcia, J. (2016, December 5). *The Whole Child, Every Child – A Story of Implementation*. Retrieved from Scholastic EDU: http://edublog.scholastic.com/post/whole-child-every-child-story-implementation

Measuring SEL (2018, December 6). *Panorama Social-Emotional Learning – Student Measures*. Retrieved from Measuring SEL: http://measuringsel.casel.org/assessment-guide/measure/panoramas-social-emotional-learning-survey/

Rulon, M. (2015, July 23–26). *IBO*. Retrieved from Educating the Whole Child for Whole School Improvement the ASCD Whole Child approach: www.ibo.org/contentassets/ef4f3c159e21444a9727ef9b7555681c/sat-11-15am-educatingthewholechildforthewholeimprovement-mikerulon.pdf

The Room 241 Team (2018, May 14). *Why We Really Need SEL (Social-Emotional Learning) Now*. Retrieved from Concordia University-Portland: https://education.cu-portland.edu/blog/leaders-link/social-emotional-learning-defined/

Part VII

Collaboration

19 Administrators and Teachers

There are a lot of important things to remember when you are a first-year school counselor. Collaboration offers support. The administration provides invaluable insight and resources about school policy. Administration provides oversight for school counselors who may be the only one in their building.

The goal of the school counselor is to provide students with the resources they need to learn in the classroom. Teachers are the heart of the school and having a relationship with them is vital. I learned early on that students will try to get out of class and abuse the system. School counselors are not an excuse to get out of class, unless it is necessary. They can work with teachers on integrating what the students are learning into our guidance lessons. This chapter will cover working administration to collaborating with teachers on curriculum. This chapter will draw from school counselors' experiences, peer reviewed or journal articles, and professional references.

Collaboration

First, I would like to start off by defining collaboration as a school counselor. In the *ERIC Digest* an article titled "School Counselors Collaborating for Student Success" states (Allen, 1994):

> Collaboration is the process whereby two individuals or groups work together for a common goal, a mutual benefit, or a desired outcome. Trust, respect, openness, active listening, clear communication, and risk taking are fundamental requirements for collaborative efforts. In order for collaboration to happen participants must share a common vision and agree on a common mission. The motivation for a common mission may be the need to identify or solve a problem, to focus on the issues, or to achieve consensus. Initiating and maintaining collaborative efforts is an appropriate role of the school counselor in educational reform.

This is a great definition of collaboration, because it focuses on having a common mission and vision. When you are collaborating with administrators and faculty it's key to relate what you are doing in the counseling office back to the mission and vision of the school. There might be disagreements on your role within the building, but there shouldn't be any disagreements about the mission and vision of the school. A school counselor wrote an article titled "Lessons in Collaboration in School Counseling" stating (Mathieson, 2017):

> Collaboration is to work with all stakeholders, both inside and outside the school system, to develop and implement educational programs that support students. It's a challenging task that first requires us to understand and appreciate the contributions others make to educating all children. Next, we need to build effective teams and working relationships.

Administrators

Chapter 16 goes into depth about advocating your position to the administration, but in this chapter, I'm addressing collaboration. There is a fine line between collaborating and advocating for your role. Sometimes those two are synonymous, but often collaboration doesn't mean you get to implement the programming you want. Collaboration means you're working together to carry out the mission, vision, and goals of the school.

In 2009, the College Board, ASCA, and the National Association of Secondary Principals created a survey of the counselor and principal relationship. The survey covered the important elements and barriers in the counselor–principal relationship, perceptions of respondents' own counselor–principal relationship, views on counselors' activities and improving academic outcomes, the biggest challenges facing equity, and the roles of principals and counselors in education reform. A total of 2,286 people responded to the survey that were filtered into categories by school type, years of experience, enrollment, location, Title I, percentage of college bound students, and diversity. The conclusion to this is as follows (Finkelstein, 2009):

> Principals and counselors who responded to the survey were very similar in how they saw the principal-counselor relationship, agreeing on which elements are most important for a successful relationship to improve student outcomes. They also agreed on which activities are most important for counselors to engage in to improve student outcomes. While there were some differences in perceptions, particularly in terms of how much time counselors spend on less important activities, it is encouraging that the basic priorities of both principals and counselors were so well aligned.

- Principals and counselors both ranked **communication** and **respect** as the two most important elements in the principal–counselor relationship.
- Principals and counselors both saw **time** as being the biggest barrier to collaboration between them.

- When asked what one thing they would change that would lead to an improved principal–counselor relationship within their own schools, both principals and counselors most frequently mentioned **communication**, followed by **respect/understanding**.
- Principals and counselors agreed that the most important activities for a counselor to engage in to improve student outcomes are helping to promote student personal growth and social development and helping students with career planning.
- While both principals and counselors agreed that supportive administrative tasks are less important for counselors to engage in to improve student outcomes, principals saw these tasks as taking up less of counselors' time than counselors said they took.

My relationship with my principal has been vital to my success as a school counselor. Whether it's relying on support and guidance or knowing what the goals are for the year, communicating with the principal is important. Edutopia has a great article on how administrators can support school counselors. I've included their "7 Ways for Administrators to Support School Counselors", because it gives you a foundation of what your administration can do for you when you collaborate.

7 Ways for Administrators to Support School Counselors (Ratliff, 2013):

1. At the beginning of the school year, meet with your counselor and complete the annual agreement that outlines goals, use of time and other responsibilities. Identifying the counselors' responsibilities maximizes their effectiveness.
2. Review the list of inappropriate and appropriate duties in the ASCA National Model to rediscover any duties that are not in line with best practices, and then decide which duties can be reassigned to other personnel.
3. Allow time for direct services to students. Direct services include presenting the school counseling curriculum in classrooms and conducting small-group and individual counseling. If there is concern that students participating in counseling will miss academic time, there may be ways to build in small group counseling during student lunchtimes. This means allowing the counselor to provide services during lunch rather than monitoring the cafeteria for lunch duty.
4. Counseling is not what it was when you were in school. School counselors are Master's level professionals with specific training in counseling skills. They can be a valuable asset for helping students cope with everyday stressors that interfere with learning. They can also help students with academic and career concerns, as well as personal and social concerns.

5. School counselors are trained to evaluate if student learning is positively impacted by the school counseling program. Meet with these professionals to see what programs or activities have been evaluated, and what the outcomes are. For example, if a counselor is working with students on anger management, have behavior referrals decreased? Have student grades improved?
6. Support counselors' recommendations for changes and programs that will benefit students and the school as a whole.
7. Review the ASCA National Model's recommended roles of the school counselor. You may discover that the counselor at your school has skills that are underutilized. Counselors support the school's overall mission and can make an incredible difference if used appropriately.

Regardless of how you feel about your principal, it is important to try to collaborate if possible. You might not always work at a school where there is collaboration, but take the opportunity to build the relationship. There will be principals who have a great relationship with the counselors and those who would rather just have counselors do 'guidance'. The only collaboration they will offer will be in allowing the school to fund testing. Some principals won't collaborate on anything new unless it was their idea. Instead of griping and complaining about the principal, build trust and respect. It might be the case that you have to work at another school in order to achieve your school counseling goals, but until then that principal is your supervisor. Never underestimate the power of collaboration!

Teachers

Teachers are not the enemy in the school building. As school counselors, our work with students directly affects the classroom. We are here to help students be able to learn in the classroom and improve academic achievement. Thus, we should work together on providing support for the students. The Ohio Assessment for Educators per Study.com states (Ohio Assesment for Educators, 2018):

> There are always opportunities for school counselors to collaborate with teachers. Below is a list of ways in which counselors can support and collaborate with teachers.
>
> - Observe students who have been identified as challenging and offer suggestions for classroom management.
> - Offer resources and guidance for teachers seeking to infuse social and emotional topics into their lessons.
> - Provide counseling to students who have been identified by teachers as in need of additional support.
> - Involve staff when planning college and career events for students. It's always great for students to hear the success stories of positive adult influences.

- Attend grade level meetings to offer support and insight to teachers.
- Assist teachers whenever they have a concern about a particular student or class.

Teachers work on the front lines and see students the most. They are able to help us identify issues and concerns with students. Knowing how a student behaves in the classroom and interacts with their peers is vital information. The U.S. Department of Education posted a blog on how school counselors and teachers can work together to meet the needs of students. The author of the article recognizes that the days of 'guidance counselors' who only did administrative duties are gone. There are many ways that school counselors can be utilized by teachers. Here are ten tips for teachers to help them maximize their partnerships with counselors. This can be used for school counselors by looking at it in reverse (Brodie, 2012).

1. **Call on counselors to help you understand the whole student.** When teachers notice red flags, such as behavioral issues or grades, school counselors are prepared to help teachers gain a more complete understanding of the issues behind the actions.
2. **Consult with counselors for professional advice.** When teachers find themselves stuck with strategies that aren't working with a particular student, a counselor who is trained to problem-solve can help them gain fresh ideas to age-old problems.
3. **Tackle problems before they become insurmountable.** When teachers sense trouble brewing in class, language or behavior that causes them anxiety, they should talk with a school counselor who can help troubleshoot and prevent a situation from escalating.
4. **Offer students an empathetic listener.** When students are having problems that seem personal or sensitive or that have the potential to get them into trouble, send them to a school counselor who can provide a sounding board and help them find solutions.
5. **Guide students' decision-making.** When students act out repeatedly in class, teachers should inform a counselor who can work with them on decision-making. School counselors can also help the child reframe the situation and illustrate how different behaviors might be in their best interest.
6. **Collaborate with a counselor to integrate counseling and class lessons.** Work together to teach lessons in class about academics, careers, and personal/social issues. These lessons are preventive by design and developmental in nature to help students with their decision-making in school. For example, a lesson about bullying and harassment in a civics class could be paired with a project on laws about harassment.
7. **Work with counselors and teachers to design professional development that meets your needs.** In-service days provide great opportunities for counselors and teachers to explain their work and develop solutions to school-wide problems.

8. **Allow a counselor to make peace.** When students can't get along in class despite the teacher's attempts to separate them or diffuse tension, allow a counselor to mediate and work out a plan for how the two parties can peaceably coexist.

9. **Explore career options.** Educators may want to engage a school counselor in helping students understand how their academic work connects to specific careers.

10. **Ask a counselor to clarify the severity of a problem.** As students develop physically, rapid changes in their mood or behavior can leave teachers wondering whether certain behavior is normal or a cause for deeper concern. School counselors have been trained to ask the questions that get at the heart of what's really going on.

Collaborating with teachers is necessary in order to do guidance lessons. If you can build trust and respect with teachers, then they'll be more willing to give you their class time. If you go to them at the beginning of the year about coming into their classes, then they'll be able to plan out a time for you in advance. Teachers don't just plan their lessons daily, but by units and quarters. Some teachers plan out their entire year before the first day of school. Know the teachers and know who is going to be willing to let you take class time. Tell them thank you for their hard work and for caring about the students. Give them something small on the first day of school. Teachers can feel overworked, underappreciated, and under paid. They take their job seriously and care about the students. Sound familiar? That is why we should work together and not against each other.

Working Together to Prevent Burnout

Both professions experiences high rates of burnout. We have a lot of skills and resources to prevent burnout that we can give to our teachers. It's better for the faculty, the students, and the morale of the school to work together to prevent burnout. Here is good information from an online article (Online Counseling Programs, 2017):

> Teachers also experience many of the same factors as counselors that contribute to job burnout. School counselors are in a unique position and can provide teachers with the appropriate tools and methods of self-care that can be an integral part in preventing teacher burnout.

> Teachers are under a lot of stress and pressure to meet ever changing deadlines and educational guidelines. Rose F. Kennedy once stated, 'Neither comprehension nor learning can take place in an atmosphere of anxiety'. School counselors can assist teachers in helping them recognize their own professional impairments. Additionally, school counselors can support their educational colleagues by offering the following ten supportive methods:

1. Help teachers to understand the student as a whole being.
2. Offer professional advice regarding troublesome students.
3. Assist with tackling classroom problems, before they get out of hand.
4. Act as an empathetic listener to both student and teacher concerns.
5. Guide students in important decision-making.
6. Work with teachers to implement counseling into academic lessons.
7. Continually develop a collaborative professional relationship.
8. Offer mediation services to students in conflict.
9. Provide career guidance and exploration to students.
10. Offer professional advice, based on education, on a student's mental health.

Counselor Perspectives

The *Confident Counselor* blog posted perspectives on relationships with teachers from school counselors in the field (Confident Counselors, 2017).

During a time when I was split between two buildings, I had a teacher who expressed some resistance in regards to implementing a behavior support plan for a student. Because I was only in the building 1–2 days per week, it was sometimes difficult to be seen as a team member. In an effort to prevent this relationship from becoming negative, I asked the teacher if we could have lunch together one day and offered to pick up lunch from her favorite restaurant. We ate together and really got to know each other. She shared with me about the stress she was feeling in the classroom and how the behavior support plan felt like 'one more thing' piled on her plate. We agreed that the plan itself was not really the issue and agreed to meet outside of school to do some self-care together! Making the effort to get to know this teacher as an individual rather than just a 'resistant colleague' resulted in one of my best professional relationships and friendships. By Keri from *Counselor Keri*.

Developing positive relationships with teachers is so important. Throughout my career as a school counselor, there have been times when I have felt a teacher did not particularly care for me. Because of this, I spent a lot of time feeling upset and at a loss of what to do. One simple thing I do now, which has made a HUGE difference, is taking note of important events that are going on in their life and taking the time to acknowledge them. An example of this is at the beginning of the school year, I write down all program performances and other important class events that will take place during the coming months. On the day of those events, I will leave a note of encouragement and small treat on that teacher's desk as a way to show care and support. This small gesture has been well received and has helped me strengthen my relationships with all teachers in a positive manner. By Jodi from *The School Is In* blog.

Wrap Up

Collaboration is part of our school counseling job. If we do everything ourselves, we will be sacrificing relationships and not giving our students the best. What is the value of collaboration? Online Counseling Programs states (Online Counseling Programs, 2018),

> Throughout much of the professional school counseling literature are statements on the value of collaborations between school counselors and other school personnel to ensure the success of every student academically, in career development, and personally/social.

- Increase in skills when working with students with disabilities
- Strengthening relationships with stakeholders
- Collaborative schools promote school improvement efforts
- Relationship team building within schools
- Supporting family involvement
- Support education level transition
- Maximize use of limited school resources

Another article from ERIC Digest states (Allen, 1994):

> There are numerous benefits to be gained by collaboration. School counselors will gain increased visibility and viability by involvement in collaborative programs. Collaborative efforts reduce competition for diminishing resources, eliminate duplication of services, and provide a diversified approach to solving the problems and providing the services needed by students. Most grants for educational purposes require collaborative efforts, a history of collaboration, and the demonstration of cost-effective methods for accomplishing goals. Acquiring additional funds for a special project or expansion of services may necessitate the pooling of resources through a collaborative grant.

Lastly, we are mandated to collaborate per the ASCA School Counselor Professional Standards and Competencies. Mindset M5 states, "M 5. Effective school counseling is a collaborative process involving school counselors, students, families, teachers, administrators, community leaders and other stakeholders" and behavior B-FS6, "Collaborate with administrators, faculty and staff in their school and district to ensure a culturally responsive curriculum and student-centered instruction" (ASCA, 2018). Behavior B-SS 6 gives a bulleted list of everything that is included under collaboration. It reads as follows (ASCA, 2018):

Collaborate with families, teachers, administrators, and education stakeholders for student achievement and success

1. Partner with families, teachers, administrators, community leaders and other education stakeholders to promote educational equity, student achievement and success

2. Demonstrate understanding of the similarities and differences between consultation, collaboration, counseling and coordination strategies
3. Demonstrate understanding of the potential for dual roles with families and other caretakers
4. Facilitate in-service training or workshops for other stakeholders to share school counseling expertise
5. Supervise school counseling interns consistent with the principles of the ASCA School Counseling Professional Standards and Competencies
6. Create statements or other documents delineating the various roles of student service providers, such as school social worker, school psychologist or school nurse, and identify best practices for collaborating to affect student success
7. Establish and convene an advisory council for the comprehensive school counseling program
8. Determine appropriate education stakeholders who should be represented on the advisory council
9. Develop effective and efficient meeting agendas
10. Explain and discuss school data, school counseling program assessment and school counseling program goals with the advisory council
11. Record advisory council meeting notes, and distribute as appropriate
12. Analyze and incorporate feedback from the advisory council related to school counseling program goals as appropriate

References

Allen, J.M. (1994, June). *School Counselors Collaborating for Student Success*. Retrieved from Counseling: www.counseling.org/Resources/Library/ERIC%20Digests/94-27.pdf

ASCA (2018, December 18). *ASCA School Counselor Professional Standards & Competencies*. Retrieved from School Counselor: www.schoolcounselor.org/asca/media/asca/Careers-Roles/SCCompetencies-2018-draft.pdf

Brodie, I. (2012, June 12). *The Top 10 Ways School Counselors Can Support Teachers*. Retrieved from Ed.gov: https://blog.ed.gov/2012/06/the-top-10-ways-school-counselors-can-support-teachers/

Confident Counselors (2017, September 29). *Conversations: Improving Relationships with Teachers*. Retrieved from Confident Counselors: https://confidentcounselors.com/2017/09/29/conversations-improving-relationships-with-teachers/

Finkelstein, D. (2009, May). *A Closer Look at the Principal-Counselor Relationship*. Retrieved from College Board: https://secure-media.collegeboard.org/digitalServices/pdf/nosca/a-closer-look_2.pdf

Mathieson, B. (2017, October). *Lessons in Collaboration in School Counseling*. Retrieved from School Counselor: www.schoolcounselor.org/newsletters/october-2017/lessons-in-collaboration-in-school-counseling

Ohio Assessment for Educators (2018, December 17). *Collaboration in School Counseling: Strategies & Benefits*. Retrieved from Study: https://study.com/academy/lesson/collaboration-in-school-counseling-strategies-benefits.html

Online Counseling Programs (2017, October 2). *Working Together on Self-Care: School Counselors and Teachers*. Retrieved from Online Counseling Programs: https://onlinecounselingprograms.com/blog/working-together-on-burnout-school-counselors-and-teachers/

Online Counseling Programs (2018, December 18). *Collaborations in School Counseling.* Retrieved from Online Counseling Programs: https://onlinecounselingprograms.com/resources/school-counselor-toolkit/collaborations/

Ratliff, K. (2013, November 20). *School Administrator's Guide to Supporting the Role of School Counselors.* Retrieved from Edutopia: www.edutopia.org/blog/admin-guide-to-school-counselors-kimberlee-ratliff

20 Other Stakeholders

It takes everyone from the janitor to the parents for a school to run. That is why school counselors must collaborate with all stakeholders. There are many ways to collaborate with parents other than when their child is doing poorly in school. Share with them how well their child is doing and keep them updated on what you're doing. Then start collaborating with the other stakeholders in the building. They will be a great way for the counselor to spread their knowledge and expertise to the community. School counselors strive to meet directly with students, but indirect services are just as important.

Stakeholders

What is a stakeholder? A stakeholder is,

> a person or organization that has a vested interest in a particular program. School stakeholders include staff, students, school boards, parents, families, and community organizations. Stakeholders can be viewed as *partners* with the school. Their interests or concerns will vary, but the central focus is on the students.
>
> (Ohio Assessments for Educators, 2018)

Parents

There are going to be a range of parent personalities that you have to work with. Some you will have great relationships with and others you'll never meet until graduation. You will have parents who critique everything you do and those who never read your emails. Regardless of how much or how little the parent is involved, it's important to offer ways for them to be involved and for them to be able to contact you. It's better to be proactive than reactive in your communication. The parents should see your counseling program as a benefit versus an emergency room.

An article from *Campus Explorer* discusses ways to communicate with parents (Henshaw, 2017c):

> Effective communication starts right from the beginning, so introduce yourself to your students' parents at the beginning of the school year. Making a good first impression can go a long way towards getting parents on board with your ideas. Whether you 'meet' in person, over the phone or via email, it's important to keep a few things in mind:

- As the **American School Counselor Association (ASCA)** points out, many parents had very different experiences with school counselors as students than their children have in today's schools. It may help to reassure parents by informing them of your certifications and special training that have prepared you to help their child.
- Provide an outline or brief summary of what your counseling program provides to students. Many parents aren't aware of all the ways that counselors can advocate for and assist students in their academic and college careers.
- Make it clear that part of your job is to collaborate with parents. It can be very encouraging for parents to know that you are not here to direct or instruct them, but rather to work together to provide proper support for students both inside and outside of school.
- Give parents a way to get in touch with you (how to make appointments, your office hours, email address, etc.). When parents feel that the lines of communication are open, they will be more apt to come to you with ideas, concerns or questions.

A clear introduction that shows parents how you can help their child is a great way to start off an effective pattern of communication. Make sure parents know that you believe they are a critical component of their child's success.

There are many ways to communicate with parents; the following are some ideas (Grovner, 2015):

Technology	*Print*
Counseling website	Newsletters
Blogs	Student/parent handbook
Emails or list serves	Friday folders
Webinars/podcasts	Event flyers at other school events and to local community organizations
Suggestion box	Students create a handwritten invite to give to their parent
Mass telephone messages	
Text messages, *check with your school policy*	
Videos for missed presentations (YouTube)	

These are just a few ways you can communicate with parents and give them information. It is important that they know what is happening with their children and within the school. This is how you can avoid confrontation over sensitive topics. I had parents get upset because I didn't communicate effectively about a speaker coming in to talk about suicide awareness. They felt unprepared to answer their child's questions. This was understandable and I sent an email going over who the presenter was, their background, and why the topic was age appropriate. The parents that were upset were happy with the information and stated that was all they were wanting. This is when your Advisory Council would be helpful in giving feedback on your communication with parents and the community. As always, check with your school's policy and get the administration's approval before you do any communication with parents.

AdLit has a great article on how parents can contact school counselors. This can be beneficial for us to know what parents will typically come to you with (American School Counselor Association, 2008).

> Parents contact a school counselor to help their children with a variety of issues, such as academic achievement; new school registration, orientation and transition; test interpretation; special needs; student crisis situations; family transitions; and higher education issues.
>
> When contacting a school counselor, parents often have many obstacles to overcome, such as culture, language, their own bad experiences in school, a lack of understanding, or feeling intimidated. Some parents may feel if they speak up and disagree with educators, their child will have a harder time at school. Work schedules can also be barriers to meeting with your child's school counselor. However, schools encourage parental involvement, and the school counselor is the primary contact for many parents to connect with the school.
>
> By focusing on parents' concerns and respecting why these concerns matter to you, school counselors offer options, including better ways to communicate with your child. Both parents and counselors share information, an important part of establishing a helping relationship. School counselors are excellent resources; however, they do not provide therapy or long-term counseling. Referrals to outside agencies may be initiated at school. School counselors are also advocates for children and provide information on parents' rights, such as the right to request information.

The following are some questions you might want to ask your child's school counselor:

- How is my child doing in school?
- What are my child's strengths and weaknesses?
- Are there any areas of concerns or delayed development?
- What are my child's goals for this year?
- What are some suggestions for action at home?
- What programs are available to help my child to do better?

- Does my child get along well with adults?
- Does my child get along well with his/her peers?
- What can I do to improve discipline at home?
- Are there ways I can improve communication with my child?
- What can I expect after a change in the family (death, divorce, illness, financial status, moving)?
- If my child is (running away from home, being disrespectful, having other problems), what should I do?
- What resources are available at school?
- What resources are available outside of school?
- What do I need to do to prepare my child for college admission?
- What are the best resources for information on financial assistance and scholarships?
- What do I do? My child is (sad, not sleeping, not eating, overeating, etc.)
- What do I do if I don't like my child's friends?

Even if parents aren't setting up meetings to discuss anything with you, make sure to give them the opportunity to do so. Come across as open and available in your communication. Also, get a second opinion before sending out any form of communication to parents. You want to make sure that you're professional.

Involvement

Getting parents involved can really help promote your school counseling program. Epstein's Model for Parental Involvement is widely used in the educational community. It is a model that school counselors can use as well. We acknowledge as a school community and as school counselors that parental involvement is crucial to student success. So, we need to take proactive measures and provide opportunities. An excerpt from "School Counselor-Parent Collaborations: Parents' Perceptions of How School Counselors Can Meet their Needs" by Natalie Grubbs states (Grubbs, 2018):

The Epstein model defines six types of parental involvement. The first type of involvement is *Parenting*, whereby school officials provide parents with information on how to establish home environments that are conducive to child development and learning.

The second type is *Communicating*, where effective forms of communication between the school and the home are designed and implemented to keep families informed about school programs and children's programs.

The third type of involvement is *Volunteering*, where parents are recruited to help and to support the school.

The fourth type of involvement is *Learning at Home*, where parents are provided with information and ideas about how to help students at home with homework and other curriculum-related activities, decisions, and planning.

The fifth type of involvement is *Decision Making*, where parents are included in school decisions, developing parent leaders and representatives.

The sixth type of involvement is *Collaborating with Community*, where resources and services from the community are identified and integrated to strengthen school programs, family practices, and student learning and development.

A school that values parental involvement thinks of the spheres of influence as overlapping, with students at the center of the spheres and with caring as a key concept. Epstein described school-like families where families are involved in education, value education, and work to create home environments that build upon and support what happens at school.

There are many ways to get parents involved. One way to get your parents involved is to have them volunteer for various activities, such as (Grovner, 2015):

1. Career day/career fair
2. Parents of college students
3. Postcard survey to identify all available talents, times, and locations of volunteers
4. Mentor to other parents (first generation college bound parents, kindergarten parents, new to area)
5. Parents assist in creating counseling related bulletin boards
6. Core curriculum lessons guest speakers (or even participant)
7. Chaperone counseling related field trips

A good way to find out what parents would like to be involved in or their views on involvement is to create a needs assessment for them. Get a survey out there to the parents to get feedback on how they view your communication. You don't want them to have to come to your office to complain about the lack of communication. It can be hard to communicate with parents who are both overinvolved and under involved in their children's lives.

Students aren't the only ones who experience anxiety. Parents can be very anxious about the various life stages their child is going through. Here are a few helpful tips for communicating with overinvolved parents (Henshaw, Communicating With Overly Involved Parents, 2017b):

1. Put yourself in their shoes
   a. They may be overwhelmed or confused with the college application process.
   b. With their adolescents increasing independence, they might feel like the one they can control is the college application process.
2. Provide specific, helpful information
3. Be an advocate for students
   a. Remind parents that the more they try to control their child's behaviors the more likely they are to resist.

b. Encourage parents to provide their child with a supportive environment.

c. Discourage them to use language that lumps them in with their child.

It can be hard to communicate with parents who aren't engaged and hard to reach. Here are a few helpful steps to take when trying to connect with them (Henshaw, Communication Tips: Dealing With Uninvolved Parents, 2017a):

When communicating with parents who have been uninvolved, make it clear that you are there to help rather than to add more to an already full plate. The following tips can make for a more effective conversation:

- Figure out the best way to get in touch with them. Do they prefer meetings, phone conversations, email, etc.?
- Offer to work with their schedule. Find out the best time to contact them with issues or concerns.
- Ask how you can help. Discover what their concerns are regarding their child's performance rather than overwhelming them with potential problems.
- Be positive. While a student may need help at school and at home, it's important to show parents that you're confident that you can help and that you see potential in their child.

While it's helpful to provide specific options for parents who are generally uninvolved, it's also important to consider their concerns and ideas. These parents understand their child in a unique way and also see things at home that a counselor does not. That's why it's so important for counselors to collaborate with parents rather than directing them.

Use the following questions to make sure parents are included in a child's academic and college plans:

- How do you feel about your child's academic performance?
- In what ways do you think your child's academic performance could be improved?
- What are your goals for your child after high school?
- How does your child respond to discussions about college at home?
- What services or resources would help you the most in regards to academic performance, college planning, etc.?

As cliché as it sounds, we're all in this together! We can't assume that parents aren't involved in their child's lives because they don't want to be. Our students come from many different home environments. We have to meet the students and the families where they are and provide them with support.

Community Partners

There are many community partners that your school might collaborate with to provide support and resources to students. Your school might have a resource coordinator that facilitates these connections between families and community partners, but as a school counselor you should also know who they are and what services they provide. The community school coordinator description is as follows (National Association of School Psychologists, 2016):

> *Community school coordinator*—This person organizes and manages the various community partnerships with the school. The coordinator works closely with the principal and others on the school leadership team to identify the needs of the students and families, and then recruits and maintains community partnerships aligned with those wants and needs. A resource coordinator can be an employee of the school system or of a community agency.

Some partners that you might work with directly are social workers and mental health counselors. These professionals are typically provided by an outside agency to provide services in the school. The purpose of community partnerships is (National Association of School Psychologists, 2016):

> School–community partnerships can help meet the needs of students and their families. All students should be eligible to access services made available through school–community partnerships, with priority given to those most in need. In all cases, community partners should consult and collaborate with school staff to ensure that their services are appropriate and complementary to the academic, social–emotional, and developmental focus areas of the school.

With all of the partnerships that schools have with community resources it can become unclear what everyone's roles are. Social workers are one of the community partners that school counselors can work closely with. The role of a social worker within the school is (National Association of Social Workers, 2018):

> School social workers have a wide range of job functions. Their title is typically 'school social worker'. Qualifications for this position are often decided by the school district or employing agency and requirements can range from a bachelor's degree to a clinical license from the state in which they practice. Below is a list of possible job functions within a school setting.

- Conducting bio-psychosocial assessments and social histories;
- Assessing students for substance use, support systems, physical and emotional functioning, barriers to academic performance, peer issues, suicidal/homicidal ideation, and similar issues;

- Developing and implementing treatment plans and discharge plans that support student self-determination;
- Providing direct therapeutic services such as individual, family or group therapy regarding specific issues;
- Providing crisis management services, including assessing for safety;
- Advocating for student services and students' best interests;
- Providing case management services including, but not limited to, referrals to community resources, collaboration with other professionals;
- Providing trainings and workshops to teachers, school staff and parents;
- Conducting home visits;
- Identifying and resolving ethical issues;
- Managing and supervising staff; and
- Contributing to a multidisciplinary treatment team.

School psychologists are another partner that is part of the mental health community. With the overlap of mental health providers in the schools, it's important that we are collaborative. The Missouri Association of School Psychologists states, "As each school mental health professional has unique and overlapping areas of expertise, these professionals must work together to achieve the best outcomes for students" (Missouri Association of School Psychologists, 2018). Due to the nature of the overlap with mental health professionals it's crucial to know what each person's role is. The school psychologist's role in the school is (National Association of School Psychologists, 2018):

> School psychologists are uniquely qualified members of school teams that support students' ability to learn and teachers' ability to teach. They apply expertise in mental health, learning, and behavior, to help children and youth succeed academically, socially, behaviorally, and emotionally. School psychologists partner with families, teachers, school administrators, and other professionals to create safe, healthy, and supportive learning environments that strengthen connections between home, school, and the community.

The ways you can collaborate with school psychologists are (Missouri Association of School Psychologists, 2018):

Through this overlap between the professions and the unique aspects each profession brings to the table, there are several potential areas for collaboration. First, on an individual level, school counselors can help identify students who would benefit from **psychological assessments** and **screenings** offered by the school psychologist. In the same way, school psychologists could include school counselors in **problem-solving team meetings** with teachers and administrators. This would allow collaboration among professions in order to offer the very best recommendations and resources to the student and family.

Second, on a school community level, school counselors and school psychologists could **share data** and **responsibilities** regarding school-wide interventions. On a smaller level, they could work together to **develop, lead, and evaluate psycho-educational interventions** for specific groups of students. They could also utilize their cumulative understanding of learning theories to **provide suggestions** to teachers and staff on behavior and classroom management strategies.

Third, on an administrative level, school counselors and school psychologists could share in the inevitable burden of **paperwork** that is a necessity within each occupation. They could include each other in the **planning meetings** for upcoming curriculum, and even **attend professional development** seminars and events with the other profession. Accompanying one another to state conventions could be a great opportunity to strengthen the relationship between professionals and understand the strengths and resources that each profession brings to the table.

Building community partnerships is crucial to student achievement and success. We can work together to develop programming and implementation (Ohio Assessments for Educators, 2018):

Community organizations are essential contacts for school counselors. In order to meet students' physical needs, counselors may have to reach out for additional support from local organizations, including child protective services, financial assistance agencies, substance abuse programs, and psychological services. In order to meet students' academic needs, counselors should have regular contact with local colleges and universities, tutoring and other academic support services, and special education organizations.

It is a good practice to develop a list of contacts for community organizations. They should develop relationships with these organizations by reaching out, introducing him/herself, and establishing the appropriate course of action, should their services be needed.

Wrap Up

"It takes a village to raise a child" isn't just an old wise proverb. As school counselors, we know that it's true. We know that for our students to be successful there has to be collaboration among stakeholders and the community. There are many ways to connect with stakeholders to improve our schools. One example is from Cincinnati Public Schools in Cincinnati, Ohio (O'Brien, 2012):

In the early 2000s, Cincinnati Public Schools learned that they had the worst school buildings in the nation. They needed to pass a levy to raise money for improvements, but one hadn't passed in a number of years. To garner community support, they proposed that the renovated schools would

Table 20.1 Communication with Stakeholders

Technology	Print
Counseling website	Newsletters
Blogs	Student/parent handbook
Emails or list serves	Friday folders
Webinars/podcasts	Event flyers at other school events and to local community organizations
Suggestion box	Students create a handwritten invite to give to their parent
Mass telephone messages	
Text messages, *check with your school policy*	
Videos for missed presentations (YouTube)	

serve as centers of the community, remaining open on nights and week-ends to provide services. The levy passed, and the Community Learning Centers (CLCs) began.

Each CLC is different, based on the needs of the community in which the school is located. Annie Bogenschutz told Celebration attendees about the CLC at her school, Ethel M. Taylor Academy, where 100 percent of students receive free or reduced price lunch. The school is open from 2:15pm to 6pm and offers a hot dinner, tutoring and mentoring, enrichment, parent and family engagement activities, and more. On site, students and families can access mental health and dental services. Next year, Taylor will open a school-based health clinic. These services, and the many others that are offered at the CLC, require no new funds. Instead, the school's partners reallocated their spending.

And they have seen results. Taylor was formerly labeled as one of the worst schools in the state, but is now recognized for its "Continuous Improvement," with increased attendance, standardized test scores, and parent involvement, as well as decreased behavioral incidents.

As you begin your first-year school counselor experience, take the time to get to know the families in your school and the community partnerships. Together you'll be able to do great things in your school.

References

American School Counselor Association (2008). *Understanding the School Counselor-Parent Connection.* Retrieved from AdLit: www.adlit.org/article/25276/

Grovner, M. (2015, November 10). *Getting Parents Involved in Your School Counseling Program.* Retrieved from Georgia Department of Education: www.gadoe.org/Curriculum-Instruction-and-Assessment/CTAE/Documents/Getting-Parents-Involved-in-Your-School-Counseling-Program.pdf

Grubbs, N. (2018, August 13). *School Counselor–Parent Collaborations: Parents' Perceptions of How School Counselors Can Meet their Needs*. Retrieved from Scholar Works GSU: https ://scholarworks.gsu.edu/cgi/viewcontent.cgi?referer=&httpsredir=1&article=1096&co ntext=cps_diss

Henshaw, A. (2017a, February 17). *Communication Tips: Dealing With Uninvolved Parents*. Retrieved from Campus Explorer: www.campusexplorer.com/college-advice-tips/2C D6435A/Communication-Tips-Dealing-With-Uninvolved-Parents/

Henshaw, A. (2017b, February 17). *Communicating With Overly Involved Parents*. Retrieved from Campus Explorer: www.campusexplorer.com/college-advice-tips/D018B300/ Communicating-With-Overly-Involved-Parents/

Henshaw, A. (2017c, February 17). *How to Communicate Effectively With Parents of Students*. Retrieved from Campus Explorer: www.campusexplorer.com/college-advice-tips/41 F2A67A/How-to-Communicate-Effectively-With-Parents-of-Students/

Missouri Association of School Psychologists (2018, December 31). *Collaborative School Mental Health: Connecting School Counselors and School Psychologists*. Retrieved from MAOSP: https://maosp.wildapricot.org/Resources/Documents/Collaboration%20btwn%20SC %20and%20SP%20final.pdf

National Association of School Psychologists (2016, January). *Nine Elements of Effective School Community Partnerships to Address Student Mental Health, Physical Health, and Overall Wellness*. Retrieved from NASP: www.nasponline.org/documents/Research%20and%2 0Policy/Advocacy%20Resources/Community%20Schools%20White%20Paper_Jan_2 016.pdf.

National Association of School Psychologists (2018, December 31). *About NASP*. Retrieved from NASP: www.nasponline.org/utility/about-nasp

National Association of Social Workers (2018, December 31). *Social Workers in Schools*. Retrieved from National Association of Social Workers: www.socialworkers.org/Lin kClick.aspx?fileticket=vvUJM-JNAEM=&portalid=0

O'Brien, A. (2012, March 21). *The Importance of Community Involvement in Schools*. Retrieved from Edutopia: www.edutopia.org/blog/community-parent-involvement-essential-anne -obrien

Ohio Assessments for Educators (2018, December 24). *Stakeholder Collaboration in School Counseling*. Retrieved from Study: https://study.com/academy/lesson/stakeholder-colla boration-in-school-counseling.html

Part VIII

Supervision and Mentorship

21 Redefining Supervision as Mentorship

Every school counselor should have a seasoned person he/she goes to for advice. Supervision isn't something that can always be done in a school setting. Having a mentor can replace the supervision that a school counselor might not receive in his/her own school. This chapter will go into detail about seeking out mentors, and the importance of supervision and consultation.

Supervision

What is supervision? Supervision is "an intensive, interpersonally focused, one-to-one relationship in which one person (the supervisor) is designated to facilitate the development of competence in the other person (the supervisee)" (Desmond, 2011).

In the clinical mental health world, supervision is mandatory for counselors to obtain licensure. As school counselors, supervision isn't as strict or limited. Our supervisor can be the administration of the school we work at or the 'head' school counselor. If you are the only school counselor in your building, your supervisor will be the administration. Depending upon the school, that could mean an assistant principal or the principal. Outside consultation and supervision isn't something that is necessary in a school as it is in a mental health facility. However, consultation is encouraged through professional development and networking. Since we don't have supervision in the same way as mental health professionals do, mentorship can be a supplement. Mentorship can provide supervision from an experienced school counselor that a novice might be lacking.

Mentorship

As a first-year school counselor, it is important to have a mentor who is an experienced school counselor. This person may be another school counselor in the school you work at, your internship supervisor, or another colleague. As the only school counselor at my first job, the principal suggested I meet with another school counselor in our district who had a number of years of experience. I met with that person at least once a quarter during my first year. Her wisdom and support were invaluable during that first year.

An excerpt from a paper presented at the American School Counselor Exposition in 2009 states (Duncan, Svendsen, Bakkedahl, & Sitzman, 2009):

Mentoring programs, or mentorships, are not new. Mentoring is a relationship in which an experienced professional helps to teach, guide, and develop the skills of a trainee within an organization or profession. Many businesses and organizations offer mentoring programs designed to promote employee development. Mentors are paired with inexperienced new employees to offer needed information, to advise, and to set a good example for their less experienced peers. Mentoring has also been 'an essential element in the areas of teacher training and administrative leadership in education'. In contrast, little has been written regarding the practice as it relates to mentoring school counselors.

Research shows that in educational systems, teachers were often paired with fellow teachers, but school counselors were frequently left out of the mentoring experience or were oddly paired with a classroom teacher. This pairing of a counselor with a classroom teacher created problems because the counselor was not receiving support for counseling-related concerns. However, much of the literature states that formal orientation programs promote a smooth transition of school counselors from their graduate programs to the work place.

Although the research is limited regarding mentoring for school counselors, one study has shown an increase in self-efficacy among first year elementary counselors who participated in a district-wide mentoring program. The mentoring program also helped prevent burnout and increased longevity of counselors. Milsom and Kayler showed that interactions with a professional already established in the field led to greater self-efficacy in the mentee. A mentoring relationship increased the confidence of school counselors to work independently and they felt better prepared for their new role in the schools after the mentoring experience.

Mentorship is important to all areas of work, but there aren't many programs that are school counselor driven. You will find information on how to implement mentoring among your students and how to provide consultation to teachers, but there's not a lot of resources for school counselors to be mentored or have consultation.

The Need for Mentorship Programs

It comes as no surprise that there is a need for mentorship programs for new school counselors. In 2016, a research paper was presented to the American

School Counselor Exposition in New Orleans entitled "Mentoring Novice School Counselors: A Grounded Theory". The paper starts with the following (Johnson, Nelson, & Henriksen, 2016):

> In the 21st century, school counselors are encouraged by the American School Counseling Association (ASCA) to follow the ASCA National Model and implement a data-driven comprehensive school counseling program (CSCP). Indeed, the implementation of a CSCP can have positive impacts on students in the areas of academic, career, and social/personal development. However, novice school counselors transitioning from academic preparation programs to the school setting may experience challenges during their early years adjusting to their districts' defined role of the school counselor. Although mentoring has proven to be an invaluable resource in a variety of fields, such as education, nursing, and business, to assist in the transition process, a formal mentoring program may or may not be a part of a novice school counselor's induction into the profession.

The authors looked at literature that discussed mentoring for new school counselors and ended up conducting their own research study. They used a grounded research method to study and examine the lived experiences by new school counselors in order to explain the induction process. Their study sought to answer the following questions (Johnson, Nelson, & Henriksen, 2016):

1. What are the perceptions and experiences of novice school counselors entering the school counseling profession and the role that mentoring plays in the induction process?
2. What perceptions and experiences of novice school counselors inform the development of an updated mentoring model?

They had eight participants in the study. Seven were female and one was male. All were between the ages of 32–47. There were seven who had fulfilled their requirements for the State Board of Texas to be school counselors which included two years of teaching experience, and one person was completing their school counselor training. Five participants were in their first year and three were in their second year as school counselors.

You can read more about the instrumentation and data results collected in their paper. The results of their study showed five themes among the counselors: starting over, relying on previous knowledge/experiences, gaining/learning new knowledges and experiences, integrating previous and new knowledge, and looking forward. The themes showed that there was a lack of confidence as new school counselors and it felt like they would either 'sink or swim' (Johnson, Nelson, & Henriksen, 2016).

Participants described the need to learn and integrate new information and experiences in order to perform their new roles as school counselors. This is usually provided at district staff development sessions. However, this can be overwhelming to the new school counselor. One participant noted that in the month of October, due to required district trainings, she was only in her building full-time five days. A mentor, during regular scheduled meetings with the mentee, could assist by discussing such topics as pacing oneself, prioritizing time, and focusing on organizational skills. This could possibly assist the mentee in managing the acquisition of the necessary knowledge and experiences while carrying out their responsibilities as school counselors. This information was found to be helpful to Alpha as his fellow counselors explained to him that he would not be able to accomplish all of his daily responsibilities and encouraged him to realize that fact and to pace himself accordingly. Experienced school counselors serving as mentors can utilize information obtained from this induction process to provide assistance to beginning school counselors. School counselor educators can incorporate aspects of the findings into their courses to further equip future school counselors for the role of professional school counselor.

As you enter your first year do not be discouraged if your school district does not offer mentorship. Seek out your colleagues and ask them if they would be willing to serve as a mentor. I also felt like it was a 'sink or swim' scenario my first year. It's overwhelming to walk into a position that might not be exactly what you were trained to do. The expectations for you might be vague and it might not be clear what your job role is. Don't be afraid to reach out to your professors for guidance as well.

Districts with Mentorship

There are school districts who offer new school counselors' mentorship. These examples will provide you with a model for implementation. In the future, it might be something you implement at your own school and pitch to your superintendent for the district. Peer support can be crucial for new counselors who are uncertain about role expectations. A study that examined factors related to role stress among practicing counselors in various school settings found that "peer consultation added to lower role incongruence" (Bass et al., 2019).

Delaware's New School Counselor Mentoring Program

Delaware has implemented a mentoring program for new school counselors. The new school counselors get paired with an experienced school counselor for three years. They have a lead mentor that implements the program, assigns mentees to a mentor, and tracks progress. They work 45 hours a week and get a $1,500 stipend (Bass et al., 2019).

Their mentors are assigned three main roles: 'helper', 'colleague', and 'role model'. Mentors are assigned up to three new mentees and are responsible for meeting with them. They have to write progress reports on goals that are set and meet with the mentee at least every 30 hours to check on those goals. There are four cycles that the mentorship program encompasses. They are as follows (Bass et al., 2019):

1. Cycle 1: After they are acclimated to these policies and procedures, the initial observation takes place. Goals are set based on feedback provided and reassessed a short time later.
2. Cycle 2: The ASCA National Model's Delivery and Accountability components are reviewed in depth. In addition, the mentor reviews the Making Data Work process of data collection, Design, Ask, Track and Announce. The Delaware State Binder Requirements are discussed and the Verification of Services Form must be completed prior to the completion of cycle two. Once the first four components listed are addressed, another observation takes place. In their post-observation meeting, the pair discusses the status of the new school counselor in successfully completing the second component of the Delaware Professional Appraisal System II (DPAS II). The mentor provides constructive criticism and assistance to his mentee. One of the goals of cycle two is for the new school counselor to become more introspective in his professional progress.
3. Cycle 3: Typically takes place during the new school counselor's second year. The mentor gives the new school counselor a reading task to highlight "leadership advocacy for a growth directed opportunity". Mentors assign appropriate activities for mentees to complete in conjunction with their reading task. The new school counselor is responsible for completing 30 hours independently in relation to this assignment and must turn in a log documenting their activities.
4. Cycle 4: Is characterized by a focus on refining the new school counselor's self-analysis skills. Based on discussions with their mentor and the lead mentor, mentees develop an official "professional growth plan" that outlines long-term goals. In order to identify their goals, the new school counselors work for a minimum of 30 hours to complete activities addressing goals of the Department of Education Annual School Review and the Recognized ASCA Model Program (RAMP).

After mentees have completed all four cycles, they are eligible to receive their full school counselor license through the state.

Missouri Mentoring Program for School Counselors

Missouri has a comprehensive mentoring program that is up to date. Their program manual is available on their website if you would like further information than I provide. This program is a collaboration with the School Counseling Section of the Office of College and Career Readiness and the Missouri School Counselor Association. The goals of the program are (Ernst, 2018):

1. The program's first goal is to offer a professional development opportunity to new and returning counselors along with mentors that encourage skill development, collaboration and reflection.
2. A second goal is to become familiar with the responsibilities and administrative culture that are inherent in a comprehensive school counseling program.
3. The third goal is to support new and returning school counselors in their work with students and to build a network of new and returning school counselors.

This is a two-year mentoring program that provides goals for each month. The first year focuses on three components (Ernst, 2018):

1. Calendaring Due: October
    Create a yearlong calendar for your comprehensive school counseling program that includes activities designed to develop student skills within the three (3) content areas of the Comprehensive School Counseling Program: Academic Development, Career Development, and Social-Emotional Development. Be sure to identify system support activities.
2. Responsive Services Review Due: January
    Review your school or building crisis plan. Reflect on if it meets the needs of the students in your building today in reference to crises that could occur. Is the plan up to date with resources? What is the process for reviewing the document? What needs to be included to make the resource comprehensive? Utilize the examples below to help guide your reflection.
3. IIR Due: April
    Complete the Internal Improvement Review (IIR) document to review your school district's level of implementation of the comprehensive school counseling program. After completing the IIR, revise or create an annual comprehensive school counseling program evaluation plan. The evaluation plan should be based upon program objectives aligned with the CSIP, student performance data, identified instructional competencies/learner objectives and any areas of improvement needed as determined through completion of the IIR.

Then there is an evaluation component and contact log to keep track of progress. The second year entails:

4. Principal/Counselor Agreement Due: October
    Complete the Principal/Counselor Agreement using the resources provided to enhance or establish a positive relationship between parties that values two-way communication.

5. CSIP Plan Due: January

   Locate your school district's Comprehensive School Improvement Plan (CSIP). Make note of goals, objectives, strategies, and action steps that relate to the School Counseling Department in your school. Note how these goals, objectives, strategies, and action steps relate to student outcomes including student achievement.

6. Evaluation Due: April

   Working from the model of Program (Comprehensive Curriculum) + Personnel (School Counselors) = Results, school counselors evaluate their programs to improve counseling services for all students, to advocate with policymakers for the support needed to fully implement effective programs, and to increase one's ability to be reflective, investigative practitioners.

A person must apply for the mentoring program, whether they wish to be a mentor or mentee. They pair the applicants based on elementary, middle, or high school preference and whether they would like someone within the district. These mentorship pairs are expected to meet twice a month in September and October and monthly for the remainder of the school year. The program requires a contract between the mentee/mentor and offers the opportunity to file a grievance report if necessary.

New Jersey School Counselor Comprehensive Mentoring Program

The New Jersey School Counselor Comprehensive Mentoring Program follows a one-year, three-cycle plan. The first-year requirements are (Hall & Conway, 2014):

> **Suggested program requirement:** All individuals entering a school counselor position for the first time in New Jersey must complete all of the following in order to fulfill the requirements for the first year of the Comprehensive Mentor Program for School Counselors. Thirty (30) contact hours with Mentor (at least once per week for the first 4 weeks of assignment)

- Three (3) observations total to be completed at the 10th, 20th and 30th week within the of the first year.
- Completion of three 20 Professional Development hours each year related to PDP goals
- Verified knowledge for all areas listed on the comprehensive mentor program for school counselors' checklist for cycle one and cycle two. *(checklist to be used at the discretion of the Mentor)*
- Completion of the following activities from the ASCA National Model text

Their program is similar to Delaware's mentoring program where their cycles reflect the ASCA National Model. Cycle one is program planning, implementation, and evaluation. Cycle two is program delivery and cycle three is leadership and advocacy. Their requirements for being a mentor are (Hall & Conway, 2014):

> Your role is primarily a coach who supports and encourages the new educator(s) during their first year of induction. You should assist the new educator(s) in looking at their current level of practice in classroom environment, planning and preparation, and instruction. You are to provide feedback based on the evidence of practice that you observed. The three roles you play are as follows: role-model, helper, and colleague.

Mentees are expected to keep a log on their meetings and progress. They are evaluated throughout the cycles and not just at the end of their first year.

North Carolina School Counselor Association Mentoring Program

The last example I'm sharing is from the North Carolina School Counselor Association. The NCSCA Mentoring Program is less detailed and structured than the other three examples I gave. It is an application-based program and requires a minimum of a year, but it does not have cycles or specific goals that the mentee has to reach. The following is the outline of the NCSCA Mentoring Program (NCSCA, 2019):

> The goal of the mentoring program is to provide new school counselors with the opportunity to have a meaningful relationship with experienced school counseling professionals. As graduate students and new school counselors' transition into the field, mentors will offer:
>
> 1. Personal and professional development
> 2. Social support
> 3. Career guidance
> 4. Resource/idea sharing
> 5. A sounding board
>
> The role of a mentor is to coach, guide, nurture and support new counselors as they transition into this field. A mentor provides support, encourages development, offers suggestions and advice on a variety of topics, and shares resources. A mentor also shares experiences and wisdom to help mentees grow personally and professionally.
>
>   The mentee is a school counselor who is in his/her first three years of counseling. The most important characteristic of a mentee is the willingness to commit the time and energy to grow and learn from a mentor. A

mentee is devoted to developing skills, enhancing professional networks, and increasing his/her understanding of the role of a school counselor. A mentee should be positive and excited about the mentoring program and put forth the effort required to receive maximum results, ensuring the program is a success.

The amount of time invested in the mentoring relationship depends solely on the expectations set by both the mentor and mentee. We ask that mentors and mentees be in contact at least twice a month during their time in the mentoring program.

While the mentoring relationship is considered to be a partnership where both parties contribute equally, we ask that the mentor be responsible for initiating the first contact. When the mentor receives his/her letter of acceptance, they will receive the name and contact information for the mentee. They will be asked to make contact within the first 3 weeks of school.

Participants in the mentoring program will be asked to complete a mid-year evaluation and a final evaluation. Success of the program will be monitored based on the feedback received from mentors and mentees. Continual improvements and modifications will be made based on suggestions and comments provided by the participants.

Although, we only ask mentors and mentees to make a one-year commitment to the NCSCA Mentoring Program, we encourage ongoing communication and support beyond the one-year commitment and throughout their professional career.

Wrap Up

As I wrap up this chapter, I hope you have gained an understanding of what mentorship is and can look like for school counselors. If you are a first-year and your district offers mentorship, don't pass up the opportunity to have a mentor! One last research article to support mentoring and induction programs for new school counselors is "New School Counselor Perceptions of Their Mentoring and Induction Program" by Carol P. Loveless. This study was to understand the perceptions of novice school counselors, in urban districts, about their mentoring/induction program.

Novice school counselors fresh from graduate training may enter the field well-versed in helping skills, but may be potentially lacking in their knowledge of school culture and their particular role within that culture. Teachers may perceive new counselors who do not have teaching backgrounds as less competent than those with classroom experience. Conversely, first year school counselors with teaching backgrounds may be quite familiar with school culture, but their shifting roles within the work setting can prove stressful. Learning to relate to students and faculty from a counselor's perspective and adapting to a less structured work environment may present challenges for these former teachers. Furthermore, many new counselors perceive that their faculties expect them to be highly functioning professionals from their initial days of employment. Peer supervision from more experienced colleagues or clinical supervision from a district counseling coordinator may ameliorate some of the stress new counselors experience, if they are fortunate enough to have such support. Those new counselors who are veterans of the profession but are new to a particular school district may benefit from training in the culture of the local district, that is, what the expectations are regarding counselors and their role. Through appropriate training and support in a first-year mentoring/induction program, these gaps in knowledge can be filled and role expectations clarified.

(Loveless, 2010)

The results were largely positive, and they concluded (Loveless, 2010),

The data collected and analyzed in this study indicated that participants had overwhelmingly positive perceptions of the program as a whole, and that such a program was an effective means of inducting new counselors into the school system. Thus, new counselor mentoring can clearly play a role in the formation of professional identity for novice counselors.

The findings of this qualitative case study provide support for the mentoring and induction of new school counselors, particularly through structured programming.

References

Bass, E., Gardner, L., Onwukaeme, C., Revere, D., Shepherd, D., & Parrish, M. (2019, January 8). *An Examination of New Counselor Mentor Programs*. Retrieved from Eric: https://files.eric.ed.gov/fulltext/EJ1072658.pdf

Desmond, Kimberly, Nelson. (2011). *The Basics of Supervision for Counselors*. Indiana, PA: Indiana University of Pennsylvania.

Duncan, K., Svendsen, R., Bakkedahl, T., & Sitzman, L. (2009, March). *Bridging the Professional Gap: Mentoring School Counselors-in-Training*. American Counseling Association Annual Conference and Exposition, March 19–23, Charlotte, NC.

Ernst, A. (2018). *Missouri Mentoring Program for School Counselors*. Retrieved from Missouri Department of Elementary and Secondary Education: https://dese.mo.gov/sites/default/files/SCmentoring_manual_18-19.pdf

Hall, M., & Conway, T. (2014). *New Jersey School Counselor Comprehensive Mentoring Program*. Retrieved from New Jersey School Counselor Association: https://static1.squarespace.com/static/5a56b9aa017db276cd76b240/t/5a70824071c10bdde54d0fbd/1517322821330/NJSCASchoolCounselorMentorProgram.pdf

Johnson, G.S., Nelson, J.A., & Henriksen, R. (2016, October 7). *Mentoring Novice School Counselors: A Grounded Theory*. New Orleans, LA: American Counselor Association.

Loveless, C.P. (2010). *New School Counselor Perceptions of Their Mentoring and Induction Program*. Retrieved from Eric: https://files.eric.ed.gov/fulltext/EJ909075.pdf

NCSCA (2019, January 10). *NCSCA Mentoring Program*. Retrieved from North Carolina School Counselor Association: www.ncschoolcounselor.org/page-1535576

22 We're a Team

One of the most important things for a first-year school counselor to remember is that he/she is not alone. Some school counselors end up with positions at schools where they are the only counselor in the building. Although they might be alone, it shouldn't feel that way. The other school counselors in my school district were very friendly and helpful. They would go out of their way to invite me to events that they might be attending. I also kept in touch with my colleagues who I had gone to graduate school with. At the end of the day, a school counselor realizes he/she is never alone because we are a team! No school counselor is alone in his/her endeavors and other school counselors are willing to do what they can to help. This is so true for the first-year counselor; no one wants to see you succeed more than your school counselors!

"No Man is an Island"

No man is an island entire of itself; every man is a piece of the continent, a part of the main; if a clod be washed away by the sea, Europe is the less, as well as if a promontory were, as well as any manner of thy friends or of thine own were; any man's death diminishes me, because I am involved in mankind. And therefore never send to know for whom the bell tolls; it tolls for thee.

(Donne, 2019)

I can't count the number of times I have felt like I was on an island all by myself. I'm sure we all feel like that at times but being the only school counselor in the building had me feeling like that a lot. There were days when I would hang out with the secretaries, because I didn't want to be in my office. I got tired of only seeing my four walls. There were only certain times of the day when I could see students and some days, I would rarely see them. I would be down there in my spacious, decorated office by myself. Sure, I could get a lot of work done but it was lonely. There is only so much administrative work you can do in one day without going insane!

Unfortunately, life doesn't stop when you're a school counselor. There are going to be times when you need the support of your colleagues. Among my colleagues there have been times when personal problems would arise, and we would have to prioritize our personal lives over work. It took the support of one another to get through those hard times. The same has been true for when crisis happened within the school.

Kirsten Perry, the 2018 School Counselor of the Year, said these words when asked to give advice to first-year school counselors (Barrick, 2018):

> I always tell my interns the same thing (which was something told to me once by a professor): 'You will learn the first third of what you need to know during your coursework; you will learn the second third of what you need to know during your internship; and you will learn the final third of what you need to know during your first year as a professional school counselor.' In other words, do not feel like you need to know everything. You are still learning, and it is okay not to know what to do sometimes.
>
> If you are the only school counselor in your school, like I am, I recommend making a list of school counselors at other schools that you can call if you need advice, have questions, or want to share resources.
>
> I also recommend sitting down with your principal before the school year starts, and periodically throughout the year, to discuss your program goals and expectations. This has always worked for me. Rather than wonder, I always ask to hear feedback so I can continually improve. Be open to any feedback—there is nothing wrong with making mistakes. We all do!
>
> Finally, listen to the staff, students, parents, and your community. They will tell you what the school needs and guide your program. The first year is definitely a year of listening and taking notes. You will never have to wonder if what you are doing is right for the school, if you listen—especially to the students! They will tell it to you direct.

The Benefits of Teamwork

Isolation is not an effective way to work, even in education. An article from Edutopia titled "For Effective Schools, Teamwork is Not Optional" by Sean Glaze, discusses the importance of teamwork within in education. The article states (Glaze, 2014):

> I remember my first year as a high school literature teacher. I began by adopting those exact habits of preparing alone and working in isolation. I was a lonely superhero who went home exhausted each day without the encouragement or support of my more experienced peers. I was right next to people who had answers and ideas that could have benefitted me, but I was too proud to ask for them.
>
> It was only by the grace and generosity of a couple of seasoned teachers from my department that I was able to appreciate what I had been missing. They reached out to offer unsolicited assistance, build a relationship, and

share a few encouraging stories with me. I had assumed that I could be more effective when planning and working alone, but I eventually found that, when working with people, *efficient* is rarely truly *effective*. It took a long time for me to realize that I could accomplish more and be far more effective and energized if I was willing to share ideas, ask for help, and lean on others.

That experience of connecting with other teachers and sharing ideas throughout the year had a tremendous impact on me as a young teacher. Over the years, it is what led me to share with and reach out to others who I felt might need encouragement or ideas.

There are two main types of isolation that teachers experience:

1. **Egg-crate isolation:** This is what I call the kind of isolation that is due to the physical layout of school buildings. Egg-crate isolation is the result of physical separateness, where teachers have little contact with others and feel as if they have no support system. To alleviate this feeling, instead of being tucked neatly away in separate rooms all the time, school administrations should give teachers the time and opportunity to talk and plan together, and to share laughter, encouragement, and ideas.
2. **Avalanche isolation:** This kind of isolation is the result of teachers feeling overwhelmed by their daily responsibilities of serving lunch duty, grading papers, making copies, attending meetings, learning new strategies, contacting parents, and the thousand other things on their to-do list. The best way to assuage this form of isolation is to focus on getting rid of egg-crate isolation.

I have felt both 'egg-crate' and 'avalanche' isolation as a school counselor. My office was at the other end of the hallway from the front office. It might not have seemed very far, but I definitely felt isolated being the only school counselor. Due to the layout of the building, I rarely saw the other faculty members because they were experiencing avalanche isolation. This led to me feeling like I didn't belong and alone. I could easily go weeks without seeing some faculty members. At a large school that might be the norm, but with a faculty size under 50 it was abnormal. I tried to make an effort to eat lunch with the faculty a minimum of once a week. In a previous chapter, I talk about burnout. If you are isolated and lack the feeling of belonging, you will experience burnout.

There are benefits to having teamwork amongst faculty. These articles may talk specifically to teachers, but they are relevant to school counselors as well. "Teamwork in Schools" from the websites EducationViews states (Hozien, 2017):

Those who are part of a team are usually able to manage their classroom and to provide instruction that is more focused on the curriculum. If educators are part of a team then they are in constant communication with others that are trying to do the same thing with the same group of students in their building and they are continuously exchanging ideas on their roles, what worked and heck what did not work. These exchanges are pivotal to the education of all. Those who work as a team can communicate their ideas on effective teaching practices and this can help educators all over better understand their role. For example, if a teacher has an issue with a group of students and classroom management then the teachers can learn from their team mates how to better manage a particular class. This is one of the benefits of a team in that they can compensate for an individuals' weaknesses. Teams of teachers can provide an ongoing support network for those who are struggling to adapt to a situation and this is particularly the case with new highly qualified teachers. There are many instances when team members who are experienced educators can act as continuous mentors to younger teachers and this can help them to improve their performance. Being a member of a team means sharing information that can be helpful, and it can mean that the resources of a school are better utilized. Teachers who are cooperating can share resources quicker and with more guidance. This is very important given budgetary pressures across the education sector and the ever looming assessment deadlines. Teams can help to establish realizable goals and provide feedback that allows school leaders to identify what is going right or going wrong with instructional practice or in a school. A growing problem in the school system are the challenges posed by teacher retention. Studies have shown that if a teacher believes that they are a part of a team then they are more likely to stay in their current role. This can help school leaders to retain talented and experienced staff and reduce the costs associated with the replacement of staff members.

Even though school counselors aren't part of the teaching faculty, you can apply this example to the school counseling team. If you are the only school counselor in the building, utilize the administration and create an advisory committee. This will provide you with the benefits of working with a team.

Effective Teamwork

We know what the benefits of teamwork are, but what does it take to be an effective team? There are common characteristics that good teamwork possesses (Schoultz, 2017):

1. **Clear direction:** Decide on team goals and desired outcomes first. Use it for clear direction for the team you select. Start at the end point: what is the outcome you want and why? Leave the team flexibility to develop the best way to get there.
2. **Open and honest communication:** The most important part of communication is listening. Listening is not just a way to find things out. It's also a sign of respect.

3. **Support risk taking and change:** Good teams support appropriate risk taking and experimentation for change. They look on first time mistakes as opportunities for learning.
4. **Defined roles:** Roles might shift somewhat once the team is assembled, but understand the skill sets and thinking styles are needed on the team.
5. **Mutually accountable:** Teams accept responsibility as individuals and as a team. They don't blame one another for team mistakes and failures.
6. **Communicate freely:** The more freely you talk to your fellow team members, the more comfortable you are in sharing insights and ideas.
7. **Common goals:** A chief characteristic of any successful team is that members place the common goal above individual interests.
8. **Encourage differences:** Diverse opinions stir imagination and new ideas. Imagination and new ideas stir creativity. Unless the status quo is threatened and questioned, you won't find those crucial 'out of the box' ideas.
9. **Collaboration:** The idea is simple enough: the more you collaborate and the more you communicate, the more you create.
10. **Team trust:** Effective teams focus on solving problems. Trust is an adjunct of effective communication; there can be trust between team members only if they are allowed to air their views freely.

I taught a guidance lesson on teamwork to my students from the ACT Tessera playbook. The ACT Tessera playbook only identified three components of good teamwork: cooperation, social orientation, and concern for others. However, when you look at the list of ten and the list of three you can see where you could put all ten into one of the three topics. Another article identified five characteristics of good teamwork (Aguilar, 2015).

1. **A good team knows why it exists.**
   It's not enough to say, 'We're the 6th grade team of teachers'—that's simply what defines you (you teach the same grade), not why you exist. A purpose for being is a team might be: 'We come together as a team to support each other, learn from each other, and identify ways that we can better meet the needs of our sixth grade students.' Call it a purpose or a mission—it doesn't really matter. What matters is that those who attend never feel like they're just obligated to attend 'another meeting.' The purpose is relevant, meaningful, and clear.
2. **A good team creates a space for learning.**
   There are many reasons why those of us working in schools might gather in a team—but I believe that all of those reasons should contain opportunities for learning with and from each other. I have met very few educators who don't want to learn—we're a curious bunch and there's so much to learn about education. So in an effective team, learning happens within a safe context. We can make mistakes, take risks, and ask every single question we want.

3. **In a good team, there's healthy conflict.**

    This is inevitable and essential if we're learning together and embarked on some kind of project together. We disagree about ideas, there's constructive dialogue and dissent, and our thinking is pushed.

4. **Members of a good team trust each other.**

    This means that when there's the inevitable conflict, it's managed. People know each other. We listen to each other. There are agreements about how we treat each other and engage with each other, and we monitor these agreements. There's also someone such as a facilitator who ensures that this is a safe space. Furthermore, in order for there to be trust, within a strong team we see equitable participation among members and shared decision-making. We don't see a replication of the inequitable patterns and structures of our larger society (such as male dominance of discourse and so on).

5. **A good team has a facilitator, leader, or shared leaders.**

    There's someone—or a rotation of people—who steer the ship. This ensures that there's the kind of intentionality, planning, and facilitation in the moment that's essential for a team to be high functioning.

We teach students that teamwork is important to succeed in life. We tell them the cliché 'two heads are better than one' and make them do group work. Often times, students hate group work due to the lack of communication, someone not doing their part, and codependence. As school counselors and faculty, it can be hard to practice what we teach. It takes effort to have effective teamwork. It means going out of your way to connect with others and taking time out of your schedule to have more meetings. Sometimes teamwork is more 'work' than doing the job on your own.

Once we commit to having effective teamwork, we can evaluate where our teamwork is by understanding that there are stages of growth. Effective teamwork doesn't happen overnight or even in a week. It takes time to develop a team mentality and forge a group mindset (Nondestructive Testing, 2019).

It is important for teachers and students (the team members) to know that teams don't just form and immediately start working together to accomplish great things. There are actually stages of team growth and teams must be given time to work through the stages and become effective. Team growth can be separated into four stages.

Stage 1: Forming. When a team is forming, members cautiously explore the boundaries of acceptable group behavior. They search for their position within the group and test the leader's guidance. It is normal for little team progress to occur during this stage.

Stage 2: Storming. Storming is probably the most difficult stage for the group. Members often become impatient about the lack of progress, but are still inexperienced with working as a team. Members may argue about the actions they should take because they are faced with ideas that are unfamiliar to them and put them outside their comfort zones. Much of their energy is focused on each other instead of achieving the goal.

Stage 3: Norming. During this stage team members accept the team and begin to reconcile differences. Emotional conflict is reduced as relationships become more cooperative. The team is able to concentrate more on their work and start to make significant progress.

Stage 4: Performing. By this stage the team members have discovered and accepted each other's strengths and weaknesses, and learned what their roles are. Members are open and trusting and many good ideas are produced because they are not afraid to offer ideas and suggestions. They are comfortable using decision making tools to evaluate the ideas, prioritize tasks and solve problems. Much is accomplished and team satisfaction and loyalty is high.

Wrap Up

In 2009, a study was conducted by MetLife that examined the views of teachers, students, and principals on teamwork/collaboration in schools. They surveyed 1,003 K–12 public school teachers, 500 K–12 public school principals, and 1,018 3–12 students. The results were as follows (Fine, 2010):

> Sixty-seven percent of teachers and 78 percent of principals surveyed said more collaboration among teachers and school leaders would have a 'major impact' on student achievement. Initiatives to create more collaborative approaches to instruction have been widely discussed in recent years. The potential benefits of greater collaboration among educators, according to some observers, are a better school climate, greater career satisfaction for educators, and higher retention of qualified teachers and administrators. Yet for some educators, collaboration may raise concerns about dilution of individual accountability, infringement on independence in the classroom, or a lack of clear management hierarchies or responsibilities, the report said.
>
> The study also noted what the teachers said collaboration was.
>
> According to the MetLife survey, the most frequent types of collaboration among U.S. teachers and school leaders are: teachers meeting in teams to learn how to help their students achieve at higher levels; school leaders sharing responsibility with teachers to achieve school goals; and beginning teachers working with more experienced teachers. The activity reported least frequently was teachers observing one another in the classroom and providing feedback. Less than one-third of teachers or principals report that this happens frequently at their school, the survey said.
>
> Elementary schools are more collaborative than secondary schools, but educators report significant variations in the presence and frequency of such practices at both levels.

Schools that are collaborative, meanwhile, seem to have better morale than other schools, according to the MetLife report. Educators in schools with higher levels of collaboration are more likely to agree that the teachers, principal, and other professionals trust each other. Teachers in such schools are also more likely to say that they and their colleagues share responsibility for the achievement of all students and are more likely to be satisfied with their careers.

It is safe to say that working in a team environment is better for meeting the needs of the children. When we can foster teamwork in our schools as a faculty, we can translate that into the classroom. There are many benefits to modeling teamwork for students because they're going to have to work with others for the rest of their lives. As school counselors, we should view teamwork as support. We have a stressful job and having someone to lean on is important. Don't avoid the opportunity to work with others!

References

Aguilar, E. (2015, June 22). *5 Characteristics of an Effective School Team.* Retrieved from Edutopia: www.edutopia.org/blog/5-characteristics-effective-school-team-elena-aguilar

Barrick, C. (2018, January 2). *An Interview with Kirsten Perry, 2018 School Counselor of the Year.* Retrieved from College Board: www.collegeboard.org/membership/all-access/counseling/interview-kirsten-perry-2018-school-counselor-year

Donne, J. (2019, January 28). *No Man is an Island.* Retrieved from Poetry: https://web.cs.dal.ca/~johnston/poetry/island.html

Fine, L. (2010, February 17). *Educator Teamwork Seen as Key to School Gains.* Retrieved from Education Week Teacher: www.edweek.org/tm/articles/2010/02/17/metlife.html

Glaze, S. (2014, May 20). *For Effective Schools, Teamwork is Not Optional.* Retrieved from Edutopia: www.edutopia.org/blog/effective-schools-teamwork-not-optional-sean-glaze

Hozien, W. (2017, December 25). *Teamwork in Schools.* Retrieved from EducationViews: www.educationviews.org/teamwork-in-schools/

Nondestructive Testing (2019, January 28). *Teamwork in the Classroom.* Retrieved from NDT Resource Center: www.nde-ed.org/TeachingResources/ClassroomTips/Teamwork.htm

Schoultz, M. (2017, March 2). *10 Team Characteristics for Effective Teamwork.* Retrieved from Medium: https://medium.com/@mikeschoultz/10-team-characteristics-for-effective-teamwork-e0429b362ddd

Part IX

Professional Development

23 Get Involved

Get out of the counseling office! This can be hard, because there is so much to do. However, it is important for a variety of reasons. One is professional development. School counselors should be continuously looking for ways to develop professionally. This ties in with networking and knowing that all school counselors are a team. Everything is constantly changing, from college application forms to the research about Social Emotional Learning, it is a school counselor's obligation to know these changes. This chapter will provide resources about getting involved with professional organizations.

The Purpose of Professional Development

The pamphlet from *learningforward* states (learningforward, 2010),

> Professional development is the strategy schools and school districts use to ensure that educators continue to strengthen their practice throughout their career. The most effective professional development engages teams of teachers to focus on the needs of their students. They learn and problem solve together in order to ensure all students achieve success. School systems use a variety of schedules to provide this collaborative learning and work time for teachers. When time set aside for professional development is used effectively and parents receive reports about student results, they realize the benefits to teachers and their students far outweigh the scheduling inconvenience. When communities see their schools making steady upward progress, they applaud the role of effective professional development.
>
> Policymakers, community leaders, and parents have a responsibility to ensure that educators within their schools engage in continuous professional learning and apply that learning to increase student achievement. Learning Forward offers a clear definition and standards for measuring the quality of professional development occurring within schools. By advocating for educator professional learning that meets these standards, policymakers, parents, and community members can do their part to ensure a successful education experience for every child in their community. John

Dewey reminds us about the importance of this role: 'What the best and wisest parent wants for his own child, that must the community want for all of its children.'

Types of Professional Development *(Mizell, 2010):*

- Individual reading/study/research.
- Study groups among peers focused on a shared need or topic.
- Observation: teachers observing other teachers.
- Coaching: an expert teacher coaching one or more colleagues.
- Mentoring of new educators by more experienced colleagues.
- Team meetings to plan lessons, problem solve, improve performance, and/or learn a new strategy.
- Faculty, grade-level, or departmental meetings.
- Online courses.
- College/university courses.
- Workshops to dig deeper into a subject.
- Conferences to learn from a variety of expertise from around the state or country.
- Whole-school improvement programs.
- Proprietary programs by private vendors.

Professional Organizations

There are many professional organizations that a school counselor can get involved with. From national organizations to specific educational organizations, there are numerous organizations and they all come with a fee. Then, each of those organizations will have a conference. These conferences serve their purpose, because they will have sessions about important updates.

ASCA

The first organization to join is the American School Counselor Association. They have a large, annual conference that has sessions on every topic concerning school counselors. You can get involved by serving on one of their committees. There are a number of benefits to being a member (ASCA, 2019d):

> An ASCA membership offers you more than just periodicals, professional development and peer networking. Joining the only national organization dedicated to furthering the needs and mission of school counselors helps you grow professionally as well as personally. You'll learn about best practices in school counseling. You'll benefit from others' experience and research. Most of all, you'll know you're joining with thousands of other school counselors to share a common vision—that of turning today's youth into tomorrow's leaders.

ASCA School Counselor **Magazine:** A slick, full-color bimonthly magazine, *ASCA School Counselor* gives members a place to turn for practical, how-to articles addressing the issues school counselors face on a daily basis. A $90 value.

Discounted Publications: ASCA publishes myriad publications targeting areas such as school violence, comprehensive guidance programs, career counseling, social development and more. Stay on top of your game with discounted publications from ASCA.

Professional School Counseling **Journal:** ASCA's award-winning journal provides peer-reviewed articles on school counseling theory, research, practice and techniques. Your subscription helps you stay on top of the latest theories and advances in the field. Members have access to full-text articles and archives online. A $129 value.

Professional Development: As everyone knows, it's important to participate in regular, certified professional development opportunities. In addition to its annual conference, webinars and local workshops, ASCA also partners with other organizations to offer members training in areas such as ethics, career counseling and more.

Liability Insurance: Don't take unnecessary risks with your career and financial stability. Protect yourself with FREE professional liability insurance developed especially for ASCA professional and student members.

Free Resources: One of the best benefits of ASCA membership is access to a plethora of free resources. From sample lesson plans to job descriptions, checklists to back-to-school handouts, your membership opens the door to a world of materials to use on a daily basis, all available in the ASCA SCENE Library. Can't find what you need? Post a question on the SCENE to see if other school counselors can help.

Online Community: Looking for school counselors in your geographic area or level for networking purposes? Need to get in touch with another member you met at a training seminar? ASCA's online community, the ASCA SCENE, gives you the perfect opportunity to network with and learn from other school counselors 24/7.

ASCA Aspects: Keep on top of new projects, resources and member benefits with ASCA's monthly e-newsletter.

Committees

I served on the Position Statements Committee for two years. Three possible committees that you could serve on are:

Position Statements Committee: Committee members will work with the Position Statements Committee co-chairs on updating position statements.

Curation Committee: Members of this committee will work to produce brief, issue-specific documents for school counselors to distribute to parents, teachers, students, and community members.

Ethics Committee: Committee members will work with the Ethics Committee chair to answer school counselor ethics questions, begin planning for the next ASCA Ethical Standards for School Counselors revision and address ethical situations as they arise.

Serving on the Position Statements Committee taught me how to write a position statement, work with other school counselors across the nation, and advocate for issues that affect school counselors. Being able to work intimately with other professionals across the nation was very helpful in my own work.

ASCA Conference

This 4-day national conference gathers roughly 3,600 school counselors from across the United States. There are inspiring keynote speakers, informative breakout sessions, and a lot of networking opportunities. The ASCA Conference website states that school counselors will (ASCA, 2019):

1. Meet school counselors from across the country and around the globe you can call on again and again for help throughout the year and take home valuable, practical tips you can put into practice immediately.
2. Discover companies that can help you find the products and services you need to run a top-notch program.
3. You'll get access to educational sessions, networking events, keynote speakers, morning coffee and lite bites three days, lunch three days and more.
4. Have the chance to earn CEUs, contact hours and/or graduate credit.

State School Counselor Associations

Getting involved with your state association is a great way to be connected to other professionals. It will provide you with networking, advocacy, and important information. Being involved at the state level can be easier than getting involved with ASCA. I was on the board of the Kentucky School Counselor Association and that opened doors to be involved at ASCA. There is the opportunity to attend regional workshops and state conferences. Also, you can apply to be a presenter at the conferences. What better way to help fellow school counselors than to share what you're doing? The following are just a few ways to get involved at the state level:

- Serve on a committee
- Run for a board position
- Be a part of the mentoring program, if your state has one
- Present at conferences
- Participate in research

There are also benefits to being a member of a state school counselor association. The Virginia School Counselor Association offers these benefits to their members (VSCA, 2019):

- Membership programs and services such as—membership mailings, materials related to National School Counseling Week and Back to School, etc.
- 2 Lobbyists at David Bailey Associates, who will advocate for Virginia school counseling issues
- A toll-free number and PO Box specific to VSCA to address your questions and correspondence
- VSCA representation on the Virginia Education Coalition (VEC) who will advocate alongside leaders from other educational associations
- FREE RAMP training and consultation for school divisions
- Scholarships for RAMP application fees
- Multiple professional development opportunities throughout the state, Annual Conference and Summer Academy each year at a reduced member rate
- Socials hosted by our Regional Area Representatives for each of the 8 Virginia Regions
- A website full of resources for members only
- Access to the membership database for your networking purposes
- *The VOICE* magazine
- Level listservs on Google Groups
- Professional recognition and awards for school counselors and graduate students
- Monthly e-mail contact from school level-specific VPs to provide members with resources, ideas, monthly features and to highlight great counselors in our state
- Training on the updated ASCA Model and SMART Goals
- Mentorship for new counselors
- Social media presence on Twitter, Facebook, LinkedIn, ASCA/Virginia Scene and YouTube
- VA delegate representation to the ASCA National Conference

Some SCAs offer liability to their members as well. So, there are many opportunities and reasons why school counselors should be members of their state SCAs. You can find all of the SCAs websites listed on Schoolcounselor.org under 'State/Territory Associations'.

National Association for College Admission Counseling

As a high school counselor, attending the NACAC conference was one of the most beneficial. They have a plethora of information on college admissions, financial aid, and the application process. Their website states (NACAC, 2019);

The National Association for College Admission Counseling (NACAC), founded in 1937, is an organization of more than 15,000 professionals from around the world dedicated to serving students as they make choices about pursuing postsecondary education.

They have state affiliate chapters as well. Those can be found on their website.

Other Professional Organizations

American Counseling Association

The American Counseling Association is a not-for-profit, professional, and educational organization that is dedicated to the growth and enhancement of the counseling profession. Founded in 1952, ACA is the world's largest association exclusively representing professional counselors in various practice settings.

(American Counselor Association, 2019a)

Chi Sigma Iota

Chi Sigma Iota is the international honor society of professional counseling and for professional counselors. It was established in 1985 through the efforts of leaders in the profession of counseling whose desire was to provide recognition for outstanding achievement as well as outstanding service within the profession. CSI was created for counselors-in-training, counselor educators, and professional counselors whose career commitment is to research and service through professional counseling.

(Chi Sigma Iota, 2019)

Our mission is to promote scholarship, research, professionalism, leadership and excellence in counseling, and to recognize high attainment in the pursuit of academic and clinical excellence in the profession of counseling. Our symbols and colors were chosen to reflect our mission and values: white for virtue, blue for trustworthiness and integrity. Our Strategic Plan and Bylaws provide information about the purposes of and membership requirements for the Society.

(Chi Sigma Iota, 2019)

Chi Sigma Iota has a rich history, summarized in pictures in our CSI Scrapbook, Annual Awards Program and Year in Review, and description of activities and accomplishments of the Society, working alone and in conjunction with other counseling associations to provide services to members of the counseling profession. A listing of past-presidents is included, as these persons reflect the rich tradition of excellence that is the hallmark of Chi Sigma Iota.

(Chi Sigma Iota, 2019)

International School Counselor Association

The International School Counselor Association is a professional organization, which provides leadership and advocacy for the profession of school counseling in International Schools.

We provide resources, professional development and a collaborative network benefiting student success in our global community.

The International School Counselor Association (ISCA) is a professional membership organization dedicated to meet the unique needs of international school counselors working at international schools.

International School Counselor Association is registered and licensed in the State of Delaware.

(ISCA, 2019)

National Board for Certified Counselors

National Certified School Counselors (NCSC) are board certified counselors who offer the highest standards of practice for schools and students because they have met stringent education, examination, supervision, experience, and ethical requirements in school counseling.

(NBCC, 2019)

National Education Association

The National Education Association (NEA), the nation's largest professional employee organization, is committed to advancing the cause of public education. NEA's 3 million members work at every level of education—from pre-school to university graduate programs. NEA has affiliate organizations in every state and in more than 14,000 communities across the United States.

(NEA, 2019)

The Association for Multicultural Counseling and Development

The Association for Multicultural Counseling and Development seeks to develop programs specifically to improve ethnic and racial empathy and understanding. Its activities are designed to advance and sustain personal growth and improve educational opportunities for members from diverse cultural backgrounds.

(AMCD, 2019)

AMCD is charged with the responsibility of defending human and civil rights as prescribed by law. It encourages changing attitude and enhancing understanding of cultural diversity. Provisions are made for in-service and pre-service training for members and for others in the profession. Efforts are made to strengthen members professionally and enhance their ability to serve as behavioral change agents. Operationalization of Multicultural

Counseling Competencies by AMCD represents a benchmark for the counseling profession and the American Counseling Association.

(AMCD, 2019)

The mission of the organization, from its inception is to:

- Recognize the human diversity and multicultural nature of our society;
- To enhance the development, human rights and the psychological health of ethnic/racial populations and all people as critical to the social, educational, political, professional and personal reform in the United States and globally;
- To identify and work to eliminate conditions which create barriers to the individual development of marginalized populations;
- To develop, implement and/or foster interest in charitable, scientific and educational programs designed to further the interests of marginalized populations;
- To secure equality and access of treatment, advancement, qualifications and status individuals and families in counseling, wellness and mental health work;
- To publish a journal and other scientific educational and professional materials with the purpose of raising the standards of all who work in providing counseling, wellness and mental health.

(AMCD, 2019)

Continuing Education Credits

Continuing education credits will vary depending on the state, but just about every state requires them. If you decide to leave one state and go to another, your continuing education may not transfer or be equivalent. It's also important to note that not all conference sessions will give continuing education credits. There are small workshops that will count towards continuing education credits as well.

The American School Counselor Association offers Continuing Education Units (CEUs) or contact hours for school counselors on their website (ASCA, 2019c).

CEUs/contact hours are currently available for reading *Professional School Counseling* journal articles, attending the ASCA annual conference, attending ASCA webinars or registering for one of the ASCA U specialist training programs.

To earn CEUs for the journal articles or webinars, members must take a short quiz demonstrating knowledge of the material. Each webinar or journal article is worth 0.1 CEUs/1 Contact Hour. One CEU is equal to 10 contact hours.

After you've read a *Professional School Counseling* journal article or viewed a webinar, visit the online bookstore to purchase the accompanying CEU quiz. To access quizzes, click on 'My ASCA' (upper right-hand corner, beneath your log in) and then select 'Online Store'. Here you'll find a link to available quizzes and trainings.

Once you've successfully passed the quiz (you may take it as many times as necessary to earn 100 percent), the record of your CEUs earned will show up in your membership record.

Each state has their own requirements for school counselors in order to maintain licensure. You can find your state's information on ASCA's website. For example, Ohio and Kentucky require the following (ASCA, 2019b):

Ohio (Two- or five-year renewal certificates)

Holders of eight-year certificates issued before Sept. 1, 1998, who wish to transition to a five-year license must complete six semester hours of coursework or the equivalent as approved by the LPDC. Holders of a two-year provisional license who have not met the requirements for transition to the five-year professional license must complete three semester hours of coursework to renew that license. Holders of a five-year license must complete the equivalent of six semester hours of coursework for renewal. Each educator is responsible for the design of an individual professional development plan (IPDP) based on the needs of the educator, the students, the school and the school district, subject to approval of the LPDC. In accordance with the approved plan, the educator must complete six semester hours of coursework related to classroom teaching and/or the area of licensure; or 18 continuing education units (CEUs) (180 contact hours) or other equivalent activities related to classroom teaching and/or the area of licensure as approved by the LPDC of the employing school, district or agency since the issuance of the license to be renewed. Coursework, CEUs or other equivalent activities may be combined.

Kentucky (Five-year renewal certificate)

Provisional—An official transcript showing at least nine semester hours of additional graduate credit in the areas of counseling or guidance counseling.

Standard—Completion of 12 Effective Instructional Leadership Act (EILA) hours as specified by the Kentucky Department of Education in KRS 156.101. (It is the responsibility to provide documentation of this training to the district superintendent, who recommends renewal on the TC-2.)

Make sure you check your individual state's requirements for CEUs. Cross reference it with what you read on ASCA's website. State education websites can be confusing, and you might need to call their office for clarification. If you have any questions regarding your state's CEU requirements,

I recommend getting in touch with the DOE for your state. The Online Counseling Programs give the following information as a resource for CEUs (Online Counseling Programs, 2019).

Many practicing counselors pursue professional certification to further demonstrate their acumen in a specialized area. Whether you acquire a designation through The National Board for Certified Counselors (NBCC), American Counseling Association (ACA) or another association, you'll need to attain a set number of continuing education units (CEUs) to maintain your status.

Both general counseling associations and specialized associations offer certification programs and continuing education courses, such as:

American Association of Pastoral Counselors
American Counseling Association
American Mental Health Counselors Association
American School Counselor Association
American Institute of Health Care Professionals (AIHCP)
Association for Child and Adolescent Counseling (ACAC)
Association for Death Education and Counseling
Military and Government Counseling Association (MGCA)
Substance Abuse Practitioner Certification Program

A number of private companies also offer online continuing education courses for professional counselors. Many of the CEU courses are offered online and include webinars, podcasts, instructional videos and more.

Continuing education courses may be necessary to maintain certification or licensure. The minimum number of continuing education units (CEUs) may be set according to the standards of the state in which you practice, your employer or the association that issued your certification. Many employers will pay for you to take continuing education courses. Most associations award a five-year-renewable certification that requires the completion of a minimum amount of CEUs or professional development points. The actual numbers vary considerably by field, state and association.

When you're looking to complete your continuing education, make sure you reach out to the school counselors in your region. They might offer workshops for which you can get CEUs for attending.

Wrap Up

As a first-year counselor, I gained a lot from attending regional and state conferences. It can be hard to transition into the role of school counselor right after graduating. Putting what you learn into practice isn't always easy. The conferences and workshops gave me best practices from other school counselors. Especially since I was the only school counselor in the building, I enjoyed learning from my colleagues and knowing what worked and what didn't for them. Each year I've been a school counselor has been different. The needs of the students and the school has changed. The professional development opportunities have aided when I didn't know what pre-post tests to use, needs assessment to give, SEL curriculum or guidance lessons, or organizations and resources to give to my students. Don't shy away from attending professional developments. It can be costly if your district doesn't pay but make the case for why it's important. There are financial aid opportunities for state and national conferences. Take advantage of them. Even when it's hard to get out of the school building, it's important for our mental health and our school that we continue to learn.

References

AMCD (2019, February 7). *About*. Retrieved from AMCD: https://multiculturalcounselin gdevelopment.org/about/

American Counselor Association (2019, February 7). *About*. Retrieved from ACA: www. counseling.org/about-us/about-aca

ASCA (2019a, January 31). *About*. Retrieved from ASCA Conference: www.ascaconferences. org/#home

ASCA (2019b, February 25). *Continuing Education Requirements*. Retrieved from American School Counselor Association: www.schoolcounselor.org/school-counselors-members/ careers-roles/continuing-education-requirements

ASCA (2019c, February 25). *Earn CEUs*. Retrieved from American School Counselor Association: www.schoolcounselor.org/school-counselors-members/professional-de velopment/earn-ceus

ASCA (2019d, January 31). *Member Benefits & Info*. Retrieved from School Counselor: www.schoolcounselor.org/school-counselors-members/member-benefits-info

Chi Sigma Iota (2019, February 7). *About*. Retrieved from Chi Sigma Iota: www.csi-net. org/page/About_CSI

ISCA (2019, February 6). *Mission*. Retrieved from International School Counselor Association: https://iscainfo.com/Our-Mission

learningforward (2010). *Why Professional Development Matters*. Retrieved from learningforward: https://learningforward.org/docs/default-source/pdf/why_pd_matters_web.pdf

Mizell, H. (2010). *Why Professional Development Matter*. Retrieved from Learning Forward: https://learningforward.org/docs/default-source/pdf/why_pd_matters_web.pdf

NACAC (2019, February 5). *About*. Retrieved from NACAC: www.nacacnet.org/about/ overview/

NBCC (2019, February 7). *The National Certified School Counselor*. Retrieved from National Board for Certified Counselors: www.nbcc.org/Certification/NCSC

NEA (2019, February 6). *About*. Retrieved from NEA: www.nea.org/home/2580.htm ?cpssessionid=SID-A578F12D-F100EA11

Online Counseling Programs (2019, February 25). *Continuing Education for Counselors*. Retrieved from Online Counseling Progams: https://onlinecounselingprograms.com/ online-counseling-degrees/continuing-education-for-counselors/

VSCA (2019, January 31). *Membership*. Retrieved from Virginia School Counselor Association: www.vsca.org/membership.asp

Index

Page numbers in **bold** indicate tables. Page numbers in *italic* indicate figures.

Printed in the United States
by Baker & Taylor Publisher Services